W9-AFH-434

Microsoft

Intranets,

Productivity,

COLLECTIVE

>K_n_o_w_l_e_d_g_e>>

and the Promise

of the Knowledge

Workplace

CARL CAMPBELL BRIGHAM LIBRARY
EDUCATIONAL TESTING SERVICE
PRINCETON, NJ 08541

Robert Marcus
Beverley Watters

PUBLISHED BY
Microsoft Press
A Division of Microsoft Corporation
One Microsoft Way
Redmond, Washington 98052-6399

Copyright © 2002 by Microsoft Corporation

All rights reserved. No part of the contents of this book may be reproduced or transmitted in any form or by any means without the written permission of the publisher.

Library of Congress Cataloging-in-Publication Data
Marcus, Robert.
    Collective Knowledge : Intranets, Productivity, and the Promise of the Knowledge Workplace / Robert Marcus, Beverley Watters.
        p. cm.
    Includes index.
    ISBN 0-7356-1499-7
    1. Intranets (Computer networks)   2. Industrial productivity.   I. Watters, Beverley.   II. Title.

    TK5105.875.I6 M37   2002
    658'.05468--dc21   2001057769

Printed and bound in the United States of America.

3 4 5 6 7 8 9   QWT   7 6 5 4 3 2

Distributed in Canada by H.B. Fenn and Company Ltd.

A CIP catalogue record for this book is available from the British Library.

Microsoft Press books are available through booksellers and distributors worldwide. For further information about international editions, contact your local Microsoft Corporation office or contact Microsoft Press International directly at fax (425) 936-7329. Visit our Web site at www.microsoft.com/mspress. Send comments to *mspinput@microsoft.com*.

Microsoft, Microsoft Press, the Office logo, Outlook, PowerPoint, SharePoint, Windows, and Windows Media are either registered trademarks or trademarks of Microsoft Corporation in the United States and/or other countries. Other product and company names mentioned herein may be the trademarks of their respective owners.

The example companies, organizations, products, domain names, e-mail addresses, logos, people, places, and events depicted herein are fictitious. No association with any real company, organization, product, domain name, e-mail address, logo, person, place, or event is intended or should be inferred.

Acquisitions Editor: Alex Blanton
Project Editor: Aileen Wrothwell

Body Part No. X08-63863

Contents

Section 2

The Culture of Knowledge

Introduction

In the shift from the Industrial Age to the Information Age, the methods and practices used to create, manage, and make the right knowledge available to the right people at the right time are as elemental to productivity as oil is to the effective operation of machinery. Knowledge has qualitative *and* quantitative value. It is emerging as *the* strategic asset of our time. And still most organizations have yet to embrace this awareness, which is why we wrote *Collective Knowledge*.

Who Should Read This Book?

Business leaders, also known as business decision makers, are those who most urgently need the productivity benefits attributed to intranets. A business decision maker is an executive-level leader who has strategic and budgetary decision-making authority over teams, departments, divisions, or an entire organization.

Business decision makers are predominantly concerned with a simultaneous and systematic focus on increasing revenue while reducing cost. They believe that business objectives should drive technology decisions, and any investment in technology must be based on sound business goals and principles. They understand that revenue in knowledge-enabled organizations is increased by superior agility, improved output, and the implementation of process efficiencies, while costs are reduced by mining organizational knowledge assets, leveraging existing IT infrastructure, and lessening the need for travel and physical events. *Collective Knowledge* is for them.

The Key Benefits of This Book

Collective Knowledge was written to increase the awareness of the power and potential in a next generation intranet solution. From these pages, the reader will secure

- A thorough account of the evolution of humankind's efforts to effectively capture and manage knowledge from cuneiform to the intranet

- A compelling vision for the crucial ways in which knowledge is emerging as the defining influence of our time, thus transforming the world of work

- A comprehensive overview of the ways in which intranets add value, illustrated through real-life case studies

- A succinct strategy for creating and managing an intranet now and in the future

Chapters at a Glance

Chapter 1 describes humankind's relationship with knowledge throughout history, the value we place on consciously accumulating and managing knowledge, and the technical innovations that have emerged to support this.

Chapter 2 defines intranets, describes how they are based on the distributed intelligence of computer networks and the Internet, summarizes their key features, and introduces next generation intranet solutions.

Chapter 3 looks at portals specifically and discusses their features and benefits, illustrated with actual deployments.

Chapter 4 explains the "why" of the intranet and portal evolution by reviewing the business and technological revolutions of the past two decades.

Chapter 5 introduces the Microsoft Solution for Intranets, comprising desktop productivity with Microsoft Office XP, portal services with SharePoint Portal Server, team collaboration via SharePoint Team Services, data management with SQL Server-all running on top of Windows.

Chapter 6 looks at knowledge workers-who they are, what they do, where they came from, what their needs are-and then outlines some core competencies.

Chapter 7 describes the knowledge workplace and how it has emerged since the Industrial Revolution.

Chapter 8 explains how to build the knowledge workplace, accentuated via scenarios that highlight common daily business practices enabled by intranets.

Chapter 9 builds on what we have learned about next generation intranets by providing case studies of four deployments using the Microsoft Solution for Intranets and explains the business value benefits that have been achieved in each deployment.

Chapter 10 is designed to help business leaders avoid missteps in planning and managing an intranet deployment by examining the key factors and attributes of both successful and unsuccessful intranets.

Chapter 11 muses on the future direction of intranets, for society in general and workplace technology in particular.

Read On...

If you use a networked computer to create, manage, and access individual or collective knowledge, this book will be useful and informative. If you lead a team, division, business unit, or an entire organization that generates and utilizes knowledge, and you are determined to increase productivity and reduce costs, this book is for you.

Dedicated to Joyce Harris, who used the power of collective knowledge to serve the cause of freedom, equality, and human rights.

From Cuneiform to Intranets: Getting Here from There

History demonstrates that knowledge work is not new. Throughout time people have sought after ways to acquire, preserve, manage, and share knowledge. From where and when to plant crops to the incantations and movements of important religious rituals, even the earliest people strove to conserve knowledge. What is new is the sheer volume of information to which we are exposed in concert with an embryonic change of consciousness regarding the perception of the value of knowledge within organizations. Knowledge has become a strategic asset that drives productivity and profitability. Great energy and resources have been expended in developing workplace tools and systems to harness it.

In this first section, Chapter 1 sets the stage for under-standing where we are in the stream of the history of knowledge and information systems. After considering humankind's historical behavior with regard to knowledge, Chapter 2 introduces intranets—the Web-based internal knowledge networks that are fundamentally changing the way knowledge is created, shared, processed, received, retrieved, and disseminated—and forms the crux of this book. Chapter 3 discusses the features and functions of por-tals, Web-based gateways to the tools and contents on intranets.

To fully appreciate business and technological drivers for intranets and portals Chapter 4 illustrates the "why" of this evolution. By reviewing these drivers—the PC revolution, the business management revolution, the desktop and online publishing revolutions, the networking revolution, the client/server revolution, and the Internet revolution—the reader will be in a better position to plan, develop, manage, and evaluate an intranet as a possible solution to a variety of business challenges.

The last chapter in this section, Chapter 5, outlines the Microsoft Solution for Intranets, comprising Office XP, SharePoint Portal Server, SharePoint Team Services, SQL Server, Windows 2000, and Windows Media. This solution enables the emergent knowledge workplace through enhanced productivity and smarter, faster decision making; an environment of optimized output, where important projects come to successful conclusion sooner. The Microsoft Solution for Intranets includes integrated and tested software, prescriptive architectural guidance, and deployment services and support from Microsoft and experienced industry partners.

Information and Knowledge in an Historical Perspective

The value of information and knowledge in organizations is enjoying new-found appreciation. (See Section Three, "How Intranets Add Value," for a more in-depth discussion of this topic.) Understanding the history of acquiring, preserving, and sharing knowledge holds out the promise of improving our ability to run businesses, other organizations, and government agencies in an information intensive new economic world order. That is why the topic is of such relevance in a book on intranet solutions for the workplace.

The literature on the history of information and knowledge could fill a building, but some simple observations about humankind's relationship with knowledge can be made that are relevant to managers today. Certain basic patterns of human behavior have not changed from the beginning of recorded time to the present day. Our technologies have evolved from systems of knowledge based on human memory to hieroglyphics and cuneiform incised on clay, metals, and shells; from using various forms of the alphabet inscribed on papyrus and parchment to massive information sharing afforded by the communications and computing technologies of the late twentieth and early twenty-first centuries. Throughout these revolutions, the following observations hold true:

- Humans see value in consciously collecting, sharing, and using information.
- Writing systems were designed to augment memory systems.
- Humankind has invented physical objects for storing and manipulating information.
- Humankind perceives value in collections of knowledge.
- Every major institution in society has collected, preserved, and exploited information.
- Humankind needs to organize knowledge to assure access.

Humans See Value in Consciously Collecting, Sharing, and Using Information

Successful organizations need to be agile, capable of swift response to constantly changing market forces and customer requirements. The most effective businesses enable their workers by providing rapid access to information as well as the tools to organize and share knowledge efficiently across the organization.

Historically, humans have always recognized the value of consciously collecting and using information, and this continues unabated. Preliterate people had no way of concretely capturing and storing their knowledge of the whereabouts of good hunting grounds and water supplies, or the poisonous or nutritive values of plant species, to share with their families and communities. These early men and women had to rely on the flawed and limited powers of retention provided by their memories for their very survival. No doubt each new generation made discoveries that became common knowledge, however briefly, before these shared memories were lost.

The method used to hold onto these "gems" of wisdom involved weaving this knowledge into stories or myths that were repeated around the campfire. Tribal histories were related, and social codes were communicated and reinforced. Some of these stories were brief, some very long and complicated. All of them relied on rhythmic repetition and rhyme to provide a mnemonic effect that helped the bits of knowledge stay in faulty human memories. "Thirty days has September . . . " is a common present-day example.

Rhythmic repetition was the method used to memorize knowledge among early tribal people, but other memory systems were devised by later peoples. The ancient Greeks, whose legacies have enriched the Western world so much, invented a system for memorizing that is now called mnemotechnics. This technique is based on the association of the facts to be "stored," or committed to memory, with places and images. The usual method adopted by the Greeks involved architectural images to build memory, just like audiovisual and broadcast technologies in present-day organizations are used to build memory.

The modern memory systems we use are found in our computers. Computer memory capabilities have evolved as fast as computer processing technologies. From punch cards and magnetic disks to RAM (random access memory), ROM (read-only memory), and optical and biochemical forms, humankind has continuously striven to improve memory forms to address the need of an expanding knowledge base. The successful organizations of the Information Age rely on these kinds of memory systems to collect, store, and share important information, just as their forefathers relied on rhythmic repetition or mnemotechnics.

Writing Systems Were Designed to Augment Memory Systems

With the robust document management capabilities of an intranet solution, organizations ensure that the tacit individual knowledge employees hold in their heads becomes explicit collective knowledge accessible to everyone. This continues the trend begun thousands of years ago when humankind developed writing systems to aid in the preservation and distribution of knowledge. From early times we found ways to record pieces of information outside our memories, ranging from marks on rocks and sticks to complex languages.

One of the first writing methods was developed by the Sumerian people in the Middle East about 3000 B.C. It was based on cuneiform (wedge-shaped) elements carved on clay tablets. (See Figure 1-1.) Comprising about 600 characters, cuneiform served as a capable instrument for recording Sumerian social, political, and philosophical thinking; for maintaining accounts of schools and social reforms; and for preserving the form and content of their hymns, prayers, rituals, sacred legends, and magic formulae.

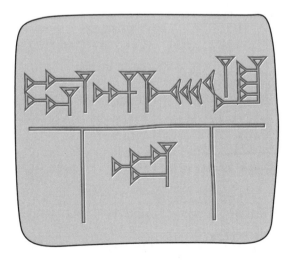

Figure 1-1   *Example of cuneiform writing*

Ancient Egyptian civilization flourished simultaneously with that of Sumer. The earliest Egyptian written texts date from the last quarter of the fourth millennium B.C., but the style of writing developed by the Egyptian scribes to suit their needs and language was hieroglyphic—a name derived from two Greek words meaning "sacred" and "to carve."[1] (See Figure 1-2.) The chief purpose of their writing was to provide lasting and impressive inscriptions suitable for monuments and temples to glorify their kings and civilization.

The Greeks adapted the Phoenician alphabet, expanding its 22 consonant symbols to 24. This Greek alphabet spread throughout the Mediterranean world and gave rise to various modified forms, including the Roman alphabet. Because of Roman conquests and the spread of the Latin language, the Roman alphabet became the basic alphabet of all the languages of Western Europe.[2]

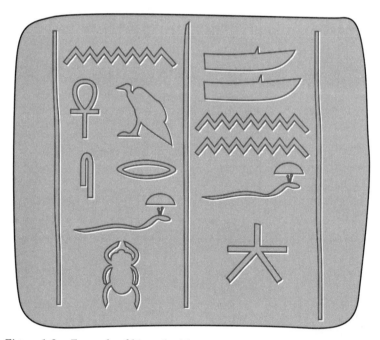

Figure 1-2   *Example of hieroglyphics*

1. J. K. Gates, *Introduction to Librarianship* (New York: McGraw-Hill, 1968), 11.
2. Alphabets, *Microsoft Encarta Encyclopedia 2000 Deluxe.*

The Chinese had independently developed their own system of writing about the fourteenth century B.C. under the Shang dynasty.[3] It had a much more extensive list of characters than the Sumerian, Babylonian, or Phoenician scripts, which they inscribed on tortoise shells and embossed on bronze vessels.

Many modern linguists complain that the world is becoming so homogeneous that the indigenous languages and writings of early tribes are disappearing, even though new writing systems, called programming languages, are appearing all the time. (See Figure 1-3.) In the half century since the invention of the computer, several thousand languages for writing software have been created,[4] especially since the watershed of Internet and Web technologies. It is these writing systems that have made it possible to store and share the vast knowledge warehouses currently found on organizational intranets.

CodeLifter 5.0   + Copy Find Save Print Clear   ✓ ! - □ x

http://codelifter.com/main/javascript/amazingframelesspopup1.html   Go ⬇ ⬆

```
function openFrameless(){
    if (beIE){
        NFW = window.open("","popFrameless","fullscreen,"+s)
        NFW.blur()
        window.focus()
        NFW.resizeTo(windowW,windowH)
        NFW.moveTo(windowX,windowY)
        var frameString=""+
"<html>"+
"<head>"+
"<title>"+title+"</title>"+
"</head>"+
"<frameset rows='*,0' framespacing=0 border=0 frameborder=0>"+
"<frame name='top' src='"+urlPop+"' scrolling=auto>"+
"<frame name='bottom' src='about:blank' scrolling='no'>"+
"</frameset>"+
"</html>"
        NFW.document.open()
        NFW.document.write(frameString)
        NFW.document.close()
    } else {
        NFW=window.open(urlPop,"popFrameless","scrollbars,"+s)
        NFW.blur()
        window.focus()
        NFW.resizeTo(windowW,windowH)
```

Figure 1-3   *Example of software code*

3. Chinese Language, *Microsoft Encarta Encyclopedia 2000 Deluxe*.
4. James W. Cortada (ed.), *Rise of the Knowledge Worker* (Boston: Butterworth-Heinemann, 1988), 6.

Humankind Has Invented Physical Objects for Storing and Manipulating Information

Customer records, financial performance, employee histories, industry regulations, product specifications, market data . . . these are all examples of databases that use computer memory to store and manipulate information and are brought to the desktop with an intranet solution. From the earliest stages of literacy, humankind has developed physical objects to store and manipulate information. Clay, papyrus, paper, and floppy disks have all been, in their time, essential for recording information. Over the centuries, thousands of other tools have appeared to carry out similar functions: notched sticks; carvings on stone; mechanical devices; movable type (in the 1400s); adding machines (1600s); typewriters (1700s and 1800s); calculators (1820s); and, beginning in the mid-1800s, a vast array of electronic machines and apparatuses, such as the telegraph, telephone, radio, television, tape recorder, and, of course, the computer.

Writing Materials

The invention of a flexible writing material about 3200 B.C. greatly advanced the progress of written, shared, and preserved human knowledge. Papyrus, which grew in abundance in the Nile River basin, was harvested, pressed, pounded, and smoothed into a writing surface and inscribed on using a brushlike pen and ink. (See Figure 1-4.) Over the course of time, other places began to import Egyptian papyrus to use for recording. This continued until about A.D. 150, when Ptolemy VII, then king of Egypt, became very jealous of the growth of the Great Library in Pergamum, an ancient Greek kingdom. This library had grown to such size and importance that it rivaled his own, and, in the hopes of halting its progress, he forbade the export of papyrus to that area of Asia Minor. Consequently a new writing material had to be found, or existing materials had to be reexamined for possible use. Parchment was made from the skin of animals, principally that of sheep or calves. Although this kind of writing material had been known to the Greeks for some time, the preferred medium was papyrus, since it was both cheaper and easier to write on.

At the height of the Roman Empire, a new book form came into prominence. The roll, inconvenient to write on, read, and consult quickly, was superseded by the codex, an early book form, consisting of bound sheaves of

Figure 1-4   *The papyrus plant*

handwritten pages.[5] In addition to improving access to the contents of the book, the codex greatly increased its chances of survival, a factor appreciated by early scholars.

For approximately 500 years the art of papermaking was confined to China, but in A.D. 610 it was introduced into Japan. It was brought into Central Asia about 750, and it made its appearance in Egypt about 800, although it was not manufactured there until 900. The use of paper was introduced into Europe by the Moors, and the first papermaking mill was established in Spain in about 1150.[6] In succeeding centuries the craft spread to most other European countries.

The Printing Revolution

The materials required for printing—a cheap and plentiful substance on which to print, an ink that would adhere to metal and transfer to paper, a

5. Codex, *Microsoft Encarta Encyclopedia 2000 Deluxe.*
6. Papermaking, *Microsoft Encarta Encyclopedia 2000 Deluxe.*

press to bring paper and metal into contact with each other, and a general knowledge of metal technology—were all available by the second half of the fifteenth century. Johannes Gutenberg is given the credit for combining these materials, processes, and skills into the invention of printing with movable type and for the concept of unlimited reproduction. His first work, known as the Gutenberg Bible, was a 42-line (meaning 42 lines per page) bible that appeared about 1456. With the increased efficiency of printing, the number of available books grew rapidly.

The printing press was one of the world's most revolutionary inventions. It led to an inestimable increase in the supply of books, a greater spread of knowledge, the dissemination of classical literature, the flowering of national literature, the development of literary criticism, and the rise of publishing as a business. Libraries increased in number and size as a natural consequence of the fact that learning, formerly confined to monasteries and universities, was now within the reach of any person who wished to pursue it. Gutenberg's invention provided a powerful shove to the democratization of knowledge.

Even as early as 1500 more than 8 million books had been printed, and by the end of the sixteenth century an estimated 200 million books had come off the busy printing presses of Europe. It is staggering to imagine, compared to the fewer than 5 million manuscripts that had been produced by scribes in monasteries prior to the invention.[7] Today more than 65,000 book titles are published annually in the United States.[8]

Encyclopedias

One of the objects humankind devised for storing and sharing acquired knowledge was the encyclopedia. In 387 B.C., Plato founded the Academy, an institution of philosophy and science that survived for almost a thousand years. One reason for its success was that its students, and potential students, believed that all knowledge could be found in one place, and that place was the Academy. The Greeks believed that knowledge was static rather than dynamic and that knowledge, once harnessed, would make it possible to control the world. They had words for this perspective: *enkyklios,* which

---

7. Fraser Stockwell, History of Information Storage and Retrieval (Jefferson, N.C.: McFarland & Company, 2000), 47.
8. International Publishers Association, http://www.ipa-uie.org (October 8, 2001).

means "circular and complete," and *paedia,* which means "education." Together these words have been translated to mean the whole circle of knowledge, or encyclopedia.

Plato believed that his Academy alone had all the essential knowledge in the world, but he never tried to capture or preserve it in any way. It wasn't until Speusippos, Plato's nephew, succeeded Plato as leader of the Academy that anyone attempted to gather this knowledge into one work. Only fragments remain of Speusippos's encyclopedia, but it is known that it was designed as a teaching aid.

The Greek concept of the circle of knowledge, preserved on parchment rolls, was attractive to the acquisitive Romans, who liked to return home with the best of everything. As might be expected, the first Roman to compile such a work was Marcus Porcius Cato (234–149 B.C.), a well-traveled general.[9] Wary of too much Greek influence on Roman culture and learning, Cato wrote *Pracepta ad Filum (Advice to My Son),* which covered oratory, agriculture, law, war, and medicine. Unfortunately, nothing of this work survives.

Of all the Greek and Roman encyclopedists, the most influential was Pliny the Elder (A.D. 23–79). He completed the *Historia Naturalis (Natural History)* which consisted of 37 parchment scrolls and 2493 articles. Handwritten copies were prized additions to every medieval library, and the work is still studied today. The encyclopedia writing of the early Romans and Greeks came to an abrupt end with the invasion of Italy by the Goths in 410. Thereafter the preservation and development of encyclopedias and other books shifted to the Christian church.

China's civil service was designed by Confucian scholars and maintained by early emperors for almost 2000 years. The first Chinese encyclopedias were written for and by these civil servants to address the needs of the government rather than to record absolute truths. There were numerous early examples of encyclopedias of every type, including historical, biographical, scientific, and literary, but they were all difficult to consult because, in traditional Chinese scholarly fashion, no indexes appeared.[10] Near the end of the sixth century, a new religion and political power arose in Arabia under the prophet Muhammad. The followers of Muhammad, or Muslims, compiled encyclopedias along with the many other Arabic books they produced. While

---

9. Stockwell, 16.
10. Stockwell, 26.

much of Christianity tended to discourage investigations and learning outside the sphere of religion, Islam encouraged the preservation of many of the early Greek and Roman texts.[11]

During the collapse of the Roman Empire, the Roman system of government and most of its other structures of society were destroyed by Germanic invaders. By 800 most of Western Europe was divided into large estates ruled by landowners. It fell to the Christian church to provide broad social structures, and, because the church had most of the literate scholars housed in its monasteries and nunneries, it supervised the collection, compilation, and transcription of all knowledge. It was in these monasteries and nunneries that medieval encyclopedias were compiled—more than 40—and it was during this period that the great shift from secular to Christian interests can be seen in the content of these encyclopedias. Science and literature were "Christinized" as the Catholic Church exerted great influence over what was written.

The modern encyclopedia—alphabetically arranged, and often with bibliographies—is usually thought to have begun in 1704 with John Harris's *Lexicon technicum* (*Universal English Dictionary of Arts and Sciences*). Inspired by this work, Ephraim Chambers published in 1728 his *Cyclopaedia* (*Universal Dictionary of Arts and Sciences*). This publication is historically important because it was the first to emphasize the use of many authorities as contributors and it introduced cross-references. The *Encyclopédie ou dictionnaire raisonné des sciences, des arts et des metiers,* or *Encyclopédie,* was one of the most influential works of the eighteenth century. Denis Diderot, French encyclopedist and philosopher, was invited to edit a French translation of Chambers' Cyclopaedia. Diderot and Jean Le Rond d'Alembert, a mathematician, converted the project into a vast, new, and controversial 35-volume work, which began publication in 1751. The famous French Larousse encyclopedias date from 1865, and the first noteworthy American encyclopedia, the *Encyclopedia Americana*, from 1829 to 1833.[12] Encyclopedias increased in usefulness in the nineteenth and twentieth centuries as knowledge in various fields grew more complex and specialized.

A discussion about encyclopedic efforts to contain the whole circle of knowledge would be incomplete without reference to the *Encyclopaedia Britannica* and its interesting history. Its reputation as the best among English-language encyclopedias is probably due more to effective marketing

---

11. Stockwell, 27.
12. *http://encyclozine.com/knowledge/encyclopedias/* (October 9, 2001).

than to content. Just as printing brought encyclopedias and other books out of the monasteries and into the hands of those who had money to purchase them, the new promotional techniques developed during the Industrial Revolution brought encyclopedias into the homes of almost every family, even those families with little or no interest in reading.[13] Published in 1768 as a small, pamphlet-sized booklet in Edinburgh, Scotland, it covered but a few topics of subject matter alphabetized under A. Thereafter, it was followed each week by another booklet, until the one hundredth installment appeared with instructions on how to bind all the pamphlets into a book.

Computer Memory

A more recent creation for physically storing and manipulating information is the computer. Computing has produced extraordinary technological and societal change in a remarkably brief time. The pace of virtually all aspects of life in the developed world has increased exponentially as a consequence, and almost inconceivable volumes of data are generated, stored, and freely roam the earth electronically.

When computers were first introduced into the workplace in the 1950s, humanitarians feared that these machines would make humans obsolete. Of course, we now know that the opposite is true. The computer industry has expanded into a colossal, global phenomenon, employing millions and generating trillions of dollars of economic activity.

Over the past 60-plus years, the computer has evolved from a roomful of vacuum tubes and wires capable of executing perhaps half a million instructions per second into a microchip of about 1 square centimeter or less that works 25 times faster. The history of computing makes for compelling reading, for it is fraught with debate over who should wear the moniker "Father of the Computer," but it is British mathematician Charles Babbage (1791–1871) who is generally credited with the idea of a digital computer.[14] Babbage spent a large part of his fortune meticulously designing his Analytical Engine, a device for solving logarithmic tables. With the help of his partner, Augusta Ada Byron, Babbage's machine, although never completed, was remarkably similar to the modern computer. Its three parts closely resemble the computer architecture of the machine's descendents: "the

---

13. Stockwell, 111.
14. Charles Babbage, *Microsoft Encarta Encyclopedia 2000 Deluxe*.

store," where all the variables were stored and where the answers resided (our current-day memory); "the mill," where the calculations were made (central processing unit [CPU]); and "internal information," or numerical data.

Babbage's machine was really more of an advanced calculator than a computer. Yet it took another British genius, Alan Turing, to envision the revolutionary concept of a machine with no fixed purpose, one that could perform one or several different tasks at the owner's command.[15] His machine, now known as a Turing machine, was intended to be used as a "universal machine" that could be programmed to duplicate the function of any other existing computing or processing machine.

It was during World War II—when machines were needed to make calculations that could be used for aiming anti-aircraft guns, breaking secret codes, and calculating ballistic artillery tables—that computer development flourished. With financial support from International Business Machines (IBM), Howard Aiken and Grace Hopper began designing the MARK series of computers at Harvard University in 1944. Used by the U.S. Navy for gunnery and ballistic calculations, the Mark I was in operation until 1959.

In 1946, electrical engineer John Mauchly and physicist John Presper Eckert developed the ENIAC I (Electrical Numerical Integrator and Calculator) at the Moore School of Electrical Engineering, University of Pennsylvania. Sponsored by the U.S. military, the ENIAC I was the first large-scale, general-purpose electronic computer.[16]

During these years, perhaps the most important of computer advances came from the work of John Von Neumann, a Hungarian mathematician who emigrated to the United States and worked at the Moore School. In 1945 he published his concept of a technique for storing a computer program in the machine's memory in "First Draft of a Report on the EDVAC (Electronic Discrete Variable Automatic Computer)." Electronic storage of programming information and data eliminated the need for more clumsy methods of programming, such as punched paper tape. His concept has characterized mainstream computer development ever since.

One of the factors that initially created demand for computing in the late 1940s was the rise in labor costs and the increase in government paperwork. U.S. President Franklin D. Roosevelt's New Deal, with its flurry of

---

15. Stockwell, 162.
16. Robert Lemos, "ENIAC: Calculated History of the Computer," *ZDNET News* from ZDWire (June 9, 1999).

public welfare programs, put an administrative burden on government and business that made computers essential. In addition, the Korean War and the rocket race in the 1950s fueled the need for higher performance machines and helped advance the computer for the commercial marketplace.[17] It was during this time that two things occurred: the UNIVAC, an important fore-runner of today's computers, appeared on the scene, and IBM made the leap from punch-card processing to computers.

As it relates to information management, computers provide storage for vast amounts of data in huge databases that make even the most complete libraries seem small by comparison. Early electronic computers in the late 1940s and early 1950s used cathode ray tubes (CRTs) to store data. (See Figure 1-5.) A typical CRT held 128 bytes, and the entire memory of such a computer was usually 4 kilobytes.[18]

Figure 1-5   *An early cathode ray tube used in computers*

17. Linda Runyan, "40 Years on the Frontier," *Datamation* (March 15, 1991), 35.
18. Computer Memory, *Microsoft Encarta Encyclopedia 2000 Deluxe*.

IBM developed magnetic core memory in the early 1950s. Magnetic core (often just called core) memory consisted of tiny rings of magnetic material woven into meshes of thin wires. Computer manufacturers first used core memory in computers in the 1960s, at about the same time that they began to replace vacuum tubes with transistors. Magnetic core memory was used through most of the 1960s and into the 1970s.[19]

The next step in the development of computer memory came with the introduction of integrated circuits that enabled multiple transistors to be placed on one chip. (See Figure 1-6.) Computer scientists developed the first such memory when they constructed an experimental supercomputer in the late 1960s. Integrated circuit memory quickly displaced core memory and has been the dominant technology for internal memory ever since.

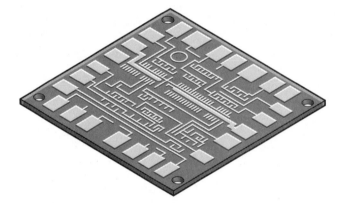

Figure 1-6   *An integrated circuit*

Since the inception of computer memory, the capacity of both internal and external memory devices has grown steadily at a rate that has quadrupled in size every three years.[20] (Computer industry analysts expect this rapid rate of growth to continue unimpeded. In the future computers will have to process hundreds of gigabytes and even terabytes of information—much more than any current CDs or DVD-ROMs can accommodate. Researchers are currently exploring holographic and molecular memory systems, using holographic images and protein molecules called bacteriorhodopsins, respectively, to store vast quantities of data.[21]

19. Computer Memory, *Microsoft Encarta Encyclopedia 2000 Deluxe.*
20. Computer Memory, *Microsoft Encarta Encyclopedia 2000 Deluxe.*
21. Maksim Len, "Memory of the Future: Two Directions," *Digit Life (http://www.digit-life.com/articles/memory/twodirections/index.html,* January 7, 2002).

When considering these examples of early objects for storing information in the light of intranet developments, the parallels are striking. Whereas early leaders, scholars, and merchants entrusted the safekeeping of their knowledge to parchment scrolls, printed books, encyclopedias, and libraries, today it is stored in secure databases, on servers, and made accessible through intranets.

Humankind Perceives Value in Collections of Knowledge

Most organizations realize that the management of knowledge resources as intellectual capital is vital to their success. This realization is directly responsible for the colossal level of investment in knowledge-management applications over the past five years.[22] Intranets are essential tools in the collecting, managing, storing, and sharing of the knowledge assets within an organization.

With the first written works came the need for a place to keep them—a place where they could be protected and preserved, used when needed, and then handed down to future generations—libraries. The first libraries were early examples of knowledge management systems. Myths in some traditions contend that libraries even predated human beings. The gods of Egypt, Greece, Persia, India, and Scandinavia were said to have had their own manuscript collections. Whether or not this is true, at all levels of society and over a very long time, individuals and institutions have made the collection of information and knowledge a high priority.

Much of our knowledge of Babylonian civilization comes from the Library of Borsippa's tablets, which were copied and preserved in the library of King Ashurbanipal of Assyria.[23] Our knowledge of Egyptian libraries is scant, but there are references to temple and royal libraries as early as the twenty-fifth century B.C. From the seventh and sixth centuries B.C., only fragments of literature from Greece remain, but we know there were libraries in Athens and Samos in the sixth century B.C. Early scholars also refer to the

---

22. Brent Thrill and John Torry, *Corporate Portals: Leveraging 51 Years of Software Investments* (Boston: Credit Suisse First Boston, May 31, 2001), 3.
23. Gates, 10.

libraries of Euripides and others in the fifth century B.C., when the civilization of ancient Greece reached its golden age under Pericles. It was a time
that saw the spread of reading as a pastime and the development of the book
trade. Aristotle (384–322 B.C.) is said to have been the first person to collect,
preserve, and use the culture of the past. His own library had an interesting
history, being passed down to relatives, hidden from manuscript-gathering
kings, sold to Apellicon of Teos for a large sum of money, and then confiscat-
ed in the conquering of Athens in 86 B.C. by Sulla.[24]

The most important libraries of ancient Greece were established in the
Hellenistic Age (approximately 300 B.C. to A.D. 300), a period that was characterized by the spread of Greek learning and culture through the conquests of
Alexander and his successors, the building of Greek cities, and the development of monarchial government.

Greek influence over the cultural and intellectual life of the Roman people was well established by the time the Romans conquered Greece in
146 B.C. Private libraries became an important feature of Roman civilization
when generals began to bring back entire libraries as spoils of war from campaigns in Greece.

During the third century A.D., the body of Christian literature had materially increased, and Christian libraries had been established in many places
throughout the Roman Empire. After the fall of the western part of the
Roman Empire to barbarian invaders in 476, learning and literature
declined, leaving only monasteries and Christian libraries as repositories of
culture and education in Western Europe.

While the western part of the Roman Empire succumbed to invaders, the
eastern part enjoyed a period of vitality and progress that was to last almost
a thousand years. In the Byzantine Empire, Constantine established the
imperial library in Constantinople, emphasizing the collection of Latin
works. (Latin was the official language until the sixth century.) His successors enriched the library with the additions of Christian and pagan works, in
both Latin and Greek, and employed scribes to copy manuscripts. By the
fifth century the imperial library had some 120,000 volumes, the largest
book collection in Europe.

During the eighth and ninth centuries, when the study and production
of secular literature was at a standstill in Constantinople, Baghdad became a

24. Gates, 13–14.

center of Greek learning and education. A "house of wisdom" was created in 830 by Abbasid Al-Mamum, as institution that combined the functions of a library, a university, and a translation bureau.[25] While the rest of the world was still writing on papyrus and parchment, with the exception of China, papermaking and book production flourished in Baghdad. In addition to private collections, libraries were set up in mosques and in all colleges. In the Library of Shiraz, founded in the later half of the tenth century, books were listed in catalogs, arranged in cases, and administered by regular staff to facilitate easy access and sharing.[26]

The golden age of libraries in Europe is considered to be sometime between the 1600s and the 1700s: the Bodlein Library at Oxford University (1598+), the library of the British Museum (1759), the Mazarine Library in Paris (1643), and the State Public Library of St. Petersburg (late 1700s). The first American library, the Harvard Library, was established in 1638. None of these early libraries were, at first, free. The books were so expensive that chains were used to attach them to shelves or desks to protect them from theft. Books could only be borrowed and taken from the institutions after depositing goods or money equal to the value of the book.

The collection of information or knowledge has long been a prestigious activity of the wealthy. A true Renaissance man is someone who knows a great deal about many subjects. The manifestation of that interest was often the private library. The great merchants of Renaissance Italy amassed great libraries of manuscripts and, later, books. Most wealthy and noble families of Britain owned libraries with thousands of volumes, as did plantation owners along the James River in Virginia in the 1600s and 1700s, despite living at the edge of a violent and rustic frontier.[27]

In the late nineteenth century, steel magnate Andrew Carnegie endowed hundreds of public libraries. In the 1990s Bill Gates, one of the wealthiest men in the world, and his wife established the Gates Library Foundation with a donation of $200 million. The Foundation will to help half of the 17,000 public library branches in the United States and Canada gain or improve access to computer resources and the Internet.[28]

---

25. Gates, 25.
26. Gates, 26.
27. Cortada, 7.
28. "Bill, Melinda Gates Deserve Our Thanks," Editorial, *The Seattle Times* (June 30, 1997), B4.

Every Major Institution in Society Has Collected, Preserved, and Exploited Information

By 2003 it is estimated that almost 100 percent of large companies (5000-plus employees) and 85 percent of midsized companies (1000 to 4999 employees) will have intranets for the purpose of collecting, preserving, and sharing their accumulated intellectual capital.[29]

Throughout history various national governments of Europe and Asia, and (more recently) large, geographically dispersed industries such as railways and large-scale manufacturing, have demonstrated that information is a prerequisite for control and expansion of operations. These institutions have always been the first in line for new information tools. The Catholic Church was incontestably the largest buyer of manuscripts and books for centuries, and every major government in the world for the past 2000 years has supported centers of knowledge such as universities, libraries, and national archives. China's civil servants were responsible for establishing the country's first libraries, which the officials used for their own pleasure and the pleasure of their relatives.

Every large and complex society has had what today are called centers of learning. Priests taught seminarians around the world, often creating new knowledge in the process in such diverse fields as agriculture, business, medicine, science, administrative practices, and military tactics and strategies.[30] The basis of these centers was to consolidate large bodies of knowledge and then use them to disseminate information through education, research, business, and consulting. Jesuit priests advised the emperors of the Hapsburg Empire in the 1600s, and today consultants from McKinsey, PricewaterhouseCoopers, and Accenture serve a similar function for CEOs of corporations.

Humankind Needs to Organize Knowledge to Assure Access

To use knowledge effectively and increase productivity, companies are relying on intranets to integrate, organize, and present mission-critical information to every desktop.

---

29. *IDC Intranet/Extranet Factbook 2000* (IDC, March 2000).
30. Cortada, 8.

In addition to the ingenuity with which we have created writing systems, writing materials, libraries, and encyclopedias, humankind has very cleverly dealt with the problem of organizing knowledge. For the Babylonian library of King Ashurbanipal, with its tens of thousand of clay tablets, organization was important. Tablets were tagged for identification and arranged by subject or type in alcoves, with a list of the contents of each alcove painted or carved on the entrance to serve as a catalog. Another early example of "information organization" was found in a Egyptian library at Edfu, where a list of the contents of all the works given to the temple priests was painted on the walls.

To keep track of the voluminous written works, the imperial Chinese court devised an elaborate classification scheme. Introduced as early as the first century B.C., it arranged the works into seven divisions. Later, in the third century A.D., a modified fourfold scheme was introduced: classics, philosophy, history, and belles lettres.

The purpose for which an encyclopedia is designed has a great deal to do with the way its text is arranged. Ancient and medieval encyclopedias were invariably arranged in a methodical way because their compilers planned them as educational tools. Designed to be read from start to finish, they provided a systematic approach to large subjects, such as God, science, literature, philosophy, and the like. Harris's *Lexicon technicum* was one of the first to be alphabetically organized. It was a popular format because of its ease of use for reference purposes, but looking up information this way appalled Samuel Taylor Coleridge, who "cried out against such an arrangement determined by the accident of initial letters."[31] Coleridge believed that fragmentation led to much repetition of information.

As the number of books increased in early libraries, so did the need to devise a rational system to organize them. For his own library, Thomas Jefferson borrowed Francis Bacon's system of classification. Books were placed in one of three categories: history, poetry, and philosophy. After Jefferson's books were purchased for the Library of Congress, this classification system remained in use, with a few modifications, until the end of the nineteenth century.

The American librarian Melville Dewey developed the Dewey decimal system, which first appeared in 1873 at Amherst College in Amherst,

---

31. Stockwell, 99.

Massachusetts. It has become a popular classification arrangement used around the world and divides books into 10 major categories, each represented by a three-decimal number between 000 and 999. Each of the 10 major groups is subdivided into more specialized groupings. Other methods to organize books include the Library of Congress classification system, devised by Howard Putnam. Based on 21 major divisions with numerous subdivisions, it was designed to handle the huge volume of books in this library.

Organizing other materials, particularly magazine and newspaper articles, was a problem of even greater complexity—we all know that article titles rarely indicate their true subject matter. One of the first acceptable periodical indexes was developed in 1847 by John Edmands, a student-librarian, to help his fellow students at Yale find debating material. The Edmands Index was the precursor of the well-known and currently available *Reader's Guide to Periodical Literature.*

In the age of the Internet, we have seen several different attempts to organize its collective knowledge. There are Web directories, search engines, and metasearch engines that attempt to arrange and facilitate access to the information on the millions of public Web pages and private intranets. Web directories slot Web pages into predefined categories and subcategories and offer the user a hierarchical approach to information gathering. A search engine compiles lists of sites that match a user query. A metasearch engine attempts to simultaneously search several search engine archives and match a query with lists of sites.

The emerging field of content management also testifies to this basic human need to organize information. Content management encompasses all business practices and technical processes that are performed for the purpose of capturing, maintaining, sharing, and preserving recorded meaning.[32] As the repositories of unstructured text grow, both on the public Web and private intranets, simple search engines continue to fail to meet all information-retrieval needs of users. Search results with thousands of hits, irrelevant and outdated content, and inflexible search protocols are just a few of these failings. Managing content metadata (essential aspects of text, such as main topics, author, language, and publication and revision dates that are assigned to the text and are searchable), profiling users, controlling access, support-

---

32. Dan Sullivan, "Five Principles of Intelligent Content Management," *Intelligent Enterprise* (August 31, 2001), 28.

ing complex search strategies, and automatically gathering content are becoming essential elements in managing text-based resources.

The document and content management features of intranets are making the knowledge resources of an organization much more discoverable, accessible, and usable, which reduce the squandering of organizational knowledge and bring about process efficiencies.

Summary

The human behaviors observed and described in the preceding pages contribute to our understanding of the interaction between man and knowledge, including the value and opportunity intranets present. From earliest civilizations humankind has demonstrated that it values knowledge; has devised systems and tools to record it; has built structures to protect it; and has formulated ways to organize, access, and share it. Today's intranets are the most sophisticated byproducts of this interdependency between man and knowledge.

The next chapter begins an examination of intranets in general and discusses what they are, what they can do, and how they function.

Intranets 101

Nothing in the recent history of computing has had as great an influence on organizational productivity than the Internet. Most organizations have found some way to link their employees, customers, and business partners via the Internet. This includes a wide range of activities and services, such as promotion, advertising, online sales, customer service, shipment, and much more. Internet usage by organizations and their knowledge workers has burgeoned appreciably over the past few years, and industry trends indicate that most companies not already plugged into the Internet are likely to be connected in the near future. Simultaneously, inside organizations, the intranet has had a sweeping impact on organizational productivity, fundamentally changing the way organizations create, share, process, receive, retrieve, and disseminate information.

The term *intranet* is of fairly recent coinage, deriving from the prefix *intra* (meaning "within") as opposed to *inter* (meaning "between"). Hence an intranet is a network within a community, and the Internet is a network between several communities. One of the earliest known printed references to the term *intranet* is in an article in *Digital News and Review* by then editor-in-chief Stephen Lawton. In this article Lawton discusses Fortune 1000 companies posting Web pages and using other Internet technologies behind the firewall.

> Vendors say they are seeing substantial growth in corporate Internets—or intranets—where groups ranging from individuals and product teams to corporate departments are posting Web pages and installing telnet and ftp servers. This is becoming particularly true at Fortune 1000 companies. . . . In many cases, intranets have grown . . . in ways that emulate the public, capital "I" Internet. . . .[1]

Some of the early pioneers of intranets were the Boeing Company, Schlumberger Ltd., Weyerhauser, and Digital Equipment Corporation. After getting their feet wet with public Web sites that promoted company products and services, these companies seized upon intranets as a swift way to streamline, and even transform, their organizations.

---

1. Stephen Lawton, "Intranets Fuel Growth of Internet Access Tools," *Digital News and Review* (April 24, 1995).

Access to business applications through Web-based technology has been possible in organizations since the 1990s. However, the organizational use of intranets is in the stages of a critical evolution as it moves from publishing static content to facilitating collaborative, interactive, and transactional environments and processes.

In this chapter we will define intranets, introduce the technologies that made them possible, explore their evolving nature, and describe the characteristics of "next generation" intranet solutions.

Intranets Defined

An intranet is a private knowledge network that provides secure collective access to integrated information, services, business applications, and communications. While the Internet and intranets share the same technologies, the biggest differences between the two are ownership and access. The Internet is not owned by any one person or entity. Anyone with access to a computer and a modem can connect to the Internet directly or via an Internet service provider (ISP). An intranet is a private knowledge network that is owned by an organization and accessed collectively by permission only.

There are other ways to describe intranets. A technical definition might look like this: an intranet is a heterogeneous computing environment connecting different hardware platforms, operating systems, environments, and user interfaces that allow for seamless communicating, collaborating, transacting, broadcasting, and innovating. An organizational definition might look like this: an intranet is a learning tool capable of integrating people, processes, procedures, and principles to form an intellectually creative culture dedicated to enhancing organizational effectiveness.[2] Any way you describe it, to understand the function and value of an intranet in an organization, you must first understand its components.

Nuts, Bolts, Bits, and Bytes

Intranets are built with technology borrowed from the client/server computing environment—which makes use of "distributed intelligence," where data

---

2. Randy Hinrichs, *Intranets: What's the Bottom Line?* (New York: Prentice-Hall, 1997), 11.

and the pieces of software required to manipulate data are spread out, shared, or otherwise distributed across a network—and Internet protocols. A more in-depth description of client/server architecture is provided in Chapter 4, "Business and Technological Drivers."

Client/Server Networking

An intranet runs on the same hardware as other client/server networks—routers, switches, wires, and cables—as well as client and server computers. Client machines (front-end devices, often desktops) make requests of network resources through servers (back-end machines). Servers store, manage, and deliver information for a private network. They can be dedicated to a specific task, such as mail service, or can be partitioned for several uses according to the types of server software installed.

What really makes client/server networking work is the software, on both the client and server sides of an intranet. The server has software to manage its functions and perform special management and administrative services. Examples include Microsoft Exchange Server and Microsoft SharePoint Portal Server. Client software varies according to the needs of the user. A browser such as Microsoft Internet Explorer or a productivity application such as Microsoft Office is a client program that can communicate requests to the server and display the retrieved information to the user.

Client/server computing has two primary characteristics: centralized file sharing and remote procedure call (RPC). RPC is the process of connecting the client to the server to execute a specific task. The intranet performs both of these functions using Internet protocols—a significant advancement that blends highly structured client/server computing with the flexibility of the Internet.

A variety of controls, scripts (a list of commands that can be executed without user interaction), plug-ins (small programs that plug into a Web browser and are activated when needed to handle a special function such as video, audio, and animation), and other small programs (applets) fall under the heading of specialty software. Some examples of specialty software components used in client/server and intranet environments include ActiveX controls (reusable software components that add specific functionality quickly, such as a stock ticker), Java scripts (used to link and automate a wide variety of objects on Web pages, including ActiveX controls and applets), and digital media such as Microsoft Windows Media Player.

Intranet Technology Basics

The original purpose of the Internet was to link together disparate types of computers and file formats in a high-speed, secure network. Data exchange protocols accomplished this by enabling vastly different computers with different operating systems to speak a common language.

An intranet offers the opportunity to achieve full integration across an organization's network through Internet-based protocols, browsers, server software, and development tools. Products that are built based on Internet protocols can interact with any other product constructed to the same standards. Typical Internet protocols used on an intranet include the following:

- TCP/IP (Transmission Control Protocol/Internet Protocol)—a stack of protocols that form the foundation of internetworking, which includes breaking messages into data packets, assigning numeric addresses, placing data packets into secure envelopes, and ensuring delivery

- HTTP (Hypertext Transfer Protocol)—provides for the movement of text and graphics

- SMTP (Simple Mail Transfer Protocol)—a protocol for handling e-mail messages over TCP/IP networks

In addition to these protocols, three additional conventions are essential for Web-based communications:

- URL (universal resource locator)—a uniform addressing system

- HTML (Hypertext Markup Language)—the language used to create documents that a Web browser can display plus some of its offspring, including VRML[3], XML, and XHTML[4]

- XML (Extensible Markup Language)—a widely used language for defining data formats for Web documents that allows designers to create their own customized tags, enabling the definition, transmission, validation, and interpretation of data

---

3. VRML is a language for displaying three-dimensional objects on the Web—a three-dimensional equivalent of HTML.
4. XHTML (Extensible Hypertext Markup Language) is a hybrid between HTML and XML specifically designed for Internet device displays.

Evolving Intranets

Intranets often begin as information-sharing networks and then evolve into profound changes in the business process. Intranets support real and complex business applications as well as simple data dissemination. The best intranets typically mature from departmental tools through which reports and data are made available to a small group of workers into vast unified systems that integrate business applications and knowledge warehouses and provide for collaboration and communication between all participants along the supply and demand chain. Intranets open up data resources, corporate processes, and knowledge applications to a broader base of users. As intranets evolve, they usually begin to focus on knowledge creation in addition to knowledge storage and access.

Intranets began as basic Web pages shared among a few technically inclined individuals and departments. These people educated a few others, and new horizons were soon perceived. Cross-functional teams sprang up, and suddenly a general awareness regarding paradigm shifts and twenty-first century business needs and processes replaced industrial attitudes. With each level of evolution, new capabilities were discovered and innovations applied.

The three levels of intranet evolution—publishing intranet, collaborative intranet, and next generation intranet—are listed in Table 2-1, including a brief description and their architecture, impact on people and processes, cost considerations, and limitations. (These characteristics will be addressed as we move through the next chapters.) As each level is attained within an organization, awareness grows about what is possible. Cross-functional teams are born, and old paradigms and business processes give way to new ones. Few intranets of the publishing or collaborative models are being built today; the focus now is on next generation intranets, and it will remain so in the years to come.

In their earliest forms, intranets were characterized by a one-way publishing model: information was submitted to a Webmaster for publication on a company's intranet. This model was well suited for the dissemination of static, paper-intensive, and administrative information such as employee handbooks, telephone and e-mail directories, medical benefits packages and forms, newsletters, training materials, and the like. Eventually users within organizations needed to collaborate in teams and share documents,

Table 2–1   Intranet Evolution[5]

	Publishing Intranet	Collaborative Intranet	Next Generation Intranet
Description	Production and access to company documents and online resources. Static.	Interdepartmental and departmental group sites and pages. Centralized intranet home-page. Advanced tool set. Dynamic.	Web-based collaborative team services. Portal for information management and discovery. Broadcast communications to employee desktops. Dynamic. Business process integration. Uses Java, XML, ActiveX, and other application programming interfaces. Dynamic.
Architecture	Basics plus publishing and document management software, search engine, and database integration facilities.	Full service intranet with directory, file, print, and mail capabilities. Integrated with project management software and e-mail systems.	Dedicated, differentiated multifunction intranet servers. Secure business process and corporate database integration. Real-time digital media broadcast functionality, including server configuration, scheduling, production, delivery, and archive of broadcast events.
Impact on People and Processes	Requires publishers, editors, and writers. Needs processes for submitting work.	Requires sophisticated infrastructure, a cross-functional Web council, Webmaster, gate-	Enables knowledge workplace. Empowers individual workers by removing Webmaster intermediary. Efficiency improvements achieved via faster, better

5. Adapted from Randy Hinrichs, "What's an Intranet?" in *Intranets: What's the Bottom Line?* (New York: Prentice Hall, 1997), 13–14.

	A centralized Web site acts as a central point of contact.	keeper, application programmers, and content providers. Needs templates, guidelines, and principles for doing business.	informed decision making, increased collaboration, and improved employee satisfaction. Process improvements via enhanced customer and partner collaboration, business process integration, and rapid access to dynamic business information.
Cost Considerations	Employee costs and tools. Increase in equipment and process.	Exponential increase in overall operating costs. Development costs are key.	Reduces costs by removing intermediaries, empowering the user to perform tasks previously requiring administrative support and easily integrating with existing systems. Rapid return on investment (ROI).

designs, and proposals, leading to the emergence of a new model for intranets. As additional ways to use intranets were devised—some companies were building dozens of project, team, and department-based intranets—their size and complexity grew. The task of mining organizational knowledge was daunting, even impossible, with no or limited search and navigation tools. As described in Chapter 1, people have continuously invented ways to improve information storage, access, and distribution and address the shortcomings of previous methods and technologies. Current intranet developments affirm this behavior and reveal the next phase in the technology cycle.

Technological advances have yielded the next generation intranet. Knowledge workers have come to expect the same performance, navigation and search tools, and personalization from their intranet as from sophisticated sites such as Amazon.com and eTrade.com. Next generation intranets deliver rapid access to information and the tools to organize and share knowledge efficiently—all in a familiar Web-based collaborative productivity environment.

Next Generation Intranets

Three core bundles of functions form the foundation of next generation intranets:

- Web-based collaborative team services
- Portals for information management and discovery
- Broadcast delivery of business communications to the desktop

   These functions are discussed in the following sections.

Collaborative Team Services

Intranets can ease the predilection toward isolationist and noncollaborative behavior in organizations. Politics and competition are only a part of this widespread problem. Collaboration has also been limited by the absence of enabling technology. Intranets provide the tools to encourage team collaboration, allowing workers to

- Collaborate on the Web with an easy browser user interface and a highly structured design that achieves simplified information discovery.
- Create and manage dynamic preformatted lists, communicate important information, synchronize activities, share contacts, and manage processes.
- Enhance output with productivity application integration by opening, saving, and uploading documents and managing contacts and events in a unified environment.
- Share content with ease via document libraries, thus ensuring uniformity through templates, controlling properties to enforce information specification, and providing automatic updates with subscription and notifications.
- Collaborate with the team, using inline document discussions, routing of documents for review, discussion boards, and online surveys.
- Manage participation, via Web-based site administration, e-mail invitations, flexible roles-based security and permissions, and tracking tools.

- Customize sites easily using browser drag and drop; filter by a set of criteria; sort, display, or hide columns; and create unique pages for custom lists and document libraries.

Information Management and Discovery

From the point of view of information technology (IT) managers, information needs to be acquired, organized, and distributed. From the point of view of knowledge workers, the main issue is access—getting the right information, when it is needed, wherever it resides. The central processes of intranets—acquiring, organizing, reviewing, editing, classifying, and distributing information—allow workers to

- Easily manage documents where they create them by utilizing a complete set of document management functionality accessible directly from the productivity application as well as the browser.

- Simplify document creation, review, and publishing: controlling documents with check-in/check-out, profiling, security, and versioning; establishing approval processes from within the document; and ensuring consistency with shared tasks, lists, documents, and calendars.

- Profile documents for superior discovery: classifying efficiently with customizable and reusable profile templates and correlating consistently with data describing the documents (meta data) and keywords.

Broadcast Delivery of Business Communications

Organizations must be able to respond rapidly to change, speed time to market, and deliver current news and updated information to a geographically dispersed workforce. Global events shake economies, competitive factors change, business strategies are altered, new products are introduced, and employees need rapid training. "Time-to-knowledge" is critical in responding quickly and appropriately to change. Increasingly, enterprises are using digital media to communicate rapidly, efficiently, and effectively to a wide range of audiences. When any one of Hewlett-Packard Company's 90,000 employees log on to the computers, they can go to their intranet and view a broadcast of chairman and CEO Carly Fiorina giving an update on corporate performance, reporting executive council proceedings, or sharing other relevant news.

Broadcast capabilities constitute a key element of next generation intranets, delivering

- Improved employee productivity with easily accessible real-time audio and video communications, automatically archived and searchable for on-demand viewing from the portal

- Cost reductions via economies on travel, events, or CD replication and increase ROI through delivery of supplementary services on existing infrastructure

- Management, production, and delivery of live broadcasts; scheduling of events on a central calendar to manage resources; productivity application integration; and the use of digital media to produce and deliver audio and/or video broadcasts optimized for any bandwidth

- Automated broadcast production and delivery with a straightforward process, automatically archiving to the portal upon conclusion

- Customization for interactivity such as chat, polling, and quizzes as well as rich-media presentations that include synchronized presentation graphics program slides or images

In combination, these three elements—collaborative team services, information management and discovery, and broadcast delivery of business communications—strengthen the intelligence and capabilities of the workforce as its members develop, disseminate, and support products and services.

Portals

The word *portal* has been integrated into Internet terminology in recent years. Corporate portals, enterprise information or application portals, and business intelligence portals are just some of the specific usages, but what really is a portal? A portal is a kind of Web site that acts as a starting point for many other sites and/or collections of information. Understood in this sense, the term originated when large, well-known Internet search engines expanded their sites to include e-mail, news, stock quotes, and an array of other functions. Some corporations took a similar approach in designing their intranet sites, which then became known as enterprise or corporate portals. "Fundamentally, corporate portals represent a Web- and role-based interface to multiple inter- and intra-enterprise applications, documents, and collaboration and community services."[6] Simply put, portals create a single point of access to aggregated information.

The portal concept has been applied to general aggregations on the Web (Internet portals), private network sites (intranet portals), and specialized online communities of interest (vertical portals, or vortals[7]). Technically speaking, a portal site includes a start page with rich navigational capability and a collection of loosely integrated features, some of which may be provided by partners or third parties. The target audience is large and diverse. The term *portal* has become a colloquialism for essentially any complex Web site involving such elements as

- Information sharing, discovery, management, and delivery
- Document management services
- Customization at the desktop

Judith Rosall, an analyst with the Aberdeen Group, has asserted that the portal is an extension of intranets.[8] A company's intranet is the structure that stores knowledge, just as a library holds books; and the portal is the conduit or index to that knowledge, just as the old card catalogue was to books on library shelves. See Chapter 3 for a more in-depth look at portals.

Extranets

One of the important new intranet strategies involves the opening up of the information on intranets to suppliers, customers, and business partners, who can then securely access select parts of internal corporate information. These "extended intranets," or extranets, can be used to access live, relational corporate databases that can be updated via a corporate intranet. Extranets simply provide secure access to certain data by certain outside users, just as intranets limit access to certain data to employees in an organization.

---

6. Brent Thill and John Torrey, *Corporate Portals: Leveraging 5+ Years of Software Investments* (Credit Suisse First Boston, May 31, 2001), 7.
7. A vortal is a portal Web site that provides information and resources for a particular topic. Vortals are the Internet's way of catering to special interests, typically providing news, research and statistics, discussions, newsletters, online tools, and many other services that educate users about a specific topic.
8. Erich Luening, "Software Firms Cash In on Portal Trend," *CNET News.com* (*http://news.cnet.com/news/0-1003-202-345390.html,* July 27, 1999).

The real benefit of an extranet is its ability to bring together all the members of an extended enterprise. A Web site no longer serves just as an authorized conglomeration of facts and data applications but as a focal point for business transactions. Bringing suppliers, partners, and even customers into the information loop is critical to productivity. A well-designed extranet can connect all businesses in a company's supply chain regardless of their locations.

The Demand for Intranets

Increasingly, organizations are building intranets. By the end of 2000, nearly 90 percent of large organizations had some type of intranet.[9] This is because corporate users have the most to gain from the internal use of Web technology as a multiplatform information-dissemination and application-deployment vehicle. By 2003 almost 100 percent of large companies (5000-plus employees) and 85 percent of midsized companies (1000 to 4999 employees) will have intranets. Large companies were the early adopters of intranet technology, and they have proven the productivity and cost-reduction benefits of having an open and homogeneous platform that allows access to collaborative and knowledge-management applications. See Section 3 for more information on how intranets create value.

For a variety of reasons—resources, expertise, awareness—smaller and midsized businesses, as well as educational and governmental institutions, have been slower to invest in intranets, but according to a study by Modalis Research Technologies, this is rapidly changing. Small and midsized businesses are highly interested in intranets as a knowledge-mining and productivity tool. According to an article in *Internet World,* only 4 percent of these companies had intranets, but 39 percent said they were very interested in building one.[10]

Of non-intranet-based organizations, more than 70 percent have expressed a desire to change to an intranet-based environment.[11] Organizations have come to realize that it is cost effective to invest in an intranet infrastructure, or to enhance an existing one, because they can

---

9. Susan Stellin, "Intranets Nurture Companies from the Inside" (*New York Times*, January 29, 2001), 4.
10. "Interest in Intranets" (March 1, 2001), 7.
11. *Intranet-Related Hardware, Software, and Services—A U.S. Market Trend Report* (Global Industry Analysts, March 1, 2001), 3.

Table 2–2   Total U.S. Intranet-Related Hardware, Software, and Services Sales[12]

Annual Projections/Estimates 1999 to 2005, $US millions

Year	1999	2000	2001	2002	2003	2004	2005
Sales	21,500	30,390	43,203	60,626	84,732	119,336	169,684
Percent Growth		41.35	42.16	40.33	69.76	40.84	42.19

more easily extend the reach of their business processes to remote users, customers, partners, and suppliers.

Sales of intranet-related hardware, software, and services initially experienced tremendous growth—between 80 percent and 90 percent per year—but demand had stabilized by 1999. It is expected that between 2001 and 2005, growth will average 40 percent to 45 percent per year. The total U.S. market for intranet-related hardware, software, and services was valued at $21.5 billion in 1999; industry analysts predict sales at almost $170 billion by 2005. (See Table 2-2.)

In a June 2001 report from Merrill Lynch, the enterprise portal software market was estimated at $2.328 billion, with a calculated annual growth rate of 49.5 percent. Further, Delphi, a market research firm specializing in the IT marketplace, has forecast that 70 percent of Fortune 500 companies will have deployed portals by 2002.

Intranets were introduced as systems that could cut costs and transcend internal organizational boundaries. They are evolving into platforms that can simply make organizations smarter about themselves, their markets, and

Table 2–3   U.S. Employees with Intranet Access 1999 to 2003[13]

In Thousands

	1999	2000	2001	2002	2003	Calculated Annual Growth Rate (percent)
TOTAL	38,051	51,777	67,763	85,630	106,281	32.0

---

12. Intranet-Related Hardware, Software, and Services—A U.S. Market Trend Report (Global Industry Analysts, March 1, 2001), 3.

13. *IDC Intranet/Extranet Fact Book 2000* (IDC, March 2000).

their products. Behind the growth of intranets are legions of knowledge workers who have grown up with e-mail and collaborative applications and who are expecting more from intranet deployments in terms of intelligence and usability. As Table 2-3 shows, the number of intranet users is expected to reach more than 106 million by 2003.

Summary

The rise of the intranet is a natural aspect of the evolution that is spawning the knowledge workplace and its components: team collaboration, rapid access to business information, intuitive document management, and live or on-demand broadcast communication capabilities. Intranets are a natural confluence of computing, communication, and content.

If we revisit the observations made about humankind and our relationship to knowledge outlined in Chapter 1, the parallels with intranet development are patently obvious. Our knowledge-based economies collect and value information. The big difference, however, is that the volume of information collected is staggering. Intranets are the latest and perhaps most revolutionary tools designed to store our collected knowledge. They are the descendents of the encyclopedias and libraries of yesteryear. In this chapter we defined intranets, introduced the technologies that make them work, and described the characteristics of next generation intranets.

In our efforts to unify and organize the knowledge residing on intranets, to assure access by knowledge workers, portals were born. In the next chapter we will examine the features and functionality of portals and offer some examples of successful deployments.

The Portal: Gateway to a World of Knowledge

Today, business leaders are challenged to find better ways to harness their organization's intellectual capital. The executives at business media company Red Herring knew they needed a more efficient means to share company knowledge and collaborate on product development and deployment. They also knew they wanted applications and information, both external and internal, aggregated and accessible from the desktop, and a personalized interface to these resources.[1] What the executives needed was an intranet portal.

A portal facilitates the creation of a knowledge workspace by providing a single point of access—a virtual front door—to aggregated information. For maximum benefit the portal is tailored to an organization's particular needs, with a highly customizable start page providing rich navigational capability, along with Web-based and personalized interfaces to multiple applications, document libraries, and collaborative services. But most importantly, the portal must be simple, intuitive, and user centered.

In this chapter we will examine the features and functionality of portals and provide some examples of notable portal deployments to illustrate their value.

Portal Features and Functionality

A core component of the intranet, a portal organizes and integrates collective knowledge and communications and makes such knowledge and communications accessible and shareable. Portals allow users to easily find, share, and publish information and typically have the following features:

- A consistent view of the organization through the use of forms-based authoring of documents, lists, reports, directories, indexes, and pages

---

1. Jennifer Mears, "Portals: The New Business Desktop," *Network World* (May 21, 2001), 34.

- Powerful search and navigational capabilities for homogeneous cross-organizational discovery of relevant content

- Highly structured information categorization and document correlation—essential to the identification and retrieval of relevant search results

- Direct and rapid access to organizational data and knowledge as well as digital media communications through the integration of diverse business applications at the desktop

- Individual, secure, and role-based access to content

A portal integrates both dynamic and static information and communications from inside and outside an organization through a single user interface. It is the center of operations for the knowledge workplace, offering search, subscriptions, document management, and digital media services, as well as the integration of business process applications—all made accessible via a highly customizable, flexible user interface.

With the development of portals, users have been placed squarely in the driver's seat. Their experiences, skills, and needs are propelling us along the technology continuum. The knowledge workplace is no longer primarily driven by the "push" of the information technology (IT) department; rather it is the "pull" of the knowledge worker.[2]

Rapid and Secure Access to Business Information

Locating information in any organization can be challenging. In addition, wading through the different forms, file formats, and storage locations (documents on file servers, HTML pages on Web servers, or e-mail on messaging servers), plus finding what you need when you need it, can be difficult. Even if a server infrastructure allows searches across multiple locations and data stores, often only limited text searches are possible. People need a consistent place to access needed information, and in a structured way that makes

---

2. See Chapter 6 for an in-depth look at knowledge workers—who they are, where they come from, and how they are a fundamental component of the information age and the knowledge workplace.

sense. Portals have become the place where such information is aggregated, organized, shared, and discoverable.

Whether searching for something specific or just browsing through a group of related documents, portals make finding information easier with several features that make searching faster and more successful:

- A single location to search for information that has been stored in many different places, such as Web sites, file systems, public folders on mail servers, and various databases. Portals improve efficiency by indexing these diverse data and enable searching multiple information sources at one time from one place.

- Full-text keyword searches—these full-text search options find all documents that match the search terms and return lists of results. "Advanced" search options are often provided; these match search terms with the document's properties, such as author, for more specific and focused results.

- Browsing by topic—for users who are unfamiliar with where documents are stored, or what keywords to use in full text searching, browsing by categories makes information discovery more successful. It groups like documents and other content, irrespective of form or location. Portals often provide category creation wizards to simplify the time-consuming task of categorizing a large number of documents.

- Subscriptions—by subscribing to relevant content, users are notified about new or refreshed information on topics that match their interests—a personalized alert service at the desktop.

Intuitive Document Management

Everyone works with documents, but not everyone has the ability to use technology to structure how they work with their colleagues on these documents. The process from document creation through intranet publishing can be a string of disjointed actions, unconnected with business processes. A portal supports features such as document locking, versioning, check-in/checkout, and publishing and makes these features accessible to the average user.

It delivers simple, document-management features that are integrated with the tools and applications that are used to create and manage documents.

Large and complex information sources can be difficult to navigate and use because there is little or no organizational structure. File shares, for example, provide only a hierarchical directory structure as a means of organizing content. There is only one navigation path to any given document, and users must know the name of the server on which the document is stored, in addition to the directory structure of the folder(s) that contains the needed document. When you add in other sources of information, such as Web sites, e-mail servers, and databases, to the mix, finding the right content is nigh on to impossible.

In addition to difficulties in locating needed documents, the inability to share documents with others, control access, and publish documents in the organization is hampered without intuitive document management. Portals offer a number of features that help to streamline document management:

- Version tracking—version control records a document's history to help monitor changes and eliminate the possibility of someone over-writing another's modifications.

- Check-in and check-out—documents can be reserved by individual users for updating and this capability can prevent others from changing the document until it is "returned" to the workspace.

- Categories—content is classified under a set of user-defined categories for better information management and discoverability.

- Application of descriptive, searchable information or meta data[3]— document profiling provides a way to add searchable information pertaining to a document. This meta data can help describe or identify the documents. By default a document profile includes basic properties such as author and title, but in addition it can incorporate, where available, organizational vocabularies or taxonomies.[4]

---

3. Meta data—data about data—describes how, when, and by whom a particular document or set of data was created or collected and how it was formatted. Meta data is essential for understanding information stored in databases.
4. Taxonomy is the science of classification. Taxonomies are lists of classified terms and concepts.

- Document publishing control—the distinction between public and private versions of a document is an important one. Document routing controls when a document can be published and ready for public viewing.

- Automated approval routes—approval routes are an easy way to ensure that a document is adequately reviewed before it is published on the intranet.

- Online discussions—Web discussions allow users to conduct online discussions about a document, without modifying it, in true collaborative fashion. With comments grouped into a single place, document authors can easily fine-tune them for publication.

- Control of document access based on roles—role-based security identifies a specific set of permissions based on assignation of roles, for example, author, reader, or coordinator.

Personalization

Portals can be customized for each individual knowledge worker. The flexibility to present information that is especially relevant to each worker, such as project-specific or workgroup-specific information, and to organize the geography of the portal page contributes to the user's sense of control and empowerment. It can also dramatically improve user productivity.[5] Portal personalization can also enrich the predefined roles of a user by facilitating the delivery of more targeted and focused content. Behaviors and stated user preferences at the desktop are tools that can be used to identify and then deliver targeted information.

Security

Security is a fundamental and critical feature for portals, given the wide range of applications and data resources portals expose and the built-in flexibility they offer to the user. Typical portal security measures include the following:

---

5. Brent Thill and John Torrey, *Corporate Portals: Leveraging 5+ Years of Software Investments* (Credit Suisse First Boston, May 31, 2001), 9.

- Authentication—verifying the identities of the members of a team to allow participation in Web-based collaboration; checking users against an internal employee directory or database

- Access control—providing users with access to application and knowledge resources appropriate to the workers' roles, departments, and other attributes

- Auditing—maintaining access logs to track portal users and utilization

Why Portals? Why Now?

The level of investment in information-management applications over the past five years has been colossal, but what is striking is that the growth rate doubled during a period in which overall technology budgets, as a percentage of revenue, remained almost flat.[6] Companies are making information management a top priority, and portals are essential to this process of harnessing and leveraging intellectual capital.

Productivity enhancements afforded by information management are well proven. According to one report, companies that invested most heavily in information technology in the early 1990s experienced the largest productivity gains in the second half of the decade.[7]

Notwithstanding the undisputed benefits of enterprise information technology, shortcomings in existing systems are substantiating the need for and powering the adoption of portals. Most notably these deficiencies include poor business process application integration and the difficult task of managing the huge quantity of electronic content being generated by organizations.

For example, business applications have been traditionally deployed in a silo or "stovepipe" manner, where each application operates in isolation from one another. This is partly because different applications were designed and developed to solve different business problems. Whether it is enterprise resource planning (ERP), customer relationship management (CRM), or supply chain management (SCM), artificial walls have separated an enormous

---

6. Thill and Torrey, 4.
7. Kevin J. Stiroh, "Investing in Information Technology: Productivity Payoffs for U.S. Industries," *Current Issues in Economics and Finance* (Federal Reserve Bank of New York, June 2001), 1.

and invaluable amount of information from employees who could leverage it to drive productivity. Such heterogeneity has created a good deal of duplication and inconsistency, which reduces productivity. And this is only part of the problem. Business process applications are complex and often designed for a specific purpose and function, with but a fraction of an organization's knowledge workers trained on how to use all the functions of one system, much less all the systems and databases that affect the workers' tasks.

Additionally, the sheer volume of information and communications generated by knowledge workers is phenomenal. An organization such as Microsoft, for example, has many millions of documents, digital media, and other electronic content to manage on its intranet. Various industry sources estimate that companies are generating more than 20 million pages of public Web and intranet content per day.[8]

The portal presents an elegant solution to both of these challenges, integrating business process applications and displaying only the most relevant data to the right individuals and effectively managing documents and communications consistently, logically, and extensibly.

Why Portals?

Portals have emerged in response to the explosive proliferation of electronic information in organizations and to address the vital need for business process application integration. Knowledge workers must have access to the right information at the right time to fuel productivity. So why portals? Primarily because they address the two key issues that inhibit productive use of available applications and information—lack of integration and access.

Make Better Informed Decisions

Knowledge workers are typically required to make operational, tactical, and long-term strategic decisions on a regular basis, perhaps daily. To make operational decisions, knowledge workers need to know when a state or condition exists and the potential outcomes and actions associated with that state. Tactical decisions require information on available resources, budget, and dynamic business intelligence. Strategic decisions involve accessing the rich

---

8. Thill and Torrey, 5–6.

possible variety of relevant knowledge. All too often, uninformed, incorrect, or no decisions are made because knowledge workers do not have the information they need to act in a consistent, timely, and well-informed manner.

Access Information from Multiple Sources

Knowledge workers need to be able to access not only documents, files, and digital media but also dynamic data from diverse business process applications, ERP systems, CRM systems, and the like. This need to traverse heterogeneous sources and systems is typically an enormously difficult, frustrating, and training-intensive undertaking for knowledge workers.

Information Overload

Product information, public relations (PR) announcements, reports, customer orders, news, digital media, updates to business processes, and numerous other items of company information are added to an organization's intranet each day. Knowledge workers require a site with well-organized content that guides users to a vast array of documents, applications, and data, both intuitively and rapidly.

Complex Navigation

Many knowledge workers have difficulty remembering how to access information that is archived, relocated, being updated, or buried deep within a corporate intranet. This shortcoming is compounded by the fact that conscious thought and a thorough understanding of the organization is necessary to logically organize and then navigate the increasing number of systems, data sources, and intranet pages.

The Expanding Online Experience

Whether enrolling in a training course, submitting compliance data, updating medical benefits, initiating and participating in communications, reviewing customer information, recording hours worked on projects, or requesting software updates, knowledge workers are spending more time online. In addition, current economic conditions—and the resulting reduced travel budgets—have necessitated more and more online meetings and communications, enabling knowledge workers to remain productive at their desktops. Making the online experience more efficient and effective through centralized access provides a clear path to improving operational excellence.

Portals in the News

The market for enterprise portals is expected to enjoy an 83 percent annual compound growth rate through the end of 2003 as companies realize the cost-saving efficiencies and productivity benefits. Here are a few examples of companies that have taken advantage of portals.

Air Products and Chemicals, Inc.

"Our end users really like it [the portal]. It's easy to use, easy to submit and retrieve documents, and easy to administer. No one needs to know HTML; they can use the familiar Windows and Web paradigm they already know."
George Witmer, Technical Data Systems Manager,
Research and Development Group, Air Products
and Chemicals, Inc.

Air Products and Chemicals, Inc., based in Lehigh Valley, Pennsylvania, is the world's only combined gases and chemicals company and has annual revenues of $5.5 billion. The company operates in 30 countries and has 17,500 employees. It needed to find a way to efficiently share information among departments to speed product development and responses to customer needs.

The problem of sharing information among nearly 18,000 employees—or even among 100 employees in a department—became acute as time-to-market pressures forced the company to find better ways to collaborate and share intellectual assets. Old, linear product-development processes weren't fast enough. Departments needed to be able to work together efficiently and in parallel to get new products out the door quickly and to respond to customers faster.[9]

---

9. *http://www.microsoft.com/servers/evaluation/casestudies/airproducts.asp.*

Air Products had about 800 gigabytes' worth of documents spread across 10 corporate file servers and had no consistent method of storing, retrieving, or retiring documents. When people could not find what they needed, they either re-created the data or spent inordinate amounts of time looking for it—both substantial time drains. Multiple versions of documents led to confusion and bad decisions. In one instance, an Air Products scientist used an old version of a technical document to design a chemical production process. When the process produced inconsistent results, it took a lot of time and money to uncover the problem. Air Products tried creating departmental Web sites for sharing information but ended up with duplicate information stores that required more work than ever and still were not accessible to everyone in the company.

Air Products' portal put an end to the problems of duplication of effort, inaccessible content, and poor document management. Robust search capabilities for word frequency and placement tailor search results to the desktop. Other sophisticated tools for discovery include an intelligent indexing engine that identifies areas where information is updated frequently so that the engine can index more efficiently; an autocategorization tool that can analyze documents and extrapolate a document type for future, automatic categorization of documents; and persistent query services to encourage users to subscribe to notifications. In addition to keyword searches, users can search by categories and properties. Categories allow Air Products to classify content under a set of groupings, such as product or technology type. Properties indicate the document type, such as trip report, memo, or lab report.[10]

Because users are able to locate the information they need more quickly, the portal allows the company to be more responsive to customers and to reduce its cost of doing business. Air Products expects to move products from lab to market faster, to save money by eliminating dozens of departmental Web sites, and to greatly leverage corporate intellectual assets through better information sharing.[11]

---

10. Ibid.
11. Ibid.

Microsoft Corporation

"The goal is to provide easy and secure access to information and services for Microsoft employees, anytime and anywhere."
Kimberley Mecham, Lead Product Manager for HR
Compensation and Benefits Planning,
MicrosoftCorporation

Until recently, human resources (HR) materials at Microsoft Corporation sat in stacks of paper forms or on several file servers, making the materials difficult to locate. Microsoft's new HR portal has streamlined processes, given knowledge workers better access to relevant materials, and provided the ability to complete employee transactions online.

Microsoft knowledge workers now have direct access to benefits enrollment and management via this portal. Vacation and sick-time reporting features automatically determine the status of a worker (such as exempt or nonexempt), display the appropriate absence-reporting forms or time cards, and calculate remaining vacation and sick-time hours. Processing time in the HR department has been sliced in half by replacing absence reporting based on paper and e-mail with the portal.[12]

The secure payroll area includes electronic features such as online direct deposit, which allows workers to specify where they want their paychecks allocated. The area also provides workers with a comprehensive view of their individual pay stubs—including earnings statements for an entire fiscal period, month, or pay period—along with W-4 tax resources for U.S. employees.[13]

Financial and investment tools are also included. The employee investment programs feature supports some of Microsoft's most valued employee benefits, including the 401(k) plan, the employee stock purchase program (ESPP), and Microsoft stock options. This feature offers workers access to

---

12. Kimberley Mecham, "How Microsoft Built a Cost-Effective HR Portal," *HR Focus* (August 2001), 4.
13. Mecham, 4–5.

secure, view-only pages that provide confidential records of their stock purchases and option-exercise histories while maintaining a real-time Microsoft (Nasdaq: MSFT) stock ticker and offering information to help the workers navigate tax-related issues.[14]

The HR portal is a busy one, with employees accessing it more than 100,000 times each month. Since its launch, it has streamlined processes, improved access to information, and reduced transaction processing time for the department by eliminating more than 200 paper forms. It has also saved Microsoft well over $1 million annually.[15]

The Boeing Company

"The whole notion was one of allowing people to experiment and decide for themselves if the portal brought business value to their department or group. That was the secret."

Graeber Jordan, Web Program Manager,
The Boeing Company

In July 2001 Boeing began deploying a portal to link all of its 200,000 employees to data and applications around the company. Integration and access to an array of information—company news, e-mail links to technical information, and personalized tools such as online calendars—was made possible. Additional benefits included the sharing of costly and valuable applications (such as aircraft maintenance programs) and access to an employee service program that connected to human resources and retirement systems. The portal also featured specialized industry content, the ability to search for specific Boeing office facilities and book conference rooms, an online library and librarian chat function, and a glossary of aerospace industry acronyms. More importantly, the portal provided a link to common data within the $54 billion aerospace giant's big three divisions: Commercial Airlines Operations, Military Aircraft and Missiles, and Space and Communications.[16]

14. Mecham, 5.
15. Ibid.
16. David Lewis, "Boeing Portal to Serve Employees, Partners," *InternetWeek* (July 30, 2001), 42.

Once fully deployed, the company plans to provide workers and supervisors on the factory floor with portal access for applications ranging from the simple checking of a work schedule to highly advanced collaboration on aircraft designs between geographically dispersed designers.

Why a portal for Boeing? There are two major benefits. (1) Business-process automation, such as automating the provision of employee and retiree benefits, holds the promise of cutting costs. (2) Executives expect to reduce the costs associated with distributing new applications to employees, including training, as well as the costs of software deployment and network management.

Summary

Despite uncertain economic conditions, the portal marketplace thrives because knowledge workers require Web-based collaborative team services, a portal for information management and discovery, and broadcast communications at the employee desktop. At the same time, businesses want better returns on intellectual investments. Portals work because they are the place to present information from multiple sources; manage workflow, events, and activity queues; facilitate collaboration and communication. They make employees more effective by providing timely access to relevant information; delivered through a customized interface; improving team and project management services; and increasing knowledge sharing between knowledge workers and groups. As well, they reduce costs associated with business operations through self-service functions while improving the manageability of the desktop. All this powers productivity.

In the next chapter we will examine the business and technological revolutions that have made it possible for intranets to become the foundation on which the knowledge workplace is built.

Business and
Technological Drivers

The 1980s and 1990s witnessed significant management and technological revolutions that transformed business and resulted in the emergence of intranets. By reviewing the various revolutions that have occurred in personal computers (PCs), business management, desktop and online publishing, networking, client/servers, and the Internet, business leaders will be in a better position to evaluate intranets as a possible solution to various business challenges.

The PC Revolution

For more than 20 years the modern corporation has been confronted by a series of challenging revolutionary forces that have ultimately made it stronger and more viable than ever before. The first major revolution was triggered by the advent of the PC. The business world was previously dominated by room-sized mainframes and cabinet-sized microcomputers, which were connected to the user via a dumb terminal. The PC was revolutionary because it united the useful components of the large computer (processors, memory, and disk storage) with the useful parts of the dumb terminal (keyboard and screen). It wasn't until a few years later, however, with the development of powerful networked machines using a graphical user interface (GUI), that PCs finally began to live up to their original promise. Thus the PC revolution came into its own.

The Search for a New Management Paradigm

Running parallel with the burgeoning PC revolution was a revolution in management theory and practice. Managers were examining their processes, assumptions, and attitudes and were questioning the standard business models of the past. The predominant theory was management according to the *bottom line.* It made sense at the time; companies divided their departments into profit or cost centers, and each was evaluated by its bottom line or management of costs.

A new way of thinking emerged in the mid-1980s: total quality management (TQM) insinuated itself into the business mind-set. It was a movement inspired by Japan's successful domination of the international automobile and electronics marketplace. By the end of the 1980s, with a major recession brewing, businesses in North America and Western Europe started to change, embracing many of Japan's own quality management practices. While TQM did not save businesses from every misstep and mistake—indeed many argue it failed to achieve many of its touted goals—it did help companies reduce their infatuation with the bottom-line approach. Managers began to reexamine how business was done and to focus on improving discrete processes. More importantly, TQM helped businesses understand the importance of empowering employees and improving communication both inside and outside the organization. What is the significance of the TQM initiative? It was one of the first occasions when management theory and practices relied on advances in information technology (IT), especially software, to achieve its goals. This drive to improve business processes and facilitate better communication infrastructures was responsible for the productivity transformation of the 1990s.

The Desktop Publishing Revolution

While managers were grappling with quality issues, yet another revolution was fomenting in the publishing arena. The publishing of company newsletters, internal memos, and reports in the 1970s relied on electric typewriters, scissors, glue, tape, and the newly invented office copying machine. Back then the phrase *cut and paste* meant just that. Final draft documents resembled ransom notes and elementary school projects.

As time progressed, publishing tools rapidly and relentlessly transformed with the development of new technologies. The typewriter was replaced by the dedicated word processor, which gave way to the PC. Other tools included PostScript (developed by Adobe Corporation), a page-description language that offered flexible font capability; laser printers; and windows-based desktop publishing systems such as PageMaker (created by Aldus Corporation), FrameMaker (created by Frame Technology Corporation), and QuarkXPress (created by Quark, Inc.).

Birth of Online Publishing and Hypertext

With these new publishing capabilities, the ancient art of typesetting was reinvented and brought to the desktop. The tedious placement of individual letters in special trays to create words on a printed page was no longer required. With the introduction of WYSIWYG (what you see is what you get) authoring technology, users could view documents displayed on their screens exactly as they would appear on the printed page. Formatting codes, such as font styles and size, did not have to be embedded in the document.

The appearance of WYSIWYG begged the question, "Why use the printed page at all?" If you can make text appear the same way on the computer screen as in hard copy, wouldn't it be more efficient and less costly to distribute reports, manuals, and many other types of documents "online"?

There were also other advantages to online publishing, including the hypertext feature. *Hypertext* refers to a collection of documents that contain cross-references called hyperlinks. These links allow the reader to jump easily from one document to another. The term was first coined in 1965 by Ted Nelson, an American computer scientist. Hypertext presents textual information that can be accessed in a nonlinear way. He used the prefix *hyper* to describe the speed and facility with which users could jump to and from related areas of text.[1]

Hypertext began appearing on desktop computers in the early 1990s, embedded directly into the operating system of PCs running the operating system Windows 3.1. WinHelp, the hypertext system for Windows, is familiar to many who availed themselves of the online help system. (Macintosh computers had a similar utility called Hypercard.) Designed to provide online help for PC-based programs, WinHelp was used by many to produce online newsletters, reports, and other documents, but it was not without its shortcomings. To format a document for display, it had to be run through a *compiler,* a computer program that translates *source code* (instructions in a program written by a software engineer) into *object code* (those same instructions written in a language the computer's central processing unit [CPU] can read and interpret). Even minor changes required recompiling. Another problem with WinHelp's hypertext documents was that the documents would not work with UNIX or Macintosh workstations. It was a victim of cross-platform incompatibility.

---

1. Hypertext, *Microsoft Encarta Encyclopedia 2000 Deluxe.*

The March to Cross-Platform Compatibility

Companies soon started addressing cross-platform issues. An early leader in this area was Frame Technology Corporation, which was acquired by Adobe Systems Inc. in 1995.[2] Using FrameMaker, a user could create a document on, say, a UNIX workstation, copy the file to a floppy disk, place the disk into a PC or Macintosh, and view and/or edit the document with no apparent conversion necessary.

FrameMaker, Interleaf, and other early desktop publishing tools had their own interchange formats—plain text representations of a document that could be moved effortlessly between different versions of the software operating on different platforms. Similarly, PostScript was a device-independent printing language that consisted entirely of coded instructions stored as plain text.

One feature that put FrameMaker ahead of its time was its ability to create hypertext links and active buttons directly on a document page. A neat, self-contained online document was created with just a few keystrokes. The significance of this innovation was that the desktop publishing file and the online publishing file were often one and the same, thereby reducing time and effort and facilitating uniformity in document production and distribution.

However, FrameMaker was not without its flaws. Though it was superior to WinHelp in cross-platform connectivity, it was inferior in its ease of distribution. If you wanted wide distribution of online documents, each user had to have a special tool (Frame Viewer) resident on his or her machine. FrameViewer was required to open, view, and print documents, but documents could not be edited.

The Author/Viewer Division

Even though these products brought with them added expense and another layer of software to the configuration burden, it was an intensely interesting development. With the advent of tools such as FrameViewer, software developers began to realize the need to distinguish between the two distinctly different functions in online publishing: authoring versus viewing. For example, Frame Technology Corporation offered two separate products:

---

2. *http://www.adobe.com/aboutadobe/pressroom/pdfs/timeline_090501.pdf* (October 2, 2001).

FrameMaker was the main authoring tool, and FrameViewer was the reading or viewing tool, also known as a browser. The former was considerably more expensive than the latter.

Other desktop publishing products adopted this model, sometimes offering the browser for free. Microsoft Corporation released in early 1995 a document browser called Microsoft Word Viewer at no charge.[3] Microsoft Word Viewer allowed the user to open, view, and print, but not edit, a Word document, even if Microsoft Word was not resident (installed) on a desktop.

Portable Document Format

In the context of the online publishing revolution, software developers at Adobe Corporation recognized the limitation of their PostScript technology. Even though it had been instrumental in opening up the field of desktop publishing, by providing a freely accessible and widely available method for printing richly formatted documents on any PostScript-enabled device, these documents were not easy to view online. File sizes were colossal, especially when they included color graphics. There was also no hypertext capability.

To address this, Adobe created an entirely new kind of file format—the portable document format, commonly known as PDF. Unlike PostScript, PDF was designed to be a compact, online publishing format that incorporated hypertext functionality. Like WinHelp, documents could be viewed online and hyperlinked from one file or World Wide Web (WWW) site to another. As with its online publishing predecessors, the viewer or browser (Acrobat Reader) was free, but the authoring software (Acrobat Distiller and Acrobat Exchange) had to be purchased.

The most interesting facet about the PDF format is that it represented the state of the art in online publishing at a time when the Internet and the Web burst into our homes and offices. In some ways the Web stole some of Acrobat's thunder because it provided many of the features of Acrobat, including the ability to access any file type, including PDF. Initially it appeared that Adobe was trying to position PDF as a replacement for the Web browser, but it has since determined that coexistence is the better route.[4]

---

3. Ryan Bernard, *The Corporate Intranet: Harness the Power of the Next-Generation Intranet,* 2nd ed. (New York: John Wiley & Sons, Inc., 1997), 44.
4. Bernard, 45.

Acrobat now includes plug-ins and controls that let Web users view PDF files inside the browser window.

The Revolution in Networking

While executives were experimenting with new management styles and PCs were proliferating at the desktop, other new technologies that would materially change information technology were emerging. In particular, networking technologies were helping to make desktop computers the machine of choice for any business application. PCs and Macintosh computers were functioning well on the desktops of the nation, but unlike the dumb terminals of bygone days, they were isolated, stand-alone machines, cut off from the central store of enterprise data held in mainframes. Then companies such as Apple and Novell found ways to connect desktop computers and mainframes into local area networks (LANs).

LAN technology provided a convenient means to connect several machines on a single floor or in a small building, but large organizations might occupy several floors in a building or have geographically dispersed locations. Each location might have its own LAN, but they were isolated from the rest of the organization until wide area network (WAN) technology connected them all together. WAN technology made it possible to connect disparate departments and scattered locations and put the entire enterprise on the same network. Multinational companies such as Chevron, Digital, and Microsoft could have their own private worldwide networks that bound together business activity centers around the world.

LANs and WANs proved to be cost-effective technologies. They facilitated the sharing and utilization of expensive resources by widely dispersed employees. The first things to be shared were hardware components, including printers and hard drives. Instead of providing each desktop with a laser printer, a company might invest in one expensive high-speed printer, connect it to a central print server on the network, and let groups of employees print to it, just as they would to a local printer. Network drives, or file servers, that could save documents and data in the same way as a local hard drive were also set up within companies.

Storage area networks (SANs) were the next innovation in the networked world. With the explosion of enterprise information and knowledge, larger and more efficient storage facilities were required. A SAN is a high-speed subnetwork of shared storage devices; a storage device is a machine that contains nothing but a disk or disks for storing data. The SAN's architecture works in a way that makes all storage devices available to all servers on a LAN or a WAN. As more storage devices are added to a SAN, they become accessible from any server in the larger network. The server is merely a pathway between the end user and the stored data.

Along with the creation of file and print servers came the question, "If you can share hardware such as printers and drives over a network, why not software and data?" Network technologists and software developers accepted this challenge, and the result was a new kind of architecture known as client/server architecture.

Client/Server Architecture

The client/server architecture makes use of "distributed intelligence." Data and the pieces of software required to manipulate the data are spread out, shared, or "distributed" across the network by splitting the processing of an application into two distinct components: a "front-end" client and a "back-end" server. The client component—itself a complete, stand-alone computer—offered the user its full range of power and features for running applications. The server component, which could be another computer, a minicomputer, or a mainframe, enhanced the client component by providing the traditional strengths offered by minicomputers and mainframes in a time-sharing environment: data management, information sharing between clients, sophisticated network administration, and security features. The advantage of the client/server architecture over older architectures was that the client and server machines work together to accomplish the processing of the application being used. Not only did this increase the processing power available, but it also used that power more efficiently. The client portion of the application was typically optimized for user interaction, whereas the server portion provided centralized, multi-user functionality.

Client/server architecture seemed to solve many of the problems of networked computing in the early 1990s. Network traffic was reduced because large database files stayed in one place instead of being repeatedly transported across the network. Centralized database files simplified the backing up of mission-critical data. Managers were able to invest in a few powerful servers rather than copies of software, larger drive space, and additional computing power for each desktop.

Then a new management formula began taking the business world by storm in the early 1990s. Corporations were experimenting with employee empowerment, teamwork, and collaboration. Client/server networking was well suited for this environment; indeed it became a key component in the reengineering revolution that refined business processes and redesigned business activity centers.

The Emergence of a Collaborative Work Environment

The key to client/server networking is distributed work and shared resources. Instead of toiling away at isolated workstations, employees were interconnected, sharing data, documents, and many other types of computer resources. New client/server applications that fostered this collaborative approach to enterprise computing began to appear. For example, products such as Microsoft Exchange, launched in 1996, were a culmination of many forces in the business world in the previous decade, especially the trend toward empowered teams and workgroups taking responsibility for business processes.

The Internet Revolution

In the midst of the new management, desktop publishing, networking, and productivity revolutions, the Internet emerged as the biggest client/server experiment in the world.

History of the Internet

The Internet, which has far-reaching and profound social potential, is also based on a technology that took time—some 40 years—to achieve broad market acceptance. Far from being a single technological phenomenon, it was spawned by multiple technologies that percolated together over several decades. At the same time a rich complex of trends and events was occurring, to the point where Internet use would increase dramatically and become part of our everyday vernacular.

In the Beginning

In 1960 the worldwide nuclear weapons arsenal attained new heights of megatonnage available, and two years later the number of warheads peaked.[5] The U.S. Department of Defense (DOD) Advanced Research Project Agency (ARPA) was charged with developing a command-and-control network that would be secure enough to survive a nuclear attack. Neither telephone nor radio was appropriate because both relied on centralized switches and transmitters, and communications would be lost if one part malfunctioned or was destroyed. ARPANET was developed as a network in which information would be digitized, broken into packets, and dispersed through a network of routers, each capable of rerouting traffic if a part of the network was damaged.[6] This packet switching system, revved up and improved, is essentially the underlying technology of today's Internet.

In 1969 the ARPANET project linked four university supercomputers and facilitated the sharing of information among scientists. Thus the seeds of the Internet were sown. Although pleased with this success, no one felt it was a momentous occasion nor realized this was the first step on the road toward the digital age and the knowledge workplace.

Today's Internet embodies a key underlying technical concept: open-architecture networking that was guided by four critical ground rules:

- Each distinct network had to stand on its own. No internal changes would be required of any such network before it could be connected to the Internet.

- Communications would be on a best-effort basis. If a packet did not make it to the final destination, it would be retransmitted from the source.

- Black boxes, later called gateways and routers, would be used to connect the networks. No information would be kept about the individual flows of packets passing through them.

- There would be no global control at the operations level.

---

5. Andrew B. Zimmerman, "The Evolution of the Internet," *Telecommunications* (June 1, 1997), 39.
6. Zimmerman, 40.

Early Years

Little by little but steadily throughout the 1970s, the Internet grew. The first public demonstration of ARPANET took place between 40 machines, and in October of the same year, electronic mail (e-mail), the initial "killer application" was introduced.

Global networking became a reality in 1973. The first international connections to ARPANET were established from the University College of London (England) and the Royal Radar Establishment (Norway). By 1974 the first public packet data service, Telnet, was opened and the term *Internet* was used for the first time in an article on Transmission Control Protocol/Internet Protocol (TCP/IP) authored by Vinton Cerf from Stanford University and Bob Kahn from DARPA.[7]

As the demand for networked computing grew, new languages, applications, and technical enhancements emerged. With each advance, such as the organization of messages by subject areas (Usenet) and the ability to transfer files, more users were attracted to the Internet. Queen Elizabeth sent her first e-mail in 1976.[8] By 1977 the number of hosts—the name for any device on a TCP/IP network—broke the 100 mark, and a network called THEORYNET provided e-mail to over 100 computer science researchers using a locally developed e-mail system. Newsgroups were established two years later, and three newsgroups were in existence by the end of 1979.

Accelerated Growth

The 1980s realized the formation of new branches of the Internet, including CSNET (Computer Science NETwork, 1981), BITNET (Because It's Time NETwork, 1981), EUnet (European UNIX Network, 1982), EARN (European Academic and Research Network, 1983), and JANET (Joint Academic Network in the U.K., 1984). TCP/IP was established in 1982 as the protocol suite for network interconnection and communication.

In 1990 ARPANET was replaced by the National Science Foundation Network (NSFNET) to connect its supercomputers to regional networks. NSFNET now operates as the high-speed backbone of the Internet. The

---

7. Dave Kristula, "History of the Internet" *www.davesite.com/webstation/net-history.shtml,* October 5, 2001).
8. PBS Life on the Internet (*http://www.pbs.org/internet/timeline/index.html,* August 20, 2001).

National Science Foundation is an independent agency of the U.S. government established by Congress in 1950 to promote the progress of science; advance the health, prosperity, and welfare of the nation; and secure the national defense.

The World Wide Web

Enabling technologies for the Internet were appearing rapidly by the 1990s, but the innovations of most consequence were the introduction of the Web, in which vast amounts of information could be linked, and then the tools that facilitated searching and accessing the Web. The Web was first implemented in 1989 by Tim Berners-Lee at the European Particle Research Center (CERN) and was based on the hypertext concept described earlier in this chapter. The innovations of Berners-Lee and his colleagues include

*   Hypertext Markup Language (HTML)—a way of marking text for online publishing that contains embedded formats, hyperlinks, and other features
*   Hypertext Transfer Protocol (HTTP)—a communication method for the exchange of hypertext documents over a network

Web Browsers

While HTML and HTTP were crucial to the evolution of the Web, it was not until a number of refinements occurred, including a more feature-filled version of HTML and a Web-browser called Mosaic, that the Web catapulted into prominence. During the mid-1990s other browsers came along—Viola, Midas, Cello, and Lynx to name a few—but Mosaic and its descendents, Microsoft Explorer and Netscape Communicator, survived. These new browsers included a number of advanced features that made them especially powerful tools for information gathering.

Unlike other types of client programs that could be used only with certain types of servers, these browsers were multipurpose clients; they could communicate with Web servers and with mail, news, and other servers. They also added unprecedented levels of convenience to file access. For instance, a Web document could contain links through pictures as well as words.

Two other characteristics contributed to the success of Web browsers. One of its most powerful features was its ability to recognize file types by their extensions (.doc, .xls) and trigger helper applications or plug-ins that facilitated file display. Although not revolutionary (as far back as Windows 3.1 it was possible to launch a .doc file from File Manager), it was a very useful addition to the Web browser's catalog of features.

The other notable characteristic of Web technology was the incredible flexibility built into the HTTP protocol that allowed nearly any kind of information transfer between client and server. Just as a file extension could launch a help application on the client side, there were ways to activate scripts or server side programs. This was made possible by a mechanism called the common gateway interface (CGI), which allowed an individual at a workstation (client) to control various applications on the server. One application was online content search. Many Web sites provided a way to search for documents with certain terms or phrases, such as "knowledge worker" or "collaboration." Typical search results were hyperlinked, and clickable lists of document titles displayed in the browser window.

Another CGI-enabled application was interactive Web pages. Containing forms with fields to be completed by the user, an individual could sign up for training courses or complete employee surveys. The information was entered by the employee and sent to the server, where it was appended to a file or forwarded to the appropriate individual. Interactive database queries were another CGI-enabled application. By typing a name in the customer database, all transactions with that customer could be displayed. The "query maker" was then able to view and edit the records, if required, and have any changes incorporated in the database records.

Java and Other Advanced Tools

Even though Web technology could handle any file type on any platform, massage and serve any kind of data, and function as a universal client for nearly any type of online application, software engineers continued to strive for improvements. They began to create advanced programming, scripting, and markup languages that could work their magic through the flexible medium of the Web, including Java, JavaScript, VBScript (Visual Basic Scripting), VRML (virtual reality markup language), and XML (Extensible Markup Language). The power of Java was the ability to send a small application via HTTP and have it operate on the client. This introduced the concept of the virtual machine—a self-contained operating environment that behaves as if it is a separate computer. For example, Java applets run in a Java virtual machine that has no access to the host operating system.

The field of Web technology is one of the most explosively dynamic and unpredictable in recent history. It has not rested since Marc Andreessen and Eric Bina invented the Mosaic browser, and it is unlikely to rest now. Due to the success of the Internet and intranets, numerous companies and individuals continue to vie for ways of improving the technology. Even more important developments are around the corner as intranets move into their role as the central foundation on which enterprise computing is built.

Summary

This chapter has reviewed the historical trends in business and information technology over the last two decades. The management revolution helped business leaders understand the importance of empowering employees, interdisciplinary teamwork, collaboration, and maximizing process efficiencies. The desktop publishing revolution was responsible for WYSIWYG authoring technologies, hypertext capabilities, and cross-platform compatibility and making the distinction between the authoring and viewing functions. The important outcomes of the networking revolution were LAN and WAN technologies, which put the entire enterprise on the same network, irrespective of location, and the client/server architecture's utilization of distributed intelligence. The important developments of the more recent Internet revolution and the enabling Web browser technologies include online content search, dynamic hypertext links, and interactivity (both forms-based and database queries), plus the ability to trigger helper applications or plug-ins and communicate with any type of server. A review of these revolutions illustrates how intranets neatly tie together these innovations and point the way to a very productive and innovative future.

Chapter 5 will present and describe the Microsoft Solution for Intranets. Arguably the most comprehensive and advanced intranet solution available, it effectively enables document management, search, subscriptions, digital media broadcast, and Web-based team collaboration.

The Microsoft Solution for Intranets

Successful organizations need to be agile, capable of swift response to constantly changing market forces and customer requirements. The most effective businesses enable their workers by providing rapid access to information as well as the tools to organize and share knowledge efficiently across the organization. This enables the emergent knowledge workplace through enhanced productivity and smarter, faster decision making—an environment of optimized output, where important projects come to successful conclusion sooner. The Microsoft Solution for Intranets includes integrated and tested software, prescriptive architectural guidance, and deployment services and support from Microsoft and experienced industry partners.

The Problem

The problem of effective information management for today's knowledge workers is all too painfully apparent. Even the simplest tasks seem to require massive effort or appear all but impossible. The only way to locate a document is to know where it was last saved. The only way to find a document someone else wrote is to request it from the author. The only way to keep track of the wide variety of online services a company makes available through its intranet is to maintain a very large "favorites" list (or bookmarks) in one's Web browser. Every time a Web-based solution needs to be created, it has to be designed and developed from the ground up; for example, in order to deliver dynamic SAP data into a portal for finance executives, an application would have to be specially written and repeatedly updated as application changes occur. When a project team is created, it is time-consuming or difficult to create shared facilities that the team can use to, for example, track tasks and share deliverables. If an executive or team leader needs to deliver an update to a broad, geographically dispersed audience, the standard ways to deliver such communication is via either e-mail (which doesn't carry the impact of the message) or an in-person event (which is extremely costly and virtually impossible for leaders of large multinational organizations). The use of digital media for corporate communications has grown in popularity, yet it has been a manual process that is difficult to administer and manage. When documents and other content, such as streaming media, are organized into knowledge management solutions, users find such systems too cumbersome to actually use and resist using them.

While individual approaches to information management remain significant, most content in the knowledge workplace is created collaboratively and accessed by distributed teams as a general-purpose resource, destined to be reused on an ongoing basis.

Knowledge workers need improved and more efficient ways to share and use information within their organizations through intranets. Microsoft has designed its products and technologies to enable this practice. Microsoft SharePoint Portal Server 2001 is the flexible portal solution from Microsoft that allows companies to find, share, and publish information easily. Microsoft SharePoint Team Services provides users with the ability to rapidly create and contribute to ad hoc team and project-focused Web sites. Microsoft Office XP provides a smarter way of working, simplifying the way individuals work, thus enabling easy collaboration and providing continual integration of additional services. Microsoft Windows Media Technologies provide the highest scalability and industry-leading audio and video quality, with tools designed specifically for an enterprise, making it easy for network administrators to centrally configure and manage the implementation of Windows Media within their organization. These products were developed as a direct result of customer feedback and research into effective information-sharing practices within business organizations. Each is a key element in the mix of technologies essential to intranets.

There's also another level. By combining the SharePoint and Windows Media technologies and Microsoft SQL Server 2000 into a single solution, customers can address the information-sharing challenges faced by both large and small groups within their enterprises. This solution gives users the ability to organize information, access that information, manage documents, and enable efficient collaboration—all in a familiar, browser-based and Microsoft Office-integrated environment.

The Solution

Next generation intranets are designed to power the productivity of knowledge workers. They enable the knowledge workplace with Web-based collaborative team services, information management and discovery, and broadcast delivery of business communications to every desktop.

Intranets provide a comprehensive solution for organizations, delivering effortless Web-based team collaboration, rapid access to business information, intuitive document management, and an end-to-end solution for broadcast communications to the desktop.

Intranets are a complete infrastructure for productivity, collaboration, and knowledge management. This includes collaboration workspaces, general-purpose portals, portals designed for specific organizational functions, document management, enterprise-wide searches, ad hoc team sites, and real-time or on-demand access to digital media content.

Intranets are, by definition, holistic and necessitate an end-to-end infrastructure. The Microsoft Solution for Intranets, which will be reviewed in this chapter, is the most comprehensive intranet solution available today, integrating desktop productivity and collaboration with Microsoft Office XP; rich portal services with SharePoint Portal Server; team collaboration via SharePoint Team Services; management, production, and delivery of digital media communications; and data management with SQL Server—all running on the Windows operating system. The Microsoft Solution for Intranets effectively enables document management, search, subscriptions, digital media broadcast, and ad hoc team-based collaboration. Its flexible portal architecture provides the facilities for constructing line-of-business (LOB) integrated portals, executive information systems, business analytical solutions, and many other applications that deliver unprecedented levels of knowledge worker efficiency, collaboration, and productivity.

Workspaces

Workspaces are an important feature of intranets. A workspace is an online presence that provides a user interface, preferably one that is customizable and extensible; a storage facility for shared content; and a set of other application services either directly hosted within the workspace or to which the workspace provides a conduit. Workspaces are also a social construct, a place for the work transactions that occur therein.

Some workspaces will have very short life cycles, having been created for brief periods of time to serve the needs of particular projects. They will handle documents, to-do lists, calendar items, member lists, and so forth.

Some workspaces will have similar requirements as project workspaces but with longer life cycles, although relevant only to relatively small teams.

Other workspaces will address the needs of larger groups of people, often providing long-term storage of document content that spans a variety of usage patterns. Such sites will also address a variety of applications at the same time, consolidating a number of functions in a portal-based interface.

Finally, a few workspaces will provide company-wide one-stop shopping to a well-defined set of services. Good examples of this include organization-wide content searching, organization-wide access to digital media (either broadcast in real time or made available for on-demand viewing by individual users), or a portal that makes human resources data viewable and (to an appropriate extent) editable by staff members.

The Solution's focus is to ensure that a comprehensive infrastructure exists for providing workspaces and organizing their content into an integrated network.

Architecture (or Infrastructure)

Figure 5-1 illustrates a fully deployed Microsoft Solution for Intranets in a medium-to-large organization. The infrastructure consists of four principal types of building blocks, organized into a manageable and coherent "hub-and-spoke" architecture.

A central corporate portal provides one-stop searching of and linking to a wide variety of content, such as divisional portals, a broadcast media portal, formally managed team sites, ad hoc team sites, and external content. It serves as a common source of company-wide information, including announcements, news stories, training, calendar items, and a catalog of other Web sites. It also provides user subscriptions for a variety of new information, in which users receive notifications of the arrival of new documents pertaining to subjects in which they are interested.

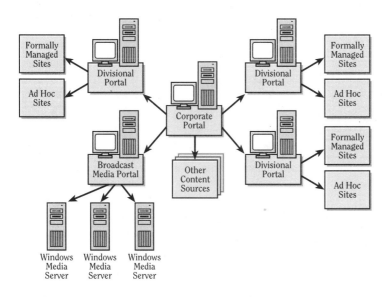

Figure 5-1 *The Microsoft Solution for Intranets*

Surrounding the central corporate portal in this hub-and-spoke arrangement is a set of divisional portals, each targeted to address the needs of up to 1000 users. Divisional portals provide document management services, search and subscription services to related team sites and external content, categorized views of content, and an application platform for integrating WebParts that provide access to a number of business applications (for example, news, events, links, LOB integration, and so forth).

Single-purpose team sites are at the outer edge of this model, each targeted at 10 to 100 users, and designed for small groups or specific projects. They are linked to and indexed by the divisional portals around which they revolve and are also indexed by the corporate portal.

It is expected that half of these sites will be formally managed and half will be ad hoc sites. Formally managed sites are administered by designated staff. They can be created only by a defined set of such administrators and are indexed by both the corporate portal and their corresponding divisional portals. Such sites may even be the official presence for a given project or workgroup.

Ad hoc sites encourage spontaneous collaboration and intrateam interaction. By default they can be created by any user when the need arises. They are not indexed by other portals, and there is no sense of the site being "published" for perusal by others. Work may well begin here before it is ready for a larger audience.

The Windows Media Broadcast component of the Microsoft Solution for Intranets provides a complete solution for managing, scheduling, producing, and delivering broadcast events, connecting employees to digital media broadcasts over the intranet. Enterprises today are using digital media primarily for corporate communications and training delivered via the intranet. As more demands are being placed on organizations to reduce costs and increase employee productivity, distributing communications to the desktop is imperative. The broadcast portal created using the Windows Media Broadcast component occupies the same position in the hub-and-spoke hierarchy as a divisional portal and enables rapid implementation of a distributed audio/video broadcast environment for announcements, meetings, training, or other content to be delivered over the organization's intranet. From the portal, organizations can configure and manage media distribution servers, optimize network bandwidth, schedule and manage live broadcast events, notify employees of events via their calendars, produce and deliver live events to employee desktops, and allow users to search for archived on-demand video presentations to view at their leisure. These capabilities have significant economic benefits over holding division or team meetings and help increase employee productivity and facilitate knowledge sharing within an organization.

Access to and control over all this content is possible via a Web browser or directly through Microsoft Office XP. The tool most appropriate will depend on what the user is trying to accomplish at any given time.

Core Constituencies

Large organizations are typically composed of business divisions that are, in turn, composed of both large and small teams. These different organizational units share information in a variety of ways: within each team, between teams, across business divisions, and throughout the entire company. This solution offers companies a way to organize, manage, and share the wealth of information generated by these teams and divisions as well as by the larger corporation.

Teams are formed to solve business problems. Team members need to be able to document, discuss, and share research in order to solve business problems. SharePoint Team Services host sites that provide a centralized and secure Web-based environment that includes document repositories, discussion groups, calendars, task lists, and site usage reporting.

Divisions are formed to unite teams within political or geographical business boundaries. Division members need to be able to track news and events relevant to their division. They also need to review content generated by other teams in their division that relates to their own team. The divisional portal provides a secure intranet site that includes division-wide news and announcements; events that affect the larger organization need to be communicated to all divisional teams and team members.

In addition, the divisional portal provides document management (supporting a variety of document profiles, categorizations, and approval routing) as well as search and subscription functionality. Users can then find the information they need and be alerted to the availability of new and relevant information.

Individual divisions may also need to provide applications to their users. A portal workspace, plus a catalog of reusable software components, makes it easy to assemble and deliver such focused solutions with high quality and low turnaround times (for example, LOB integration and business intelligence).

A corporate portal provides information at the enterprise level (news and announcements, navigation within and outside the organization) as well as access to aggregated information from the divisional and team levels (search and subscriptions). For any user in the organization, a variety of training, public information, or other material may be available either as a permanent collection of video on demand or as a series of scheduled broadcasts available to any desktop.

At all levels, content may be restricted to specific users or groups, enabling them to assume specific roles (author and reader, for example) over specific sets of content. Given that all servers authenticate from a common directory or set of domains, access control is preserved and respected at all levels of the workspace hierarchy.

The architecture described in this book supports a corporate information system that allows content to flow from various teams, up to and including the divisional portal and the corporate portal. Content generated at the team level is aggregated at both divisional and corporate levels to provide shared access. Team members and teams who currently struggle to share information effectively can use search and subscription services to take advantage of their similar and mutually beneficial efforts.

The solution presented is based on a company with 15,000 users and tries to reflect the actual demands a user base of this size would actually place on a set of servers. In a typical corporation, it is reasonable to assume that most users will interact with the intranet portal homepage. A certain percentage of these 15,000 users will be part of a division that enables information sharing and collaboration through a divisional portal. Some of these 15,000 users will participate in team-based collaboration. Over the course of time, teams will be formed and retired. At any given point in time, a subset of these users will be perusing the Broadcast Media Portal for on-demand content. During important enterprise-wide announcements, broadcasts will be delivered in real time to every user in the organization. Therefore, this architecture allows for flexibility and scales to meet the needs of a large company.

Specialized Solution Components

The key to delivering the functionality and performance outlined by this solution is the deployment of servers to deliver specialized functions. The physical architecture behind the logical model illustrated earlier is similar to the diagram in Figure 5-2.

The corporate portal is actually a single server running SharePoint Portal Server 2001 with Service Pack 1. This server hosts the portal homepage and all the prescribed WebParts, corporate-wide search, and subscriptions. It does not directly index any content sources but instead receives regular index updates from the content index server. It provides no document management services of its own, although some of its WebParts provide direct links to the divisional portals and team sites hosted on other servers.

The content index server indexes all content across the various intranet and Internet servers and forwards its results to the corporate portal, which is a physical server running SharePoint Portal Server 2001 with Microsoft Service Pack 1. It can be configured to crawl file shares, Web sites (secure and anonymous), Microsoft Exchange public folders, Lotus Notes databases, and SharePoint Team Services sites. While it is kept quite busy, all of its activity occurs in the background relative to the activities of other servers.

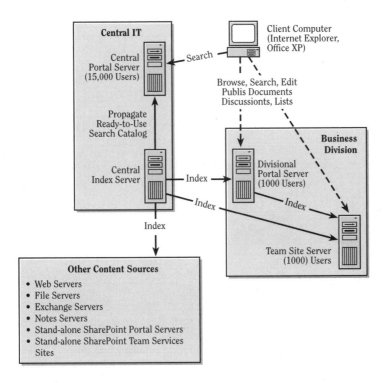

Figure 5-2 *Architecture for specialized solution components*

A divisional portal is a physical server running SharePoint Portal Server 2001 with Service Pack 1. It hosts the dashboard-based portals used by division members, processes search requests for local content as well as content in federated team site servers, and provides document management services. This server is configured to support 1000 users performing a variety of tasks. Other WebParts and sub-dashboards may be customized after deployment to provide division-specific application functionality.

The team sites for a division are delivered using a physical server running SharePoint Team Services and SQL Server 2000. This server stores the content for all team sites. It is configured to support up to 1000 users spread across 100 team sites.

The broadcast portal is a single server running SharePoint Portal Server 2001 together with a custom Active Server Pages application running under Microsoft Internet Information Server 5.0. It fits into the overall intranet architecture by having its content indexed by the content index server for use by the corporate portal. The corporate portal also provides links that carry users directly to the portal. Figure 5-3 illustrates the overall design.

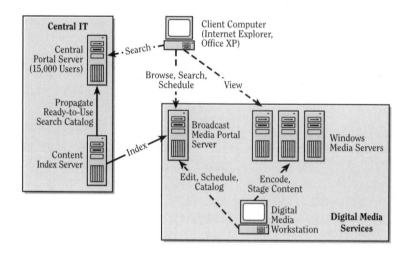

Figure 5-3   *Design of the broadcast portal*

The broadcast portal server hosts an application that provides management, organization, and scheduling functionality for digital media. Broadcast events (unicast, multicast, and on-demand) can be searched or browsed by users, and selecting a media event results in a connection to the most appropriate (usually the closest) distribution server. The portal server can also send appointment items to Exchange Server 2000 calendars that automatically handle connection to a live multicast when it takes place.

Windows Media Servers are dedicated Microsoft Windows 2000 Servers and provide the actual storage and streaming distribution of digital media content. The fact that Windows Media Services is built into a Windows 2000 Server means that you can take advantage of the operating system's reliability, scalability, performance, and cost-effectiveness.

The Digital Media Workstation provides the production console where media content is captured and encoded into digital formats and placed on Windows Media Servers. It works in conjunction with the Broadcast Media Portal to provide both production facilities and ease of logistics when making them available to users.

Knowledge Worker Productivity

No intranet solution will be successful if users avoid it. No interface is ideal for all tasks. The Microsoft Solution for Intranets encourages using the right tool for the right task at the right time. Two primary interfaces exist for accessing portal and team site content: (1) Microsoft Internet Explorer (5.0 or above) for browsing, search, and Web portal application access, which can be used to handle document management facilities; or (2) Microsoft Office XP to provide the optimal interface for document navigation, management, authoring, and administration of content maintained on the divisional portals. Office XP also provides several facilities that leverage the corporate portal's search facility from within Microsoft Word, Excel, and PowerPoint.

While many if not most document management tasks *can* be performed exclusively within a Web browser environment, using SharePoint Portal Server and Office XP together makes documents more discoverable; the business process around finding, sharing, and publishing documents thus becomes more mainstream. Support for SharePoint Portal Server ships with every copy of Office XP. Consider the following:

- With Microsoft Office XP's client for SharePoint Portal Server 2001, the workspace's content is as easy to navigate as the folders on a user's local disk drives. All extended document information can be seen via task panes, used as column headings in folder views, and edited via property pages.

- Within Microsoft Word, Excel, and PowerPoint, document check-in/check-out, publishing, categorization, versioning, and profiling become as easy as opening or saving a file. Document management functions appear on menus and toolbars, and dialog boxes that prompt for categories and profile information appear from within these native applications.

Consider the alternative, which would involve accessing the portal with a browser, downloading the document to one's local disk drive, editing it with one's word processor, saving it, returning to the portal from one's browser, uploading the new version of the document, providing additional profile and category information, and then saving the new information with the uploaded file. The difference in effort and time is more than a matter of convenience—it is a matter of productivity.

Office XP also allows for the unified searching of documents from within its File menus, allowing a single search to examine local drives, Microsoft Outlook message content, and anything a SharePoint Portal Server can index (e.g., network places, file shares, Web sites, Exchange Server public folders, Lotus Notes databases, SharePoint Team Services servers, and other SharePoint Portal Servers). This is done from within the native application; no separate trip to a Web browser is necessary.

Smart tags, a technology in Office XP that allows for custom, context-specific code to appear on demand when specific text is present, are available to directly link to SharePoint Portal Server categories and searches from within Office XP documents. Moreover, Office XP isn't just a tool for using the content of a SharePoint Portal Server workspace; it can help create the portal as well.

Documents created in Office XP applications and saved using the "Save as WebPart" functionality can, in turn, become part of a portal. This allows users (if so authorized) to contribute to a divisional portal's home dashboard and even create entire personal dashboards composed exclusively of Office XP-authored content. A set of spreadsheets, for example, can be saved as WebParts to create a business intelligence application hosted within a divisional portal—with very little time and effort necessary to go from a document to a WebPart that can be used and reused by a variety of portals.

Usage and Performance Profiles

The Microsoft Solution for Intranets reflects a practice-based, open-ended architecture for providing collaborative workspaces and other knowledge management services. It was designed to provide specific hardware and configuration specifications in order to yield a well-tested, well-measured level of well-defined performance.

Each type of server is provided with a specific usage scenario that translates into a given server load. This prescriptive architecture delivers performance numbers that meet the demands of these usage scenarios. For details on how these usage profiles translate into specific server operations, such as peak vs. average usage calculations, consult the Microsoft Solution for Intranets and Windows Media Broadcast Prescriptive Architecture Guides available at *http://www.microsoft.com/solutions/MSI/techinfo/solutiondocs/default.asp* and the Capacity Planning Guide available at *http://www.microsoft.com/sharepoint/techinfo/planning/Cap_Plan.asp*.

The corporate portal is the central information source for an organization and delivers a single corporate portal that has been tested to address the activity of 15,000 users searching across 1,000,000 indexed documents. To create the test scenario for this solution, a number of organizations were studied to determine their use of the main pages of their corporate portals to create performance targets; this data was then doubled. The study entailed visits to the portal homepage, the viewing of corporate announcements, executing searches, and examining search results.

Generally, a corporate portal is visited by almost every user in the organization within a one- or two-day period, but few if any users spend a great deal of their day-to-day activities at such a site. Most of the access is read-only, as the ability to edit the corporate portal is most likely restricted to a defined set of users.

Divisional portals are created along formal and/or functional boundaries within an organization, and this solution offering tested each divisional workspace to serve 1000 users, managing a total of 50,000 documents.

The divisional workspace's portal is intended to host the homepage and the central repository of information for large teams within a business division. Teams within the division can store and manage documents within the workspace, meaning that updates to the site take place frequently and by many users. Most users probably visit this portal during any given day.

The typical activity under which this scenario has been tested involves multiple visits to the homepage, browsing the document library, browsing category listings, searches, opening documents, saving documents, and performing check-ins/check-outs.

Team sites help project groups and ad hoc teams share information; the architecture supports up to 100 team sites, with 10 users per site, on relatively modest hardware. The scenario expects most of a site's users to use the site during a given day and further assumes several visits to the homepage, several document postings and retrievals, and several list perusals and contributions.

The broadcast portal, like the corporate portal, can be visited at any time by anyone in the organization, but the total number of users accessing the portal at any one time usually falls short of the company's total population. The exception to this is, of course, a company-wide real-time broadcast. In addition, client time spent at the portal is usually a fraction of the time spent connected directly to the Windows Media Server-hosted content the portal makes available. For real-time broadcasts, scaling to (and beyond) 15,000 users is quite possible, particularly when multicasting (one transmission sent out to multiple receivers) is leveraged aggressively. For on-demand content, redundant copies of media placed on multiple servers allows for both load balancing (when the servers are co-located) and minimizing wide-area bandwidth (when the servers are geographically dispersed).

Summary

Intranets are, by definition, comprehensive, flexible, and adaptive. While each of the component products delivers discrete value, a completely integrated solution produces a productivity benefit greater than the logical sum of the parts. Intranets, by definition, are composed of flexible portals with powerful search and document management capabilities, ad hoc team collaboration sites, and live or on-demand digital media broadcast capabilities—all made accessible and manageable with a powerful desktop productivity application. None of these technologies can be individually described as an intranet. Seamlessly integrated, the technologies coalesce to define the category.

In order to meet the needs of knowledge workers in today's knowledge workplace, the intranet must provide the full span of productivity applications offered, with Web-based collaborative team services, information management and discovery, and broadcast delivery of business communications to every user desktop. These are the fundamental building blocks of the knowledge workplace. In the next chapter we will look at the audience for whom intranets are intended.

The Culture of Knowledge

Why is there such an expansion of interest in the subject of knowledge? Why concentrate on a subject that has in some form been around since the pre-Socratic philosophers? Is this subject to be in vogue for a brief time and then soon forgotten? We don't think so. When all is said and done, there is no sustainable advantage for the modern organization other than what it knows, how it utilizes what it knows, and how fast it can learn from what it already knows. But this does not answer our original question, "Why now?"

There are some very broad trends that contribute to the current emphasis on knowledge workers and the knowledge workplace. They are as follows:

- Proliferation of information creation and dissemination through computing, networking, advanced communications, and the advent of the Internet

- Globalization, which is forcing businesses to improve their agility, innovation, processes, and time to market

- Specialization of knowledge and work brought about by the substantial advances of the past 100 years, thus producing more complex professional and organizational functions, processes, and routines.

- Valuation of knowledge as an assessable and measurable managed asset that drives productivity and the bottom line

- Education or e-learning via inexpensive networked enterprises that provide us with a tool for working with and learning from each other[1]

---

1. Laurence Prusack, "Why Knowledge, Why Now?" in James W. Cortada, ed., *Rise of the Knowledge Worker* (Boston: Butterworth-Heinemann, 1998), vii–viii.

To truly harness an organization's collective knowledge and thereby facilitate productivity and wealth creation through intranets, the agents of that knowledge and the environments within which it is collected, manipulated, and applied are worthy of our attention. In this section we consider the "knowledge worker" and the "knowledge workplace," two emergent phenomena that drive the engine of twenty-first century productivity.

In Chapter 6 we look at today's knowledge workers—who they are, what they do, where they came from, what their needs are, and where they are going—and then outline some core competencies. In Chapter 7 we define and explore the knowledge workplace and discover how it has emerged through the tectonic forces of the Information Age.

The Knowledge Worker

Knowledge workers have been around for thousands of years, and knowledge work—historically performed by shamans, teachers, and lawyers equipped with tools such as brushes, tablets, books, and pens—for just as long. What is new is the general awareness that knowledge workers constitute a well-defined and discrete population that when enabled by key technologies, practices, and processes merges to form the foundation of postindustrial productivity.

What Are Knowledge Workers and What Do They Do?

Peter Drucker coined the phrase *knowledge worker* in his 1959 book *Landmarks of Tomorrow.* He described knowledge workers this way: They are not satisfied with work that is only a livelihood. Their aspirations and their views of themselves are those of the "professional" or "intellectual," and they demand that knowledge become the basis for accomplishment.[1]

Drucker also identified four characteristics of knowledge workers:

- They have specialized knowledge.
- They are able to acquire and apply theoretical and analytical knowledge.
- They are anchored in the habit of lifelong learning.
- They are effective in teams.[2]

While Drucker's characteristics are useful in understanding how knowledge workers function, the characteristics do not adequately put boundaries around the concept. Several definitions of the term *knowledge worker* have surfaced over the past few years. Perhaps the most cogent, put forward by the Gartner Group, describes the knowledge worker as one who

---

1. *Knowledge Worker Manual* (*http://navcenter.borgess.com/KworkerManual/ePages/front_ page/kw_def.html,* October 31, 2001).
2. Peter F. Drucker, *Managing in a Time of Great Change* (New York: Dutton, 1995), 226–243.

gathers, analyzes, adds value and communicates information to empower decision-making. The nature of "k-work" is ad hoc, demand-driven and creative (both in the ability to create new knowledge greater than the sum of its parts and in the ability to present the knowledge in a highly communicative way).[3]

Some narrowly define the knowledge worker as an individual involved in information technology—such as a software engineer, a programmer, a systems analyst, and so forth—but this is too limited. A truer representation of a knowledge worker goes beyond that and includes professionals in just about every field, from advertising to teaching to medicine to librarianship.

One way to better understand knowledge workers is to examine the different types of knowledge work they perform. Knowledge work involves the creation of knowledge and much more. There are several key types of knowledge work activity:

- Creating and collaborating on original knowledge
- Performing routine or administrative knowledge tasks
- Discovering knowledge
- Recycling knowledge
- Communicating knowledge

The Internet and intranets arguably represent *the* most powerful enabling technologies for knowledge workers. While there has always been an assumption that knowledge work cannot be automated—it requires creativity, and computers, servers, and software are only as clever as we make them—intranets do, in fact, facilitate the creative process. When the personal computer (PC) was a solitary, stand-alone machine on the desktop, this assumption might have been more relevant. But Internet and intranet technologies have changed everything. As interconnections between computers and individuals become easier to use, faster, and more valuable in terms of the services and content they support, they offer knowledge workers access to not only their individual work but to the collective work of colleagues across a company and the work of many others around the globe.

---

3. The Gartner Group, *Knowledge Worker State of the Market* (July 2000).

Interconnections provide a venue for sharing and communicating company knowledge and a means for encouraging creativity and innovation.

Let's take a closer look at each of the key knowledge work activities.

Creating and Collaborating on Original Knowledge

Original knowledge creation has not historically consumed a large portion of the knowledge worker's day, but information technologies, particularly productivity applications such as Microsoft Office XP, changed that. From desktop publishing to spreadsheets to CAD/CAM (computer-aided design/computer-aided manufacture), individual knowledge workers are empowered to create original knowledge. Electronic mail and instant messaging power the collaborative process. Web-based collaborative forums—with inline document discussion (the ability to embed comments, suggestions, and corrections to text), group survey features, seamless document and data integration, and the like—provide for the exchange of opinions from colleagues and introduce the opportunity for team innovation.

Performing Routine or Administrative Knowledge Tasks

The advent of the PC has had a major impact on routine work, especially on administrative and clerical activities. Networking technologies and intranets in particular have had a multiplier effect in this regard, reducing the complexity and time required to complete routine work and contributing to a shift in the configuration of skills in the modern workplace. Whereas a worker previously would have typed and formatted a report, an intranet allows individuals to write and publish reports themselves. Web-based forms, desktop publishing, document sharing, and many other features of intranets have continued to reduce the demand for clerical positions, freeing up staff and resources for other tasks.

Discovering Knowledge

Knowledge creation requires rapid discovery of relevant information. How can you build a better mousetrap if you cannot first find the design for the previous incarnation? Intranets enable this with advanced search and document management features, in addition to easy categorization and navigation through a hierarchical corporate taxonomy. As an organization grows, it tends to become more complex. Its knowledge workers create, manipulate, and analyze more company knowledge, which in turn must be archived and accessed by others. Employing automatic content categorization and correlation via meta data assures that relevant information is shared between knowledge workers, thus leading to better informed and faster decisions. In addition, because the portal aggregates disparate business process information at the desktop, knowledge workers have easy access to previously unavailable content.

Recycling Knowledge

The output of knowledge workers—each document written, presentation prepared, spreadsheet developed—represents an intellectual asset with distinct value. Each time that output is lost to the collective organization, money is lost. Each time that output is preserved, managed, and made discoverable, it may be reused or recycled and thereby developed into greater value.

Intranets facilitate knowledge mining and information gathering. For example, Whirlpool loads on its intranets the engineering specifications of many of the components used in its appliances. An engineer in Brazil who wants a specific design element for a new refrigerator can then search the site and borrow an idea that has already been thought up for a product in, say, the United States or France. It has been estimated that this kind of sharing of existing knowledge could increase the productivity of designers by 30 percent.[4]

Communicating Knowledge

Intranets are emerging as a universal communications workspace. Just as audio and video are integrated with text and graphics, the process of communicating knowledge throughout a company has been integrated with the process of creating knowledge. Departments or individuals might use digital media technologies to broadcast information to another department or to the entire company. As mentioned in Chapter 2, when any one of Hewlett-Packard Company's 90,000 employees first log on to their computers in the

4. Kit Sims Taylor, "The Brief Reign of the Knowledge Worker" (paper presented at the International Conference on the Social Impact of Information Technologies, St. Louis, Missouri, October 12–13, 1998).

morning, they can view a broadcast of Chairman and CEO Carly Fiorina giving an update on corporate performance, reporting executive council proceedings, or sharing other relevant news. These broadcasts might include Q&A, chat, polling, and quizzes to make them interactive. PowerPoint and other Microsoft Office applications can be synchronized with digital media for online and just-in-time learning scenarios. For example, the features of a new product could be highlighted in a PowerPoint presentation and then broadcast to each desktop.

Knowledge workers are also the recipients of training materials, in their continuous quest to build on their knowledge to be more effective in their work. For example, Hewlett-Packard distributed online learning to its sales force to educate them on a new product line release in advance of its launch. A return on investment (ROI) study showed an 1800 percent ROI in one year.[5]

Communicating results and know-how is an important part of the company-knowledge equation. All the features of intranets—desktop publishing, document sharing, automatic content categorization and correlation, aggregation of disparate information at the desktop, superior search engines, collaborative tools, and digital media communications—support this work pattern and establish it as one of growing significance in organizations.

Where Did Knowledge Workers Come From?

Historians, sociologists, and economists agree that the amount of information and diversity of skills needed to perform nonmanual or professional work has been rising steadily throughout the nineteenth and twentieth centuries. This is in proportion to the ever-increasing complexity of the tasks at hand. An increasing number of people in the industrialized world now make their living through work that does not require them to be on an assembly line or to plant and harvest crops. In addition, more and more jobs that are not typically regarded as "knowledge work based" depend on knowledge-worker skills, for example, the floor supervisor at an appliance assembler who must consult inventory databases and scheduling tools to support decidedly physical tasks. As we have seen from the definition provided earlier, a knowledge worker is a person who deals with data, information, and ideas to solve problems and generate knowledge-based output.

---

5. *http://www.microsoft.com/windows/windowsmedia/archive/casestudies/hewlett/default.asp.*

And as we have also discussed (see Chapter 1), there have always been knowledge workers—medicine men, lawyers, professors, and, of course, teachers. Every culture, whether agricultural or industrial, has had its individuals whose stock-in-trade was information and intellectual activity. Some knowledge workers have performed the same work for centuries but have only recently been characterized as such. When one starts to catalog all types of knowledge workers, they appear today to represent a substantial proportion of the workforce—evidence of a remarkable shift given that people have been employed in agriculture for the majority of humankind's history and only for the last two centuries in industry.

It is also true that as a culture grows and becomes more complex, the number and variety of knowledge workers expands and diversifies. So too do their respective tasks, responsibilities, and the requisite work tools. As an example, in the 1700s and 1800s, as the population of Europeans in North America increased, so too did the once-tiny number of actual knowledge workers: editors, writers, teachers, lawyers, and others. They represented the not-yet-identified knowledge industry; these people identified with their chosen professions and did not think of themselves as knowledge workers per se. As the North American economy of the 1700s and 1800s grew, it was able to support more people in such professions (for example, more teachers), specialization within professions (for example, elementary vs. high school teachers), and new professions all together. New industries produced new knowledge workers as old knowledge gave way to new. For example, in 1800 there was an industry for cutting ice from frozen New England lakes in winter and shipping it to the southern United States for ice cubes in beverages. By World War I that industry was gone, replaced with another for making motorized ice makers and refrigerators.[6]

With the rise of industrialism in North America beginning in the 1840s and continuing through the 1920s, in addition to more editors, writers, teachers, lawyers, and the like, new waves of knowledge workers swelled the economy. These included office clerks, operators of new information-handling equipment (such as telegraph and telephone operators), and individuals making a living generally handling information—economists, consultants, and experts on topics that had been of only minor interest a century earlier, such as dentistry.

6. James Cortada, "Introducing the Knowledge Worker" in James W. Cortada, ed., *Rise of the Knowledge Worker* (Boston: Butterworth-Heinemann, 1998), xiv.

The expanded reliance on science and technology that began to influence North American and European economic activity after the 1850s
(following the first World's Fair and the laying of the first transatlantic telegraph cable) created not only entirely new industries but new professions
and complex bodies of knowledge to support them. The following professions
appeared once the Industrial Revolution came into full swing: social critics
who put food on the table by selling their writings, inventors who supported
themselves with business and patent activities, accountants, secretaries,
office workers, and consultants. The most dramatic example, of course,
occurred in the latter part of the twentieth century: the computer industry
burst on the scene and was employing millions of workers by the end of the
century.

Prior to its invention in the late 1970s, few could envision the usefulness of the computer. A decade later these machines populated government and business offices where people knew little or nothing about the
technology, and thus organizations had to hire experts who could help
them use the machines and troubleshoot problems. But by the 1990s, with
the complex networking of these disparate machines, the need for
telecommunications and PC experts had burgeoned further. Computer
programmers had been generalists in the 1950s, but by the end of the
1960s they were specialists in specific languages, applications, and types of
software. The increasing complexity of computers contributed directly to
the creation of more knowledge work.

To understand the forces behind the increase in knowledge workers,
we can make the following observations. A class of knowledge worker
comes into existence when a body of information must be collected,
applied, and built upon for subsequent action.[7] In addition, as the volume
of information about a particular subject grows, so too does the probability that the workforce that gathers, sorts, manipulates, analyzes, publishes,
and otherwise communicates that information will become specialized.
Take the example of the knowledge-management workforce. As the
discipline evolved and the body of literature supporting and developing
knowledge management expanded, its members developed specialized
communities of practice. For example, there are those who specialize in
intellectual asset management as a business strategy; others who focus on
the application of knowledge-sharing strategies on the frontlines; and still

---

7. Cortada, 12.

others who consider the corporate, physical, human, and technological structures that combine to form the infrastructure of knowledge-based enterprises.

Each new knowledge-handling technology also creates a new kind of knowledge work and a new class of knowledge worker. Examples abound. We previously mentioned telegraph operators who emerged after the invention of the telegraph, and likewise telephone operators after the invention of the telephone. With innovations in office equipment such as typewriters and adding machines, secretaries emerged in large numbers. The introduction of computers and software made it possible for men and women to make a living programming computers and writing software code. And there are many other examples.

The central features of this work specialization include

- An intimate understanding of how a new technology functions

- An appreciation of how to apply a new technology to work processes, for example, using the telephone as a sales tool or an adding machine to attend to new forms of accounting

- An expansion of the body of knowledge and a contribution to improved work processes and performance[8]

Another observation about the growth of knowledge workers is their number increases when the volume of work or the size of the organization grows. The enormous increase in the number of clerks in offices in the twentieth century was a direct result of the growth in organizational size, both in the public sector with the expanded role of government and in the private sector with the rise of corporations. The same thing happened in China between A.D. 1300 and 1400. The emperors were ambitious conquerors who succeeded in amassing great territories for China. This expansion and the necessity for control called for vast armies of civil servants who could administer the empire in an efficient manner, so the ranks of these early knowledge workers swelled.[9]

As our economy and industries expanded and became more complex, the number and type of knowledge workers required to support these activities grew relationally.

8. Cortada, 13.
9. Ibid.

Today's Knowledge Workers

Thomas Davenport, author of *Human Capital: What It Is and Why People Invest It* (San Francisco: Jossey-Bass Publishers, 1999), recently commented that many North American organizations are stifling their key "knowledge workers" with well-intentioned but outmoded management approaches.[10] In some ways the jobs of top management are becoming easier: supervising knowledge workers and their activities does not constitute a big part of management's daily responsibilities because the nature of knowledge work is mostly private, intellectual, and unsupervisable. What is more crucial—and what presents a major new challenge—is motivating members of this sophisticated workforce to be as creative and productive as possible. This can be especially frustrating for those members of a management team who rose through the ranks under the old management paradigm that shaped the way they think about work, about managing their businesses, and about reacting to the challenges that arise in day-to-day situations.

The skills associated with the old model of management that originated in the 1920s—skills such as planning, controlling, and organizing—need to be replaced with new skills of leadership, which involve such things as helping, inspiring, listening, respect, and trust.

Knowledge workers are seeking several things from the workplace. They are looking to invest in their long-term knowledge careers through constant learning, innovation, and collaboration. In a recently published study, research on employee attitudes shows that one of the knowledge worker's most valued attributes in an employer is the ability to encourage innovation and new thinking.[11] Knowledge workers also value an environment in which a balance between work and life is a given. As individuals feel an increasing ownership of their lives and careers, living skills—such as learning, communication, independence, citizenship, leisure, physical fitness, and well-being—become just as important as professional skills.[12] The corollary of this is that knowledge workers, in exchange for investing time and knowledge in a company, desire customized deals, not just the standard employment packages most employers still offer.

Knowledge workers are seldom motivated by traditional management strategies. Knowledge workers react stubbornly to force and other methods

---

10. Virginia Galt, "Firms Seen Stifling Key Employees," *Globe and Mail* (July 3, 2001), B1.
11. Galt, B1.
12. Louisa Wah, "Workplace of the Future," *Management Review* (January 2000), 9.

of coercive control. Appraisals and rewards need to be more creative, and the workplace environment is important.[13] Even though the stock phrase "Our employees are our best assets" finds its way into almost every annual report and many print and other media advertisements, the phrase rings hollow with knowledge workers themselves. The term *assets* implies ownership and lumps human beings together with buildings, computers, and trucks. The phrase also suggests that work is a one-way exploitation of an asset by an owner, rather than a two-way exchange of value.

Knowledge workers strive for autonomy, freedom, and flexibility. Intelligent, educated, and motivated employees want to do their jobs their way. Roper Starch Worldwide, a U.S. market research firm, recently conducted a study of *Fast Company* readers about the aspect of work that provided them the most personal satisfaction. "Knowing you had a really productive day" rated higher than a compliment from the boss, a larger-than-expected raise, and a faster-than expected promotion.[14]

True knowledge workers will only be willing to share their knowledge with their company when there is a solid basis of trust. This trust will lead to the belief that the company, and thereby the knowledge workers themselves, will benefit from the knowledge.[15] Building trust requires a "knowledge attitude" throughout an organization—one that convinces knowledge workers that they are working on their own knowledge careers, that their sole responsibility in addition to job performance is to learn and keep on learning. And when it comes to sharing, the main value is respect for someone else's knowledge, ideas, and thoughts. Creating and maintaining a knowledge-centric mind-set in an organization is a formidable undertaking. It is more than investing in training programs, establishing company-wide communications and information networks, and writing mission statements that stress how important lifelong learning is to the organization. The engagement will be against the old workplace paradigms grounded in individual rather than collaborative efforts and in the status quo vs. change as the creative imperative.

Core Competencies of Today's Knowledge Workers

It is people who make knowledge work. That is why it is vital that today's knowledge workers possess competencies that allow them to work with

13. Galt, B1.
14. Ibid.
15. Rene Tissen, Daniel Andriessen, Deprez Andriessen, and Frank Lekanne, *The Knowledge Dividend* (London: Financial Times/Prentice Hall, 2000), 166.

knowledge and achieve greater personal satisfaction from a job well done. These competencies support their learning and, like most competencies, can be learned.

Today's knowledge worker must be able to sense and respond to unstructured knowledge, create and produce structured knowledge, and connect the two to bring added value to the organization. Knowledge workers must continuously update their individual knowledge bases with specialized education and training, plus create and maintain connections with other individuals, within and without the organization.

There are three main groups of competencies: competencies that help knowledge workers learn from information; competencies that help them improve their thinking; and social competencies that help them interact better with their colleagues, customers, and suppliers.

Learning from Information

The ability to learn from information draws on sourcing, questioning, and awareness. Sourcing is a competence for knowing how and where to look for needed information. Questioning is all about turning data into information by making certain it provides an answer to a specific question; it involves knowing what question to ask and recognizing when the "answer" is complete. Awareness means being responsive and open to new ideas and information; it means postponing judgment on any matter until all information is available and listening with an open mind, observing, and perceiving.[16]

Improving Thinking

Steps to improve one's thinking include analysis, creativity, and reflection. Analyzing is a competency that is based on logic, systems thinking, and mental modeling—a rational and systematic approach to thinking and making decisions. It helps to identify missteps, discontinuities, and gaps in process and in knowledge when making decisions. Creating requires a more emotional approach and an acceptance of "thinking outside the box." It needs the freedom and support for having "bad ideas." Reflecting is the ability to ponder lessons learned and thereby grow[17] and is the basis for much of what we master.

---

16. Tissen et al., 163.
17. Tissen et al., 165.

Social Competencies

Networking, teamwork, and dialoguing are valuable competencies for the knowledge worker. Networking is vital. It helps the knowledge worker build a close circle of trusted colleagues and customers who support creativity and productivity. Teamwork assists in developing the ability to collaborate and share knowledge, and is often the catalyst for innovation. Dialoguing is the ability to listen with full attention and entertain positions and advice from all team members, suppliers and customers, regardless of one's preconceptions.[18]

Summary

Enabling knowledge-worker creativity is both the principal opportunity and challenge for today's organizations—an opportunity because of the inestimable value that emerges through the treatment of knowledge as a managed asset, and a challenge because it requires management and cultural change. How can this be accomplished? What can be done to direct an organization toward this vision? We believe that the following "rules for the workplace" are a good place to begin:

- The nature of knowledge work dictates that knowledge workers have to manage themselves more or less autonomously.

- Continuing innovation is central to knowledge work and motivates and excites knowledge workers.

- Knowledge work necessitates continuous learning as well as constant teaching and sharing of this learning with colleagues.

- Knowledge-worker productivity needs to be rewarded in creative ways.

In the next chapter we look at the larger context in which these knowledge workers exist: the knowledge workplace and the knowledge-centric society in which we live. There is no question that the workplace has been transformed by the information revolution and computing. The consequence for business leaders is that they must respond to the needs of the twenty-first century knowledge worker in the context of the new workplace and provide the necessary tools to manage intellectual capital to drive productivity.

---

18. Ibid.

CHAPTER

7

The Knowledge Workplace

To understand how workplace intranet solutions can bring value to an organization, the nature of that workplace must be considered, which is the goal of this chapter. We will first look at the big picture: the nature of the information society, which is the larger context in which the knowledge workplace exists. Then we will explore how the nature of "work" has changed as we moved from the Industrial Age into the Information Age. Then we will look at how the knowledge workplace has been transformed by highlighting how some old workplace maxims, such as "treat employees consistently" and "people need jobs," have been updated. Finally we take a look at the formal discipline of knowledge management and show how to "make knowledge work" in an organization.

From the Industrial Revolution to the Information Age

Today we live in the Information Age, where knowledge is generally accepted as a foundation for any business process, product, service, strategy, event, or relationship. This Information Age evolved from the Industrial Revolution, where labor and machines combined to form the basis of economic activity. What lies between the ore cars and smokestacks of the nineteenth century, and the satellites and microchips of the twenty-first century, are forces that have transformed our economy and world of work.

In the 1950s an eminent sociologist, Daniel Bell, a professor at Columbia University and then Harvard University, described three kinds of societies: a preindustrial society, an industrial society, and a postindustrial society. A preindustrial society can be described as a "game against nature," wherein humans attempt to extract resources from the natural environment. Primary sector occupations and industries such as hunting, fishing, farming, mining, and logging dominate the economy, and custom and tradition severely limit the supply of land and resources.[1]

An industrial society is a "game against fabrication" that centers on the human-machine relationship and uses energy to transform the natural into another good. Economic activity is focused on manufacturing and processing industries, and the challenge is to mobilize sufficient capital to establish such enterprises. The central occupations are secondary sector occupations such as the semiskilled factory worker.[2]

A postindustrial society—the Information Age—is a "game against persons," a game in which intellectual technology (based on information) rises alongside machine technology. This society involves industries from three sectors: the tertiary sectors of transportation and utilities; the quaternary industries of trade, finance, and capital exchanges; and the quinary industries of health, education, research, public administration, and leisure. Because the generation of information is the key economic issue, and because science, technology, and other research disciplines are the most important sources of this information, the central economic challenge is collecting, storing, and protecting that information.

The industrial society experienced several transformations in the 1950s and 1960s. Bell identified several characteristics of the Information Age that set it apart from previous societies:

- The *centrality of knowledge* will become the primary source of invention as big science institutionalizes the process for innovation.

- A *new intellectual technology* will be created as experts exploit computers to make use of mathematical techniques for the purpose of engineering more efficient and rational solutions to economic, material, and even social problems.

- A *knowledge class* will emerge from the ranks of the rapidly growing technical and professional workforce.

- The economy will *shift from being goods based to being service based* (even by 1970, 6.5 out of every 10 workers were engaged in the provision of services).

---

1. Malcolm Waters, Daniel Bell (London: Routledge, 1996), 109.
2. Ibid.

- *The character of work will change* and will challenge previous conceptions about management, reward, loyalty, individual behaviors, and more.

- *The role of women will expand* because the service sector has afforded them employment opportunities and encouraged economic independence.

- *Science as imago*—science and technology will become more bureaucratized and tied to the payoffs derived from its applications.

- *Meritocracy*, which rewards education, knowledge, intelligence, and skill, will replace inheritance, property, and cultural advantage in society.

- *Information and time will become scarce* and take their place beside the old scarcities of material resources.

- *The economics of information* will attend to the growing need for cooperative strategies to guarantee the optimal distribution of knowledge throughout the society.[3]

Bell was prescient in his observations about the changing nature of work, the transformation of the workplace, the mission-critical nature of knowledge, and the pivotal role of technology in the interplay of these forces. Our current preoccupation with knowledge management and collaborative and productivity tools in the workplace is a testament to his foresight. It is the context in which we must consider the business value propositions of intranets.

The Changing Nature of Work

One of the first scholars to appreciate the changing nature of work was Fritz Machlup, a Princeton University economics professor. In the 1950s he began to look at knowledge much the same way that an economist would examine a product—by documenting its creation, distribution, and significance. His research led others to view knowledge work as something distinctive, something different from other types of work. He estimated that information

---

3. Waters, 111-112.

activities had absorbed 29 percent of the gross national product (GNP)[4] and 31 percent of the workforce by 1958. He demonstrated that the information sector had grown at twice the rate of the GNP between 1947 and 1958 and concluded that the complexity of business processes and the need for better-educated and better-trained employees fueled the growth in the knowledge-worker sector.[5]

Two communication professors, Jorge Reina Schement and Terry Curtis, undertook more recent research on the size and dimension of knowledge workers in the United States. They concluded that information-handling activities were being broadly incorporated into ever wider sets of occupations than in previous generations.[6]

Every new kind of work requires new tools and techniques; different understandings and insights lead to new experiences, values, and dynamics. Put another way, the rise and recognition of knowledge work and knowledge workers is leading to a redefinition of work. New tools, insights, and technologies have been developed to make knowledge productive, reusable, and profitable.

From Manual Work to Knowledge Work

In Chapter 6 we said that knowledge workers have always existed, but the twentieth century witnessed an exponential growth in their number. Peter Drucker observed in 1980 that in the world of work, the center of gravity had shifted from manual work to knowledge work. While in 1920 the ratio of manual workers to knowledge workers was 2:1, the reverse was true by 1980.[7] This shift to knowledge work was accompanied by two additional shifts in the workplace: (1) control of work moved away from the supervisor or manager and to the knowledge worker, and (2) the focus of work moved from the worker to the work process.

---

4. The value of an economy's total output of goods and services.

5. Fritz Machlup, "Knowledge Production and Occupation Structure," in James W. Cortada, ed., *Rise of the Knowledge Worker* (Boston: Butterworth-Heinemann, 1998), 89.

6. Jorge Reina Schement and Terry Curtis, "The New Industrial Society," in James W. Cortada, ed., *Rise of the Knowledge Worker* (Boston: Butterworth-Heinemann, 1998), 133–150.

7. Fred Nickols, "What Is in the World of Work and Working: Some Implications of the Shift to Knowledge Work" (*http://home.att.net/~nickols/shifts.htm,* October 28, 2001).

There are several differences between manual work and knowledge work. Manual work is materials based, whereas knowledge work is information based. The results of manual work (a conversion of materials from one form to another) are tangible, whereas the results of knowledge work (a conversion of information from one form to another) are frequently intangible. Consequently, the working behaviors of the manual worker are public, while the working behaviors of the knowledge worker are more private because the work of the knowledge worker is done "in the head" and cannot be readily seen. Although it is true that both manual workers and knowledge workers use information and knowledge, only the latter works *on* it.

Public behaviors and the visible, often immediate, consequences of those behaviors make it comparatively simple to determine the success or productivity of the manual worker and his or her tools. This, in turn, simplifies managerial control and supervision. Conversely, the private nature of knowledge work makes it difficult to ascertain linkages between behavior, tools, and results and presents a challenge for supervision.[8] It also calls into question the traditional management techniques predicated on a different work paradigm (more on this later).

The Locus of Control Shifts to the Worker

For hundreds of years the means of control or "power" in organizations were defined by two variables: knowledge and discipline. In factories of yesteryear, managers at the top closely held onto knowledge; in today's modern organization, knowledge is widely known. Discipline was previously achieved through the "chain of command." With materials-based work, the linkages between behavior and results were observable by individuals other than the worker. Modifications to behavior were communicated to the worker via sets of instructions and were enforced through supervision, incentives, and penalties. Because much of what knowledge workers do is private and "unsupervisable," an important link in the chain of command has been broken. The manager is no longer the locus of control.

The nature of knowledge work is such that it demands a significant amount of self-control over work and working habits. According to Peter Drucker, knowledge workers configure their responses to work situations

---

8. Ibid.

instead of acting out prescribed ones. They have almost total authority over the matching of their work methods against specific tasks. The days when a stern warning from the overseer prompted increased productivity are history. The typical knowledge worker of today acts on behalf of his or her employer, not at the behest of the supervisor. This represents a shift from compliance to contribution and from instrument to agent in the world of work. Thomas Peters and Robert H. Watermen, in their watershed book, *In Search of Excellence: Lessons from America's Best-Run Companies,*[9] acknowledge this transformation when they identified "autonomy and entrepreneurship" and "productivity through people" as two of the eight properties of excellence. A consequence of all this is that the locus of control has moved away from the manager and to the shoulders of the knowledge worker.

The Focus of Control Shifts to the Work Process

A corollary to this shift in the locus of control is a shift in the focus of control. Owing to the nature of manual work, management focused on the worker when determining productivity and efficiencies, but this is not the case for knowledge work. To make knowledge work productive, control must be exercised over the work process, not the worker. The corollary is that it is incumbent on organizations to provide knowledge workers with the best tools possible to realize productivity gains, tools such as intranets.

> The task of making knowledge work productive will be the great challenge of the century, just as to make manual work productive was the great management task of the last century.[10]

While Drucker made that pronouncement in 1973, it still holds true today.

Transformation of the Workplace

Constancy does not exist in the Information Age; we see vast transformations in the nature of work and continuous change in the work environment—hallmarks of the knowledge workplace.

---

9. New York: Warner Books (1982).

10. Peter Drucker, *Management: Tasks, Responsibilities, Practices* (New York: Harper & Row, 1974).

A new reality exists. Unlike all previous foundations for wealth-land and natural resources in the preindustrial age and capital and machinery in the industrial age-knowledge can be given away but also retained at the same time. We have shifted from a zero-sum game, where one side always wins and the other side always loses, to a win-win game, where all sides can potentially win through knowledge sharing. This has had an understandable effect on the rules of the workplace game. To succeed in maintaining and growing the knowledge capital of an organization, old structures, such as jobs and management paradigms, must be reinvented and transformed.

This section will describe seven observed transformations in our working environment. Table 7-1 presents knowledge workplace maxims contrasted with those of the industrial age.

Knowledge Workplace Maxim #1: Promote Change as Creative and Imperative

The need for and the inevitability of change has never been as prominent an issue for the business leader as it is today, and we have a whole new discipline as proof: change management. Organizations are called on to respond to, indeed leverage, changes in the workplace, the global marketplace, society at large, and our technological capabilities. While implementing change may be disruptive, it can also be thrilling, challenging, and the catalyst for innovation.

Agility in responding to changes on the business landscape is a hallmark of a successful organization. Flexible and dynamic tools such as intranets

Table 7-1 Industrial Age vs. Knowledge Workplace Maxims[11]

Industrial Age Maxim	Knowledge Workplace Maxim
Preserve the status quo.	Promote change as creative and imperative.
Resist organizational movement.	Encourage organizational movement.
Engender rugged individualism.	Inspire connected teamwork.
Command and control workers.	Lead by facilitating utmost creativity.
Organize for uniformity.	Respect worker individuality.
Divide and control.	Collaborate and innovate.
People need jobs.	Value each contribution.

11. Adapted from Doug Wesley, "Retaining Workers in the Knowledge Economy, *Information Outlook* (October 2000), pp. 35–40.

must be in place to make this possible. Rapid access to relevant business information, real-time collaboration, and broadcast communications are necessary to inform the knowledge workplace and facilitate the generation and implementation of creative responses.

Knowledge Workplace Maxim #2: Encourage Organizational Movement

When losing an employee meant losing knowledge capital, organizations fought to keep the employee as long as possible. High employee retention and low staff turnover were key goals, but what if an organization could capture the knowledge of exiting employees and build on the continuous use of their contributions to the organization? It is possible to lose employees but preserve value in the knowledge workplace. The sophisticated document management capabilities of intranets are instrumental in this regard.

If the organization is in the business of learning, then we can expect to see an increase in the wealth of the enterprise with personnel turnover. It was previously assumed that old-timers would teach apprentices; indeed, the master had an obligation to do so. With increased circulation of knowledge workers between organizations, the new employee can often teach something to his or her colleagues in return.[12]

The knowledge workplace comprises systems that capture individual knowledge and makes it available to the collective. But why would workers agree to part with this knowledge? For the reason that, in return, they are provided with access to the knowledge of the organization, other innovative people, training opportunities wherein they can enhance their skills and personal knowledge, and tools that support this. Someday the most important part of the job interview will be not "Where did you work and for how long?" but "What did you learn?"

Knowledge Workplace Maxim #3: Inspire Connected Teamwork

When individuals operate in isolation within an organization, the organization is less productive. Things fall between the cracks as a result of overspe-

---

12. Wesley, 35.

cialization and professionalism as well as the inherent human tendency to hoard information. Businesses thwart fulfillment of customers' needs because "it's not my job" or "it's not this department's responsibility." We have all learned to ask for the manager because we know that few workers have the authority to solve unusual problems or ones that cross organizational borders. Most knowledge workers would rather solve the problem and leave the customer satisfied than hand it off to someone else.

Business success now depends on the connections between customers and the organization and between employees themselves. The connections between the customer and the organization are best maintained by small teams of employees who are responsible for the relationships and who respond quickly. The value of these connections is widely recognized, which is evidenced by the growing emphasis on customer relationship management tools and techniques.

The connections between employees are also vital for business success. These connections are enabled in work environments that value collaboration, teamwork, and knowledge sharing.[13] When highly focused and unimpeded by technological or geographic barriers, these connections give power to the organization. They bring about the conversion of intellectual assets into profit-generating products and services and process efficiencies.

In the 1980s students devised a solution for information overload: study groups or knowledge networks. Students pooled their knowledge, engaged in team projects, and studied together. Today's knowledge workplace is populated with many of these graduates who are very comfortable with work group collaboration and welcome the tools that make it possible.

Knowledge Workplace Maxim #4: Lead by Facilitating Utmost Creativity

With an educated, specialized workforce, new organizational structures appear: intranets support many management tasks and encourage a continuous learning environment; small, self-managed teams no longer need supervisors and managers to motivate them to achieve peak performance.

The role of management has moved away from command and control and is becoming centered on leadership as defined by facilitating the creative

---

13. Wesley, 36.

process, enabling the free flow of the organization's knowledge capital, and promoting a culture of individual responsibility and accountability. This is accomplished by cataloguing known knowledge capital, utilizing and applying it in creative ways, archiving it within the organization where it can be shared among all employees, and engendering a nurturing and learning culture wherein it can grow.

This new workplace maxim redeploys managers' skills. It takes the "bossing" out of managing and replaces it with leading, encouraging, inspiring, and facilitating.

Knowledge Workplace Maxim #5: Respect Worker Individuality

Even before the Information Age began, consumerism in North America (especially in the United States) coerced Industrial Age businesses into changing the way they conducted their affairs. The first fruits of globalization in the 1970s provided consumers with more choice; it was possible to get the products we wanted when we wanted them at a reasonable price. This forced businesses to revisit their notion of selling identical products to sheeplike mass markets. The "custom" part of the customer took on new significance as enterprises began to treat each customer as individuals.[14]

This trend has spilled over into the workplace. Just as there is no longer a mass consumer market, there is no longer a homogeneous labor market. Employees are increasingly making independent, individual decisions about what they want from the workplace and the organization. Compensation and reward systems are becoming more individually tailored, appreciating the differing work and life needs of the twenty-first century knowledge worker. This need to personalize has also been incorporated into the desktop and the intranet. No one interface is standard across an organization. Customization of desktop geography, identification of priority items, and personalized subscription services are all essential.

Knowledge Workplace Maxim #6: Collaborate and Innovate

Today's business mantra is no longer "divide and control"; rather, it is unite and collaborate. When an organization's performance was rooted in stan-

---

14. Wesley, 37.

dardized machine and production systems, it made sense to force employees to comply with established rules and procedures. Even though individuals on the front lines might have had suggestions on how to improve the process and effect better performance, employee suggestions were not always encouraged, let alone implemented.

Not so in the knowledge workplace. Not happy to check their brains at the door, today's knowledge workers want to contribute ideas and see them work in a knowledge-sharing environment. They want to participate in problem resolution, innovation, and the strategic direction of the enterprise through Web-based collaboration: on-line forums, document sharing, broadcast communications, and the like. Just as global markets have enabled free trade across national borders, so must we emancipate knowledge workers to freely cross internal boundaries to combine talents and innovate.

To succeed in global free markets, organizations must constantly invent and reinvent. They can no longer afford to squander knowledge worker output, which is, of course, knowledge itself. To earn the loyalty and maximize the innovative contributions of these workers, old workplace paradigms must give way to the new.

Knowledge Workplace Maxim #7: Value Each Contribution

Organizations can no longer afford to employ only parts of the individuals they hire. The twentieth century's wizard of industry, Henry Ford, mused in his 1923 autobiography, *My Life and Work*,[15] about the more than 7,800 specialized jobs required to make the Model T:

> 949 specialized jobs required strong, able-bodied and practically physically perfect men, 3338 needed men of merely ordinary physical strength, most of the rest could be performed by women or older children, and we found that 670 could be filled by legless men, 2637 by one-legged men, two by armless men and 715 by one-armed men and 10 by blind men.[16]

---

15. with Samuel Crowther; Garden City, NY: Garden City Publishers.

16. Ford and Crowther, 108.

It appears as if organizations have followed in Ford's footsteps by institutionalizing organizational designs that employ only certain parts of people. To reverse this pattern, organizations must begin to deal with the softer, more complex issues of emotion, family demands, conflicting needs, and obligations. To earn the right to integrate the whole person, organizations must respect each person's contribution as individual and essential. Knowledge workers must be allowed and encouraged to shape their own work and afforded significant autonomy and power over the tools and resources at hand to achieve high performance and personal satisfaction.

If organizations are to be successful in harnessing and leveraging their growing knowledge capital, knowledge workers must cooperate and actively participate in this process. To earn that cooperation, organizations are now realizing that they must reinvent their relationship structures with and between their knowledge workers and invest in strategic knowledge tools such as intranets to support the new workplace maxims.

Knowledge Management

Knowledge management has emerged as a discipline that treats intellectual capital as a managed asset. Its aim is delivery of the organization's intellectual capacity to the individuals who directly contribute to the success or failure of an enterprise. The hypothesis of knowledge management is that in a fast-moving, increasingly competitive marketplace, an organization's only enduring source of advantage is its knowledge-the knowledge of its employees and the knowledge that is built into the organization.

In some respects knowledge management and the knowledge workplace are synonymous. The field of knowledge management has been somewhat limited by the intellectual and academic debate over "what it is." This tendency to intellectual abstraction has slowed its progress and limited its impact in the real world. Our view is that the debate is moot because the knowledge workplace is not a theoretical concept but a real, emerging phenomenon. Nevertheless some reference to knowledge management is important here.

Central to the theory of knowledge management is the concept that the organization is a social institution. It draws value from the individuals within it and from its ability to harness their knowledge. However, individuals also draw value from the organization in more ways than a paycheck. They learn from their colleagues and receive satisfaction from completing tasks they would otherwise be unable to complete. As social beings, employees enjoy sharing their experiences and being part of a group, project, and team. There is value in creating structures and systems that enable, not constrain, social activity and knowledge sharing, and knowledge management can be seen as a set of techniques and practices that facilitate the flow of knowledge into and within an organization.

There are two key requisites for the effective management of knowledge work: (1) The organization must accept the concept of "teamness" and encourage individuals to interact, work together on projects, and share their ideas informally. (2) Systems are needed to collect, archive, and codify the knowledge of individuals so that others can learn from it.[17]

Knowledge Work Tools

The primary "tools" applied in the practice of managing knowledge are organizational dynamics, process engineering, and information technology (IT). These three tools work in concert to streamline and enhance the capture and flow of an organization's data, information, and knowledge and deliver these things to individuals and groups engaged in accomplishing a specific project.

Organizational Dynamics

A large part of knowledge management is simply about facilitating the natural interactions between people. One approach is to design the physical layout of the office so that social interaction is encouraged. New work styles do not necessarily work in buildings designed for the old top-down corporation. For example, in the late 1990s ALCOA abandoned its aluminum tower in Pittsburgh for a new complex on the banks of the Allegheny River. Their new workplace operates with open cubicles and includes "communications centers" with televisions, faxes, newspapers, and tables to encourage impromptu meetings and exchanges.[18]

Another approach is to design formal structures of interaction around key knowledge flows. Cross-functional teams are a good example of this

---

17. Julie Birkinshaw, "Making Sense of Knowledge Management, Ivey Business Journal (March 1, 2001), 32.
18. Joan O'C. Hamilton, "The New Workplace: Walls Are Falling as the Office of the Future Finally Takes Shape," *Business Week* (April 29, 1996), 106.

approach, with prescribed meetings to ensure all individuals involved bring their relevant knowledge to bear on a task.

A third approach is to facilitate information interactions through what are often called "communities of practice": groups of individuals with common interests and problems that are dispersed throughout the organization. It is argued that these individuals will actively seek one another out to share experiences and learn from one another.[19]

Process Engineering

A number of specific knowledge management tools can be used by organizations to hone the knowledge collection and dissemination process. One is the transfer of best practice, a structured process for taking a practice in one location and transferring it to another. Everyone recognizes how important this is in principle, and organizations have been very clever in attending to this, using best practice databases and benchmarking tools.

As an example, the Ford Motor Company's Ford Motor Benchmarking Clearinghouse created a process benchmarking Web site on the company's intranet. Designed for a quick eyescan, the site contains core benchmarking how-to information and has been very successful in creating benchmarking and best practices awareness through the organization.[20]

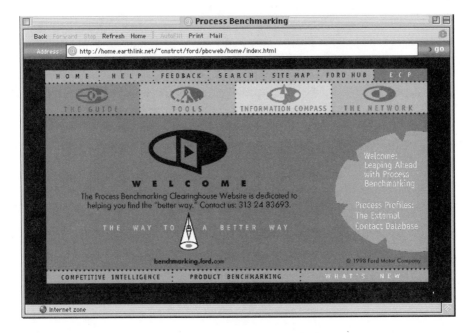

Another management tool for the knowledge workplace is the creation and designation of centers of excellence, which are groups of individuals whose expertise is recognized and communicated throughout the enterprise so that other members of the organization may access it when needed.[21]

Information Systems

Knowledge management has evolved from information management because knowledge and information are so closely linked. Intranet solutions enable virtually every aspect of knowledge management with Web-based team collaboration, search, document management, and digital media communications. McKinsey and Accenture, for example, have highly sophisticated databases that provide libraries of information about their proprietary methodologies, clients, and previous engagements.[22] These are essentially repositories of codified knowledge. They have captured the collective memory and experience of their knowledge workers so others can learn.

While it is true that technology drove the initial interest in knowledge management in the United States, knowledge workers and their organizations now realize that an effective approach also addresses people and processes.[23] The tripartite focus on people, process, and technology has enabled the planning and adoption of solutions to meet an organization's business goals.

It is now worth noting the existence of two related concepts: organizational learning and intellectual capital. These two concepts somewhat overlap with knowledge management, yet each maintains its own nuances. The underlying premise is similar: knowledge is a scarce and valuable resource, so organizations must become better at learning and sharing knowledge to succeed in the ever-changing global marketplace. The difference is that organizational learning is about managing the processes of learning, while knowledge management is more concerned with techniques for capturing, building, and applying stocks of knowledge.[24]

---

19. Birkinshaw, 34.
20. Vicki J. Powers, "Ford Creates Clearinghouse, Virtual Network, Web Site to Support Its Benchmarking Efforts, *Benchmarking in Practice* (#15, First Quarter, 1999).
21. Birkinshaw, 34.
22. Birkinshaw, 35.
23. Greg Dyer, "The State of KM," *Knowledge Management* (May 1, 2001), 31.
24. Dyer, 33.

The intellectual capital movement took shape at about the same time as knowledge management. It emerged from the world of accounting as an attempt to identify and quantify intangible assets. By distilling a firm's intellectual capital into such elements as human capital (skills and capabilities of employees), customer capital (existing relationships), and structural capital (patents, operating systems, and practices), useful measures were devised that could be monitored and evaluated over time. The best-known example of this was the Navigator model developed by Skandia, a Swedish insurance company, in which the elements of intellectual capital were identified, measured, and reported in a supplement to its annual report.[25]

Putting Knowledge to Work

Putting knowledge to work in an organization means improving the way it is shared and applied. It means adopting the knowledge workplace maxims described here and bringing people together with information technologies. There is no rapid way to implement such a system in an organization. It requires a continuous learning style of working to create a workplace that best suits the organization's objectives, culture, processes, and IT environment.

The most innovative organizations have already embarked on this journey, without associating directly with knowledge management per se, through empowering knowledge workers and adopting enabling technologies. Leading organizations in virtually every sector have shown, through an ever-growing number of case studies, that more effective use of knowledge and insight gives them a competitive advantage. Business success is not about amassing assets; it is about putting them to work. Now is the time for those who are in the "early majority" to take action, closing the narrow but fast-growing gap between themselves and innovators.

There are no quick solutions for creating or changing knowledge attitudes within an organization, but there are steps to take to make it work better. Begin by assessing the competencies of knowledge workers, which can assist them in working more successfully in the knowledge workplace. Questions such as "What is the knowledge attitude of my organization?" "Do workers respect each other sufficiently to want to share and listen?" "Do they

---

25. Birkinshaw, 32.

trust the organization with their knowledge?" and "Is there a willingness to put their knowledge in the system?" need to be asked and answered.[26]

Then methods to improve these competencies and attitudes should be defined. There are numerous training courses for improving knowledge competencies, but changing attitudes require more thought and attention. The approach will, of course, depend on the severity of the situation. If there is no respect for or trust in the management team, the process will be a long and challenging one.

Summary

The knowledge workplace is emerging as a result of advances in information technology, knowledge proliferation, and profound societal and organizational change. It is enabled by next generation intranets that deliver the productivity benefits, process improvements, and reductions in cost, which are essential to postindustrial businesses. For organizations to remain agile and succeed in a constantly changing marketplace, new vision is required. This includes integration of knowledge management theory, but it is not limited to its constraints as an academic discipline. In the next chapter we move into a discussion on the benefits of identifying and measuring the business value proposition for intranets and describe how a few organizations have effectively measured returns on their intranet investments.

---

26. Rene Tissen, Daniel Andriessen, Deprez Andriessen, and Frank Lekanne, *The Knowledge Dividend* (London: Financial Times/Prentice Hall, 2000), 210.

How Intranets Add Value

The challenge for business decision makers is to engender a workplace that promotes creating, sharing, and leveraging knowledge resources. The challenge is also to identify appropriate tools and demonstrate the value these tools will bring to the organization in terms of productivity enhancements, cost savings, process efficiencies, or increased functionality. This section is all about how intranets—one of the essential knowledge-building tools of our time—can bring value to an organization. Chapter 8 discusses the "how" and "why" of identifying and measuring value, including a look at both qualitative and quantitative approaches. It also profiles how some organizations have quantified the returns on their intranet investments.

The productivity and knowledge-enabling potential inherent in intranets is best demonstrated with actual case studies. Chapter 9 examines four intranet deployments and describes the business value benefits that have been realized. Enlightened by the experience of others, business decision makers are better positioned to make choices about the intranet solution best suited to their workplaces.

The Business Value Proposition for Next Generation Intranets

In the changing workplace and with newfound consciousness regarding the value of knowledge, business decision makers (BDMs) face the challenge of building the knowledge workplace, a dynamic environment of maximized productivity and enhanced process efficiency. BDMs must also provide evidence that the tools they use have quantifiable value, which is the focus of this chapter. We describe the challenges and benefits of identifying and measuring the business value proposition for intranets, which includes a discussion of both qualitative and quantitative value, and profile a few organizations that have effectively measured returns on their intranet investments.

Advances in communications and computing technologies, the advent of the Internet, and the proliferation of advanced, high-speed computer networks and systems are producing a new order in business collaboration and productivity. This revolution will affect every aspect of life in some manner. The global village envisaged by Marshall McLuhan is undoubtedly emerging: an information-centric environment, where individuals work in concert with technology to streamline and enhance the capture and flow of an organization's data, information, and knowledge and deliver it to individuals and global teams engaged in accomplishing specific tasks. These individuals, or knowledge workers, are indispensable resources and represent the productivity engine of the twenty-first century world of business.

The shift to knowledge work has produced a revolution in organizational behavior that has led to a reinterpretation of success, of a business' fundamental value.

"Today, the long-term success of organizations comes from their knowledge-based assets-customer relationships; innovative products and services; operationally excellent processes; the skills, capabilities, and motivation of their people; and their databases and information systems."[1]

Similarly, the trend toward globalization has produced a vast transformation in business practices and in the day-to-day transactions that knowledge workers are required to perform in order to be successful. Location, distance, and even time zones in today's world are of reduced importance as communication and collaboration become easier, faster, and less expensive. Markets are becoming global as electronic media now reach most people in the world. Boundaries-national, social, economic, and otherwise-are fading as information flows. Businesses are reshaping around networks that allow them to take advantage of otherwise unavailable opportunities, such as teaming employees who live and work in scattered locations.

Intranets can provide entrée via virtually any online device to a vast repository of information. Rapid access to methodically and logically ordered and dynamically updated information can mean the difference between success and failure in an economy where nanosecond responsiveness is vital. Information or knowledge is an extraordinarily precious intellectual property and the lifeblood of the nascent knowledge workplace. Providing effective management over and straightforward access to that knowledge has the potential to yield unprecedented levels of individual and organizational productivity.

Emergence of the Knowledge Worker

As we have previously indicated, the productivity emphasis in the postindustrial economy has shifted away from a demand for a large quantity of inexpensive, physical and industrial laborers, as industrial production moved to developing countries with abundant unskilled labor and low wage rates. For the first time in recorded history, vast numbers of ordinary workers no longer earn their living through largely undifferentiated manual labor. This significant shift began to occur in the period following World War II and peaked in the 1990s. Supported by improvements in education and unprecedented technological advances, a colossal number of workers left fields and factories and became producers and consumers of intellectual property:

---

1. Robert S. Kaplan and David P. Norton, *The Business Scorecard: Translating Strategy into Action* (Cambridge, MA: Harvard Business School Publishing, 1996).

industrial designers, computer engineers, human resource professionals, trainers, marketers, media specialists, communication technologists, medical researchers-the catalog of knowledge workers is quite long and begins to represent a substantial part of the population. These "knowledge workers" now power our developed economies.

Emergence of the Knowledge Workplace

The new economy gave birth to the knowledge workplace, an information intensive environment structured around a new discipline that treats intellectual capital as a managed asset. The knowledge workplace rationalizes and enhances the management and flow of an organization's knowledge. The goal is to deliver the intellectual capacity of the organization to the individuals who make the day-to-day decisions that, in aggregate, determine the success or failure of an enterprise.

The knowledge workplace is not defined by a central repository that is somehow a complete replica of all that is known by employees or that is embedded in the systems they use. It is a web of interactions that take place between employees, their customers and suppliers. It embraces a diversity of individual and shared knowledge sources and cultivates that knowledge in situ on a dynamic basis, while at the same time capturing its context and giving it greater meaning through its relation to other information from within and without the organization.

In essence, the knowledge workplace is about fueling what we do best as knowledge workers, what Bill Gates refers to as "thinking work." It is about making technology a partner with culture and business processes and using it as the vehicle to manage and deliver the business information and coworker expertise to the most fundamental driver of business growth: the knowledge worker.

The Economy, the Knowledge Workplace, and Productivity

The organizational and technological revolutions of the late twentieth century unleashed an unprecedented increase in productivity. The measure of this rise in output is characterized by the "productivity growth rate," which calculates the increase in yield from each hour of work. In order to increase productivity, companies must generate higher revenue, raise profits and wages, reduce expenses, and not increase prices.

The advances in organizational behavior and technological systems we have witnessed over the past 10 years enabled the robust expansion of the global economy in the 1990s, produced an extraordinary rise in prosperity in the United States and other parts of the world, and led to an increase in business expansion that caused companies to use labor more efficiently than ever before.

Many believe that these productivity gains will continue to expand, possibly indefinitely. Even noted experts, including Alan Greenspan, Chairman of the Board of Governors of the Federal Reserve System, predict with bullish optimism that the efficiencies of the Information Age, as companies increase their investments in computer-based technologies and the Internet, will continue to yield a strong increase in profits, incomes, and employment for the foreseeable future.

Although the United States and other nations now face a recession-stock prices have fallen, the budget surplus has evaporated, and the new economy is losing its luster-many economists believe that this downturn will be brief. Implicit in such reasoning is the conviction that the foundation of the productivity miracle remains intact. Thus the knowledge workplace is a keystone in the architecture of twenty-first century productivity. For those organizations that recognize the opportunity inherent in building and engendering the knowledge workplace, the probability of enduring gains in output is high.

Building the Knowledge Workplace

The knowledge workplace, and the intranets that enable it, is a key means by which productivity can continue to expand. For knowledge-enabled organizations in a knowledge-centric world, creating and efficiently utilizing intranets to capitalize on intellectual assets and streamline the process and flow of information may potentially emerge as *the* significant productivity driver.

This potential applies in equal measure to organizations that are on the leading edge of high technology and computing use, as well those that are only just beginning to deploy these systems in their workplaces. Over the past decade or so, businesses that have embraced high technology have invested in communications and networking infrastructure, software, and hardware, with an emphasis on operating systems, the desktop, and collaboration systems for messaging and Internet access. Many organizations are still in the process of integrating these technologies and shifting their business practices accordingly.

In either set of circumstances, organizations have rarely, if at all, begun to leverage their infrastructure investments into true knowledge-enabled productivity assets. Actualizing this grand vision necessitates the seamless integration of the continuum that extends from the operating system to the desktop; a largely Web-based and highly collaborative workplace that provides rapid access to business information, intuitive document management, and broadcast communication to each desktop-the shape of a true knowledge workplace.

The Leaders

Business leaders, otherwise known as business decision makers, are those who are most urgently in need of the productivity benefits attributed to intranets. A BDM is an executive or other leader who has strategic and budgetary decision-making authority over teams, departments, divisions, or an entire organization. A BDM is typically a consumer of information technology (IT) but is unlikely to be an IT professional.

BDMs are predominantly concerned with a simultaneous and systematic focus on increasing revenue while reducing cost. They believe that business objectives should drive technology decisions, and any investment in technology must be based on sound business goals and principles. They understand that revenue in knowledge-enabled organizations is increased by superior agility, improved output, and the implementation of process efficiencies, while costs are cut by mining organizational knowledge assets, leveraging existing IT infrastructure, and reducing the need for travel and physical events. These productivity improvements must be achieved in a constantly changing environment of fluctuating economic cycles, both positive and negative. It becomes all the more challenging in times of economic difficulty or recession because additional profit must be extracted with fewer resources.

BDMs also face the challenge of leading highly distributed organizations in the face of unprecedented global competition, where responsiveness to customer need and time to market unite to form the hinge on which the business cycle swings. Projects must be successfully stewarded to conclusion with a team that is dispersed across the globe, in different time zones, at different physical locations, and working from different baseline information systems; all require rapid access to the right information at the right time in order to drive the project forward. When relevant knowledge is centrally and sensibly made accessible to the entire team, collaboration can continue around the clock, while the productivity cycle takes on a perpetual characteristic.

BDMs are acutely aware of the gap that exists between their needs and the limitations of existing systems. Business process applications lag behind technology advances, and integrating or customizing these applications has historically proven to be costly and difficult. Intranets have surfaced on an ad hoc basis and are consequently fragmented and reliant on rigid user interfaces, thus making information access and management extremely difficult.

The combined impact of these and other constraints limit the processes that enable productivity. In order to build the knowledge workplace, it is important that BDMs collaborate with their IT colleagues. The two groups have different and equally legitimate agendas and concerns. Whereas BDMs are primarily focused on productivity, IT professionals are focused on stability and long-term goals of system permanence, continuity, security, and reliability.

The Benefits

Agility is synonymous with productivity for BDMs. A fast-moving, agile organization means lower costs and higher profits. Agility helps achieve customer centricity, bringing in new revenue by reaching new customers and aligning the business with, and making it more responsive to, customer needs. It reduces costs and gains internal and external flexibility, enabling fluid responses to changing business conditions. It empowers employees, increasing individual output by enabling rapid action and decision making at any time, from any place, and from any connected device. Time is of the essence in an agile organization; the only sustainable long-term competitive advantage comes through implementing fast, incremental, and short-term solutions. Immediate access to knowledge enables the intelligent decision making that powers the agile organization.

Faster and better decision making has the derivative benefit of forcing process improvements that further facilitate productivity. A logically structured knowledge workplace not only expedites the successful conclusion of projects but also imposes new disciplines in terms of the process for information capture and management. In addition, it automates, for example, workflow as a means of driving efficient document review.

Scenarios

The potential of the knowledge workplace is perhaps best described through various scenarios: descriptions of common daily business practices enabled by intranets.

Scenario 1: Sales

The sales process is as geographically distributed and information intensive as it is dynamic. Sales organizations need rapid, unfettered access to a variety of updated information at any time and in any location. A sales intranet may contain current or past requests for proposals, sales tools, details on sales initiatives, target forecasts, lead aggregation information, and real-time sales tracking data. Consumers of this information might include field sales, management, manufacturing or production, and benefits teams. The sales intranet streamlines processes, enhances operations, tightens management, and generally improves customer responsiveness. One key benefit of a sales intranet is the ability to mine for competitive and comparative information. The sales professional can drill down through categories of products, services, reports, and analyses and harvest very useful information to close a sale.

Scenario 2: Marketing

Marketing is extraordinarily information intensive, whether developing market research initiatives, planning advertising campaigns, designing promotional activities, or tracking competitors' products and performance. A variety of collateral and sales support content can be made available on a marketing intranet to describe both proprietary and third-party positioning, strategies, and tactics including brochures, fact sheets, news stories, white papers, case studies, videos, reports, business forecasts, and internal documents.

The information is consumed by marketing and sales teams, product development, and the attorneys responsible for legal review. The marketing intranet can provide rapid access to information and facilitates the easy reuse of knowledge and the self-service collaboration on ad hoc projects.

Scenario 3: Finance

Financial information must be dynamic yet support archiving of historical performance data. Finance intranets have typically included payroll, revenue forecasts, budgets, profit and loss statements, sales reports, accounts payable and receivable, financial statements for specific business divisions and product lines, cost statements for cost centers, cash flow forecasting, exchange rates, tax rates and compliance information, and performance reporting data such as sales volumes and marginal profit by customer. All employees consume the information, but with roles-based permissions the security of confidential data is guaranteed. The finance intranet can disseminate information rapidly to the entire organization and obviates the need for one-to-one support to management and employees.

Scenario 4: Operations

The operations group delivers a variety of dynamic information to the whole organization. Operations intranets might include status information on voice mail, unified messaging, the network and phones, fulfillment and distribution, purchasing, security, facilities, the helpdesk, and other departmental support functions. The entire organization consumes this information. For the operations function of an organization, an intranet disseminates information rapidly at low cost and provides access to dynamic information such as support resolution and tracking.

Scenario 5: Manufacturing

Manufacturing is all about process improvement. Manufacturing intranets may contain inventory, component data, quality assurance, product specifications, material safety data sheets, order tracking, and fulfillment and scheduling information. Users of this site include manufacturing teams, management, and operations. A manufacturing intranet delivers tight inventory control, just-in-time support, and effective management insight.

Scenario 6: Human Resources

Human resources (HR) is information intensive. HR intranets are used by the entire organization and may contain career planning tips and sites, the company handbook, benefits forms and programs, and training information. Some organizations have also included "lifestyle" sections on their HR intranets that incorporate advice on substance abuse, health prevention, parenting, caring for seniors, moving, and the like. The HR intranet delivers rapid, self-service information dissemination at low cost as well as legal compliance.

Scenario 7: Research and Development

Research and development (R&D) is process and information intensive. R&D intranets may contain test tools, business plans, budgets, research methodologies, project schedules, and team-specific data, along with third-party alerting services that track new developments in selected fields. This information is used by R&D, marketing, and manufacturing. Benefits include improved information dissemination, enhanced collaboration in the R&D cycle, and tighter project coordination and management.

Scenario 8: Live Broadcast

Broadcast delivers live or on-demand Web-based audiovisual communications to the desktop. Broadcast is typically on a one-to-many basis and is particularly well suited to the needs of executives. A typical broadcast might comprise a new product launch, information about a corporate acquisition, or an earnings announcement. Broadcast improves employee productivity and focus; reduces costs via economies on travel, events, or CD replication; and increases return on investment (ROI) through delivery of supplementary services on existing infrastructure.

Scenario Summary

These scenarios have illustrated just some of the productivity, communication, and collaborative benefits associated with next generation intranet solutions. While each of the scenarios is presented as a functionally discrete application of the intranet, greater productivity gains are achieved through the bringing together of knowledge from unrelated areas of an organization:

marketing can find value on the R&D intranet site, finance can make use of the sales intranet, HR could learn from the manufacturing site, and so forth. By removing barriers between functions and creating connections between departments, enterprise-wide intranets afford opportunities for truly creative and collaborative knowledge work. The next section will look more closely at assessing the business value of intranets in the knowledge workplace.

Assessing the Business Value of Next Generation Intranets

Intranets are widely valued for driving operational efficiencies, streamlining business processes, enhancing communications, building collaborative work-places, and reducing the cost of internal business functions. Virtually every business, division, unit, or department within an organization can benefit from the power, flexibility, and bottom-line value of an intranet. While implicitly understanding an intranet's value is second nature for many organizations, measuring its value remains a challenge.

Calculating technological payback has bedeviled organizations for years, particularly when it comes to investments such as intranets that are designed to provide a foundation for both qualitative and quantitative invest-ments. If you view intranets as interfaces to critical information residing on disparate enterprise systems, then companies of all sizes are probably either implementing them or have plans to do so.

The greatest benefit of intranets is increased productivity, according to a recent survey of Meta Group teleconference participants. Also ranking high in the survey were employee retention and improved sales. One company found more than 10 distinct areas of financial gain across several categories.[2]

Many organizations understand the implicit or explicit value of intranets and portals and are therefore willing to make investments in this regard. According to the Meta Group, more than 85 percent of Global 2000[3] compa-nies have implemented or are developing intranets, not just large multina-tional companies. According to a 2001 Modalis Research study, more than 70 percent of all small and midsized businesses, including government agen-

2. David Yockelson, "ROI Can Be Found in Enterprise Portals," *Internet Week* (October 8, 2001), 28.
3. Global 2000 corporations are defined as the 2000 largest capitalized corporations.

cies and not-for-profit institutions, believe that having an intranet is a strategic asset and either have one or are planning to deploy one.[4]

Appraising the value of intranet investments is an imperfect science. Most analysts contend that precise ROI measurement is not always possible due to the expansive and far-reaching nature of intranets and the qualitative changes they effect in the workplace. Yet there are means by which many organizations quantify potential and existing ROI. A number of studies have been conducted on intranet projects, with ROIs ranging from over 1,000 percent to a more modest 20 to 40 percent. Why the huge range in ROIs? It depends on who did the study, who and what was studied, and, more importantly, what variables were considered in calculating the return.

There is a very simple formula for ROI,[5] but applying it in complex strategic decisions will involve participants' assumptions and comfort levels more than straight arithmetic. Surfacing these assumptions and discomforts are critical. However you determine the variables that will be used, three steps must be completed:

1. Explicit objectives of the intranet solution must be stated.

2. Appropriate measures for the objectives have to be identified.

3. Baseline data must be collected before proceeding.

Generally speaking, intranet ROI can be grouped into one of two categories: quantitative and qualitative. Quantitative returns include savings from, for example, cost avoidance of printing or distributing documents, travel expenses for employees, and reduced staff time on repetitive tasks, while qualitative returns, for example, come via enhanced access to business information, improved communication and knowledge sharing, agile response to changing business conditions, and increased productivity.

Quantitative Returns

Company executives increasingly demand evidence of quantifiable benefits from their investments. They want to know the business impact of IT

---

4. *Intranet ROI: Appraising the Value of Intranet Investments* (Toronto, ON: Prescient Digital Media, 2001), 3.

5. $\text{ROI} = \dfrac{\text{incremental revenue or savings} - \text{investment}}{\text{investment}} \times 100$

investments vis-à-vis investments in other strategic parts of the business, such as R&D, manufacturing, sales, and marketing; some companies even require that investments be mapped to shareholder value.

Historically, our economy has measured value directly as profit. For example, the equation for determining profit in manufacturing is typically calculated on the basis of sales price minus the cost to produce. Organizations have traditionally valued IT investments on a quantitative basis exclusively, measuring cost reductions, often within the IT group and system exclusively. Methodologies have tended to focus on total cost of ownership (TCO), whereas the strategic role of IT in driving new opportunities for the business is largely ignored. Thus IT's broad impact on the business can be difficult to quantify and, as a result, is often omitted from the equation.

In addition, because IT is relatively new, its importance as an asset may not be as thoroughly understood as, say, real estate. Business managers are then predisposed to view it as a utility with limited intrinsic value, disassociated from its ability to return value or create opportunity. In boom times this narrow perspective has little impact on the bottom line, but in times of economic recession, when management seeks improved profit but cannot raise prices, the focus turns to cutting costs; trimming the size of the staff needed to manage IT systems; and reducing the cost of software licenses, support, hardware, and the like.

This approach does not consider the impact that a strong and agile IT infrastructure can have on an organization's productivity, even if the influence is difficult to quantify. This is especially true of intranets, where a profit equation for the knowledge workplace must include qualitative characteristics, determining value on the basis of increased productivity as a benefit minus cost.

We have encountered three ways for measuring intranet ROI:

- Assign the intranet a value equal to the TCO, dollar for dollar. This is the easiest approach to adopt, which is why organizations tend to rely on it so heavily despite the fact that it is often not the most important factor for an organization's long-term health. It does not account for any quantitative (dollars) or qualitative (intangibles such as increased productivity, employee retention, increased collaboration) benefits.

- Ascribe a nonmonetary value to the intranet as a collaborative communication and information management tool in the same way you might value the telephone system.

- Measure and assess specific benefits from implementing an intranet.[6]

Qualitative Returns

While appraising the ROI of an organization's intranet is critical for most BDMs, a great deal of untapped, qualitative ROI exists that may be of far more value than can be measured in dollars and cents. A professor at Harvard Business School, David Upton, indicated that organizations were foolish to measure the value of either an intranet or portal in terms of cost savings or cost avoidance alone; intranets have the potential to lead to new business models. He further suggested that BDMs think in terms of a financial investment and the options such an investment will bring to the organization. Upton refers to these options as the organization's ability to do things it has never thought of before.[7]

Others are of the same mind-set. "Most of our intranet is about top-line growth, not the cost reduction associated with a ROI," said Martin Armitage of Unilever, the multibillion dollar Anglo-Dutch maker of food, home, and personal products, ranging from ice cream and tea to shampoo and deodorants. "Intranet applications often provide a new way of working...and how do you measure that?"[8] Mitre Corporation is a nonprofit technology company that services several U.S. federal agencies. Its chief information officer (CIO), Al Grasso, said in an interview with *CIO Magazine* in May 2000, "Our most important gain can't be easily measured-the quality and innovation in our solutions that become realizable when you have all of this information at your fingertips."[9]

---

6. *Intranet ROI*, 5.

7. Megan Santosus, "The Trouble with Numbers: Why the Harvard Business School Doesn't Worry About Its Intranet's ROI," *CIO Magazine* (October 1998, *http://www.cio.com/archive/webbusiness/100198_hbs.html*).

8. Charles Waltner, "Intranet ROI," *Information Week* (May 24, 1999), 90.

9. Debby Young, "An Audit Tale," *CIO Magazine* (May 1, 2000), 156.

Of course, there are many other important, qualitative benefits that cannot be measured, or are very difficult to measure, that deserve attention. A well-planned and deployed intranet can enhance an organization's reputation in the marketplace. Companies such as General Electric have received millions of dollars worth of free publicity and media coverage because of their in-house efforts to reduce costs and increase operation efficiencies via intranet technologies.[10] While the attention brings with it enhanced revenues and greater long-term profitability, the free advertising also serves as valuable recruiting tools. Innovators and technology leaders attract talent and help retain what they already have.

Most employees inherently know and understand the value of a telephone system. It is a mission-critical instrument in an organization, and no ROI is needed. Likewise many employees implicitly realize the value of their intranet and consider it a critical business tool. That's the thinking of Unilever Corp. Of the dozens of intranet applications the company is developing to tie together its 300 subsidiaries operating in over 80 countries, most are not justified by ROI but by their ability to improve the flow of information throughout the company and, as a result, to improve elements such as time to market and increased local sales effectiveness.[11] A positive end user experience is a key benefit of an intranet. It translates into users returning to the intranet site to access knowledge or utilize the services offered there, and it will produce improved employee satisfaction and loyalty. Either benefit is too difficult to measure explicitly, but both clearly have a positive impact on productivity and, ultimately, revenue and profitability.

Return on People, Process, Knowledge, and IT

As previously mentioned, intranet ROI has been calculated largely on cost-benefit criteria related to IT deployments: the cost of purchase plus the cost of deployment minus quantifiable improvements often measured in time or method efficiencies. This approach to ROI, while helpful to IT professionals, fails to effectively address concerns vital to BDMs: the significant productivity-centric transformation of organizational culture that occurs when knowledge that was once squandered is converted into a high-value asset. The calculation and interpretation of these vitally important benefits ascribed to

---

10. *Intranet ROI*, 22.
11. Waltner, 91.

this change can be categorized in terms of a "return on people," "return on knowledge," "return on process," and "return on information technology."

- Knowledge-enabled organizations may increase their return on people through efficiency improvements achieved via faster, better informed decision making and improved employee satisfaction. The knowledge workplace frees knowledge from the confines of the silos within which individuals tend to work.

- Knowledge-enabled organizations generate an increased return on process through enhanced knowledge worker collaboration tools, effective business process integration, and rapid access to dynamic business information. The knowledge workplace achieves synergy between the often conflicting goals of the IT and BDM communities.

- Knowledge-enabled organizations achieve an increased return on knowledge through streamlined collaboration practices; efficient capture, management (especially content management), and discovery of knowledge as a reusable strategic asset; and integration of dynamic data.

- Knowledge-enabled organizations demonstrate an increased return on information technology by leveraging existing network and other infrastructure investments, as well as through improved manageability, reliability, security, and training.

It is crucial that intranet ROI be measured in an expansive framework that recognizes and measures the value of a return on people, process, knowledge, and IT. Intranets that effectively reduce the constraints imposed on productivity through recognizing and addressing the limitations on people, process, knowledge, and information systems experience measurable benefits that can be factored into any relevant ROI analysis. The removal of these barriers will lead organizations to increased productivity and reduced costs.

Perhaps the best way to demonstrate how to measure intranet ROI is through examples. Four ROI profiles of organizations who sought solutions to business and technology challenges through deployment of an intranet will now be presented. In each profile we describe the organization; the productivity, process, or technology issue; how the intranet addressed the problem; and how the ROI was calculated. We conclude each profile with a three-year financial analysis.

ROI Profile 1: Children's Hospital Boston

Since its establishment in 1869, Children's Hospital Boston has grown to become the largest pediatric medical center in the United States, the primary pediatric teaching hospital of Harvard Medical School, and the world's largest pediatric research facility. Scientists at Children's have set the pace in pediatric research, by identifying treatments and therapies for many debilitating childhood diseases, including polio, measles, leukemia, and sickle cell disease.

The 325-bed pediatric health center has a clinical staff of 800 active medical and dental staff, 700 residents and fellows, and 3000 full-time employees, not to mention the 850 volunteers. Children's Hospital has approximately 18,000 inpatient admissions each year and more than 150 outpatient programs that care for more than 300,000 patients annually.[12]

Although it deployed a document publishing environment several years ago, Children's Hospital lacked facilities for online documentation and collaboration, which are critical processes in a research environment. The hospital needed a system that could support a large volume of different types of documents, including clinical practice guidelines, regulatory compliance information, HR documents, and nursing guides. It also needed easy-to-use management tools so content owners could maintain their own documents.

Moving from a document publishing environment to an intranet-enabled environment provided many direct and indirect benefits, including improved support for collaboration and information sharing and a devolution of responsibility for content from the IT department to the individual authors and departments. Children's Hospital realized a return on technology with its improved technology management. It was able to support growing document management and content maintenance with current personnel, while increasing the amount of information available via their intranet.

The hospital also experienced a return on process with reduced paper and printing costs. The availability of online information reduced the number of documents that had to be printed, leading to significant direct savings. A return on people was also generated. Productivity enhancements and an increase in document-based collaboration were realized without the need for additional training. Personnel currently responsible for editing and updating

---

12. "ROI Profile Microsoft SharePoint/Children's Hospital Boston," *Research Note,* #B28 (Nucleus Research, Inc., 2001), 1.

content were freed to move on to other higher-level tasks, such as mentoring and information architecture. A return on knowledge was also demonstrated with streamlined collaborative practices and efficient capture, management, and discovery of the hospital's intellectual capital as a reusable asset.

An analysis of the three-year costs of the intranet solution for Children's Hospital-hardware, personnel costs, consulting, and software-was performed. It was discovered that software made up the greatest percentage of the total because of relatively low costs for hardware and consulting. Key returns quantified in this analysis included a reduction in the need to hire additional IT staff to maintain content plus a conservative estimate of savings in document printing costs; only printing costs recognized by the technology department were considered. It was demonstrated that the ROI for Children's Hospital Boston over a three-year period (see Table 8-1) was 409 percent, with a payback over only three months.[13]

Table 8-1 Children's Hospital Boston: Three-Year Financial Analysis

Total Benefits:	$1,538,868
Total Costs:	$638,000
ROI	409%
Payback:	3 months
TCO:	$212,667

ROI Profile 2: Anderson Power Products

Anderson Power Products (APP) was founded in the 1877 to support the railway and mining industries.[14] Today the company has evolved into an industry leader in the design and manufacture of high-power interconnects and accessories, supplying components to back up the power, telecommunications, data communications, and materials handling industries. APP components are often used in electric vehicles, power stations, personal and network computers, and telecommunications and data communications switches.

---

13. *Research Note*, #B28, 3.
14. *http://www.andersonpower.com.*

With facilities in the United States and Ireland, APP is an ISO 9001 certified company designing and manufacturing versatile high-power interconnection products and components. The company works with a worldwide network of sales representatives and distributors to ensure high-quality products, on-time deliveries, and a high level of customer service.[15]

Like many large distributed organizations, the challenge for APP was to provide a means for small tactical teams to share information, collaborate on specific deals and projects, and establish a broader platform for enterprise-wide sharing of product and customer information. As in many organizations, APP tried to address its needs with two different and separate systems.

APP's document management system for document versioning and approval had limitations. Users did not find it intuitive, and its maintenance requirements put a significant burden on IT staff. APP had a first generation intranet, but its poor information architecture and lack of central searching tools made it difficult for users to find what they needed. As the number of documents on the intranet grew, so did replication and versioning problems, the cost of adequate storage, and user frustration. APP needed an intranet solution that would facilitate better organization of information and better support of small teams as they collaborated and shared information.

APP realized both direct and indirect benefits from its intranet deployment. Their return on process included improved information organization and access and tactical collaboration. The searchable central document repository and intuitive Web-based interface provided employees with an easy, intuitive, and efficient way to access information, which reduced the time they spent searching for and re-creating information, which then increased productivity. Their intranet generated a return on knowledge with an easy, informal process for teams to centralize and share projects and team information and archive that information for future consultation by different teams pursuing similar efforts.

The reduction in IT management costs constituted their return on technology. By eliminating a costly document management system and a high-maintenance first generation intranet environment, APP could focus some of these resources on intranet deployment and other strategic projects.

---

15. "ROI Profile: Microsoft SharePoint/Anderson Power Products," *Research Note,* #B30 (Nucleus Research, Inc., 2001), 1.

Key cost areas involved in APP's deployment included software, hardware, consulting, personnel, and training. Consulting in the initial years of the project included both outside and in-house services, and these services drove much of the early project costs. Productivity increases on the part of team members made up the largest part of the quantified benefits. Returns were calculated based on a time savings estimate adjusted by a correction factor to account for the inefficient transfer of time and multiplied by the fully loaded hourly cost of an employee. Other benefit areas included a savings in the time needed to manage the old system along with associated hardware and support costs. Not included was the expected benefit from the use of current documents. Employees previously printed and saved hard copy documents, which increased the likelihood that an out-of-date document would be used. The company expects that the intranet's greater ease of use will reduce this tendency and therefore decrease the potential for mistakes and rework. Based on a three-year period (see Table 8-2), APP demonstrated an ROI of 267 percent with a payback in five months.[16]

Table 8-2   Anderson Power Products:
Three-Year Financial Analysis

Total Benefits:	$1,210,873
Total Costs:	$255,159
ROI:	267%
Payback:	5 months
TCO:	$85,053

ROI Profile 3: Law Firm

The organization described in this profile is one the United States' leading law firms practicing in the area of intellectual property and technological law.[17] For more than 100 years, this firm has helped its clients safeguard their intellectual property through patent, trademark, copyright, and trade secret protection. With more than 1000 clients and offices nationwide, this firm helps to protect ideas, nurture innovation, and bring new concepts to the market. Its attorneys are specialists in high-tech litigation, as well as in

16. *Research Note,* #B30, 3.
17. Note: This law firm has requested anonymity.

dealings with the U.S. International Trade Commission, the Federal Communications Commission, and the Food and Drug Administration.[18]

Like most legal firms, this company has significant document management challenges. Because of the technical nature of its litigation, each client dossier includes hundreds of thousands of documents; larger clients and more complex cases may generate millions of documents. Documents stored in client dossiers include research, discovery, and brief documents. Many of these documents are received from external sources and must be scanned and entered into the system, although some are created by the firm's case teams.

There is also a significant amount of non-client-specific information and documentation stored in the databases. This firm had a document management system, but because client teams were often dispersed among other offices and work sites, a way to provide secure, managed access to information over the Web, as well as an environment for document-based team collaboration, was needed.

This firm also recognized an important opportunity in the way technology could be used to interact with its clients. Like any law firm, billable hours are the key to revenue generation. From a strict revenue perspective, technology that increased efficiency would reduce billable hours, yet the firm acknowledged the value of providing high-quality and efficient services to its clients. The trade-off was lower costs for clients, along with a long-term increase in the amount of business referred to the firm. As part of this effort, the firm wanted to provide its clients with secure extranet access to their case materials, to keep them better informed and reduce internal case management burden. Other key requirements included document security, audit trails, integration of research databases, and enhanced search and discovery capabilities.

With their intranet deployment, this firm effected a number of key benefit areas, including a return on process in the increased productivity of its attorneys. They were able to deliver successful litigation to clients for a smaller number of billable hours, providing cost benefits to clients. This firm also realized a return on people; the increased efficiencies of case managers enabled the firm to grow its caseload without the need to hire additional managers. A return on knowledge was achieved because of better manage-

---

18. "ROI Profile: Microsoft SharePoint/Legal Firm, United States," *Research Note,* #B26 (Nucleus Research, Inc., 2001), 1.

ment of the research teams and databases, which improved the collection and dissemination of intellectual capital in the firm.

The need to enhance security capabilities, integrate databases, and develop an appropriate interface made consulting the largest cost area for this deployment. Other cost areas included in the ROI calculation included software, hardware, personnel, and training. The largest benefit area was the increased efficiency of its case managers. Other quantified benefits included reduced administrative overhead and paper and printing costs, although these were minimal in this instance. Based on a three-year time frame (see Table 8-3), the ROI was 161 percent, with a payback of less than one year.[19]

Table 8-3   Law Firm:
Three-Year Financial Analysis

Total Benefits:	$990,000
Total Costs:	$397,500
ROI:	161%
Payback:	0.97 years
TCO:	$132,500

ROI Profile 4: Aanza, Inc.

Aanza, Inc., of Lynnfield, Massachusetts, is a software company whose products help companies rapidly and efficiently define, develop, and launch products in the marketplace. Their goal was to create a product life-cycle automation tool that would facilitate the management of its customers' entire product life cycle, from new product development to obsolescence, with a unique customer-focused approach.

The challenge was to develop a product life-cycle automation application that would provide benefit to both Aanza and its customers. Aanza's intranet solution helped customers reduce time to market and, therefore, increase product revenues, while at the same time reducing product development costs. It facilitated collaboration, workflow management, knowledge management, and central document storage, with easy access to best practices, templates, and how-to instructions. With interactive project scheduling with

---

19. *Research Note,* #B26, 3.

alerts, plus chats, discussion boards, and real-time status reports for better portfolio and risk management application, Aanza realized direct and indirect benefits from its intranet.

Key benefit areas were primarily return on process. They included reduced development costs and time. The ease and speed of development enabled Aanza to create its product with significantly less development expense and shortened the time needed to develop and launch its solution, which enabled the company to shorten its time to market and begin reaping sales revenues from its solution sooner. Key cost areas used to calculate the ROI were related to the cost of product development-hardware, software, and personnel and training costs. In calculating the ROI for Aanza's product development project, benefits from product revenues in the first three years were quantified (see Table 8-4), as well as reduced costs of development efforts. Costs included development and other miscellaneous charges. With a payback of approximately 34 months, Aanza demonstrated an ROI of 463 percent.[20]

Table 8-4   Aanza, Inc.:
Three-Year Financial Analysis

Total Benefits:	$2,060,000
Total Costs:	$996,000
ROI:	463%
Payback:	0.27 year
TCO:	$332,000

Profile Summary

To find and measure value, intranets should be rigorously planned, with benchmarks and measures for future success, and thoroughly assessed by stakeholder and user groups to set requirements and expectations. These are the hallmarks of successful intranets. By committing to formal planning and assessment up-front, the uncertainty and risk associated with new technology are reduced or eliminated, and intranet and portal ROI goals are planned in advance.

20. "ROI Profile: Aanza, Inc.," *Research Note*, #B25 [Nucleus Research, Inc., 2001), 3.

Summary

Making the transition from an infrastructure-based IT worldview to one founded on recognition of the intrinsic value of knowledge as a managed asset requires a departure from the traditional approach to quantifying value. This has created a need for a broader method to evaluate IT investments, one that can identify and quantify qualitative ROI across functions and departments and the knowledge value chain over a period of time.

The long-term agility and performance of an organization comes from its knowledge-centered resources: customer relationships, innovative products and services, streamlined business processes, the skills and motivation of knowledge workers; and integrated and available intellectual capital. Chapter 9 provides case studies of how a few leading organizations have invested in success by accepting the challenge to build a knowledge workplace. Their best practices provide examples of how these powerful, collaborative, and productivity-enhancing business tools can work for your organization.

Case Studies: Successful Workplace Intranets

Nothing demonstrates more effectively the potential inherent in intranets than actual case studies. Building on what we have learned about what makes an intranet successful, this chapter examines four intranet deployments and explains the business value benefits that have been realized by each company.. Informed by the experience of others, business leaders will be better positioned to make knowledgeable decisions about intranet solutions for their workplace.

H&R Block Delivers Superior Customer Services

A business value assessment confirmed that the Microsoft Solution for Intranets enabled H&R Block to consolidate access to content, tools, and services information from a number of existing intranet sites and applications into a single intranet-based work platform, thereby unlocking silos of information and creating a truly functional corporate knowledge base. Financial advisors at H&R Block now have the ability to easily access key tools and services, search the knowledge base, and map client financial information to new products and services, thereby increasing the advisor's own efficiencies while improving client satisfaction. The platform provides personalized access based on the user's role within the company and each user's identity and enables key information to be pushed directly to the financial advisor's workspace. The new Windows Media Broadcast component provides a vehicle for pushing out real-time and on-demand media events for training, product launches, corporate communications, and executive messaging and in so doing decrease the costs associated with training, travel, and internal communications. The Advisor Workspace is the company's initial step toward an intranet-based work platform that will eventually enable thousands of financial professionals with diverse specialties and needs to easily and simply access the information and services necessary to deliver superior service to their clients and in that process position H&R Block as a global leader in financial products and services.

Executive Summary

As the market leader for tax preparation services and the nation's seventh largest accountancy[1], H&R Block has been an innovator in the use of information technology (IT) to achieve its business goals.

Extensively utilizing corporate intranets and network applications, H&R Block has known the importance of timely information access for its financial professionals. An increasingly diverse and specialized workforce of financial advisors, tax professionals, and other sales associates were being served by a variety of decentralized information management and communication platforms. As good as the existing intranet sites were, they did not provide comprehensive product information, aggregation of user systems, or homogeneous enterprise-wide search capability. They also did not begin to leverage the potential of bringing content, tools, and services together for each user based on that user's needs. To serve this geographically dispersed but functionally interlinked workforce, H&R Block was looking forward to using the latest advances in video broadcast technology with the Windows Media Broadcast component to reduce costs, improve distance learning, and enable cost-effective and company-wide executive broadcast.

The first business unit within H&R Block to take advantage of the most current advances in intranet technology through the Microsoft Solution for Intranets was the financial services division of the company, H&R Block Financial Advisors.

Bernie Wilson, Senior Vice President of H&R Block Financial Advisors, noted:

> A core focus of the company is creating a community between management and financial professionals and their clients. We wanted an online space where our advisors could easily form a community based on their ability to share information and ideas. Further, we needed a platform solution that enabled all of our financial advisors to easily and quickly search, access, and manage information on our products and services yet also provide centralized administration and secure access. Using the Microsoft [intranet] solution we were able to get up and running quick-

---

1. Based on H&R Block, Inc., ownership of RSM McGladrey, Inc., a national accounting, tax, and consulting firm with 100 offices nationwide, as well as affiliations with 550 offices in 75 countries as U.S. members of RSM International.

ly and have near instant functionality that enabled us to transform our ability to support advisors in their interactions with clients. The speed of deployment and flexibility of the [Microsoft] solution is already showing promising returns.

As described in chapter 5, "The Microsoft Solution for Intranets," this solution is the next generation intranet designed to power knowledge-worker productivity. The solution enables the knowledge workplace with Web-based collaborative team services, information management and discovery, and broadcast delivery of business communications to every employee desktop.

H&R Block Financial Advisors implemented the Microsoft Solution for Intranets throughout the organization and expects that nearly 2,400 financial advisors will be using the service by the end of 2001 and over 5000 advisors by the end of 2002. They anticipate usage of the platform to potentially grow to thousands of financial professionals from different business units within H&R Block, including financial advisors from H&R Block franchisees, advisors in other countries, tax professionals, and mortgage officers. By establishing an intranet based on industry standards, the group anticipates influencing the growth of a centrally administered common work platform for the company.

Global Information Access Spurs Financial Advisor Productivity

Serving as the financial partner to mainstream America, H&R Block's competitive advantages include year-over-year relationships with over 19 million clients in more than 10,000 worldwide offices. Knowing that the life-cycle value of each client is a multiple of that client's spending on tax services, H&R Block Financial Advisors needed to optimize its use of client data by integrating disparate bits of historic client information in different databases into true business intelligence. Providing a central repository that defined the company's various products and services enabled any advisor to access vital information no matter where the advisor was located, including the corporate headquarters; a corporate regional office; a franchisee office; or a nondomestic office located in Canada, Australia, or the United Kingdom.

John Thompson, Director of eBusiness for H&R Block Financial Advisors, noted:

> Our prior service was an amalgam of nonintegrated information that was organized by business unit, not by topic or function. By developing the Advisor Workspace-the name for H&R Block's service-using the Microsoft Solution for Intranets, we essentially created a one-stop-shopping environment organized by topic and function for our advisors to access information about the complete range of the company's financial products and services. We are able to search the entire archive and find the right resources for our advisors using a variety of search criteria. Using the Microsoft Solution for Intranets, we have transformed bits of data existing in silos into a truly usable knowledge base that adds value far beyond the sum of its parts.

The new Advisor Workspace pulls together or displaces a variety of divisional and departmental intranet sites and leverages existing content with new search, communications, and collaboration tools to increase operational synergy and in the process improve advisor productivity. The site is a centrally administered, secure document repository where document posting is restricted and managed by an executive committee composed of senior financial advisors, product planners, and management. Advisor access to the intranet is currently controlled downstream of the application; follow-on activities will utilize the Active Directory service of Windows 2000 Server for user authentication and expanded personalization services.

One key to the success of the Advisor Workspace is that the initiative was driven by business executives within the Financial Advisors group. Defining factors critical to the project's success were based on business criteria, such as the increased number of calls per day to clients, the increase in new clients, overall revenue increase, and the increased amount of assets under management; more traditional IT-defined values, such as uptime, availability, and user support, helped develop a functional specification for the project that assured its success.

Selected collaboration, document management, and business intelligence features of the Microsoft solution that helped H&R Block are as follows:

- **Web-based collaboration**-an easy-to-use level 4.0 browser-based user interface and structured design using template-based Web sites

- **Search with incomparable ease**-unified search capability, automatic information sorting, and organization of group information by common schema and index content using industry-leading technology

- **Access business information easily**-integrating information from inside and outside the organization into a single portal user interface and receiving information customized to end user preferences based on subscription services

- **Rapidly deploy a customizable portal**-Web parts based on Extensible Markup Language (XML) that are delivered as a user-defined and/or role-defined digital dashboard

Thompson continued:

We knew that if we enabled our advisors to operate more efficiently, then they would be more productive, which in turn would improve client satisfaction and increase revenue. The more we anticipate the needs of our advisors and proactively design products and services that meet their requirements, the more capable we will become in effectively competing for new business. The new intranet solution enables our financial professionals to more effectively leverage our knowledge base, serve our clients, and create new revenue.

Video Broadcast to the Desktop: Simple, Elegant, and Effective

As H&R Block has grown into an international powerhouse in tax services, its Financial Advisors business has undergone rapid growth and transformation. With it has come the need for new product development, increased training, and more direct exposure to the corporate mission and culture as embodied by H&R executives. Escalating travel costs, a geographically distributed workforce, and new IT-based conferencing tools have finally converged in a cost-effective solution for company-wide video broadcast and push media.

The Microsoft Solution for Intranets opens new ground by integrating the Windows Media Broadcast component with the Windows Media Player client for an all-inclusive video broadcast capability to the desktop. Executive management can now improve communication effectiveness by delivering video product or training updates to employees in real time or as on-demand media. Users can view broadcasts without leaving their desks, thereby increasing productivity. This helps H&R Block reduce costs and maximize its return on people. Customization, including chat or quizzes along with the ability to synchronize with the Microsoft PowerPoint presentation graphics program, enables richer, more interactive communications for improved learning and retention.

IT network administrators can easily configure and set up broadcast events, specifying distribution servers required to reach a geographically distributed audience. Since Windows Media Broadcast is configured as a WebPart, it can be easily integrated with Microsoft SharePoint Portal Server, utilizing calendar and document management functionality. Centralized event management and a scheduling notification link to the Microsoft Outlook messaging and collaboration client, or other calendaring applications, easily enable a Web broadcast to be scheduled like any other meeting. Broadcasts can be easily produced and delivered with a four-step wizard and automatically archived on the intranet portal site.

Jim Powers, Director of National Sales for H&R Block Financial Advisors, exclaimed:

> With multiple applications, such as training and professional development, product launches, product and services training, and executive messaging, the Financial Advisors group is a rich environment in which to apply the Windows Media Broadcast component. We use Windows Media Broadcast to replace meetings throughout the management chain and as a simplified way to communicate with all financial advisors. While product and sales trainings drive our broadcast initiative, we envision numerous uses for this multimedia rich experience. Video broadcast to the desktop is simply the most elegant and cost-effective approach to corporate communications and a tremendous addition to the Advisor Workspace.

Structure Enhances Advisor Productivity; Analytics Aid Management

Delivering a structured sales process for tools, services, and products to the H&R Block field organization should result in operational efficiencies throughout the company's internal value chain. Equally as important to generating new leads, following up on customer inquiries, and servicing existing clients is management's ability to oversee financial advisors and administer their activities and success on a day-to-day basis. Management of each financial advisor is based on the role he or she plays within the organization and his or her need for management and direction. Less experienced advisors would have access to different content and services than a more experienced advisor. Advisors who need specialized applications based on their qualifications, for example, access to tools and services for selected products such as annuity sales, would have them. Field management would have access to information necessary to manage that portion of the business.

Real-time analytics and intranet monitoring enable management to review usage patterns of each section of the Advisor Workspace and assess how effective any particular section is in helping advisors reach their new business and revenue goals. Monitoring usage patterns also helps executive management understand the overall operational efficiency of the Financial Advisors group, which helps in strategic planning and market positioning. Monitoring tools enable tracking from business intelligence tools to direct customer delivery and every point in-between.

According to Bernie Wilson, Senior Vice President,

> Gaining client respect and with it increased confidence in our ability to manage [the client's] complete portfolio is only part of the game. We must also recognize our client's needs in advance and train our advisors in effective account management so that there is consistency in each customer's experience. Real-time monitoring and analytics helps us spot usage trends, which in turn enables us to direct our attention to those situations, individuals, or Web site content that require assistance, guidance, or support. It enables parity in our value chain by providing executive support for our advisors and in the development of products, services, and value for our clients by ensuring we are offering them the very best services and range of products.

Business Driven, IT Success

"The fact that the business unit stepped up to the plate and really drove the project ensured our success," noted Jenny Sherman, Project Manager with G.A. Sullivan, a Microsoft Gold-certified solution provider and system integrator for the H&R Block Advisor Workspace. A key element that makes the Microsoft Solution for Intranets so beneficial for IT departments is the portability and extensibility of the technology. Because the inherent architecture of the Advisor Workspace is not proprietary, other business units or the IT group can quickly used the template-based structure as the container to organize and publish new and existing content. This enables H&R Block to rapidly expand its existing Advisor Workspace by utilizing the same basic architecture and functionality and rapidly incorporate the content of other business units.

Sherman continued:

Because the business sponsor worked closely with the IT team, there were few surprises. Our goals were clear, and the path to those goals was well defined. From a project management perspective, we were able to meet the business objectives of the Advisor Workspace with minimal IT resources, specifically due to the integrated and comprehensive nature of the Microsoft solution. We had IT implement the infrastructure and configure the solution; the business units were then empowered to build the platform.

Access to Knowledge Leads to Success

Timely access to knowledge is an important ingredient for the success of H&R Block Financial Advisors. Therefore, getting the new Advisor Workspace up and running quickly was a key to enabling that success. Creating the Advisor Workspace on an easy-to-build, easy-to-integrate, and easy-to-use standards-based platform helped to launch the project in a brief four months.

Jim Powers noted:

The Advisor Workspace is a stratospheric step toward defining a community-driven capability for our organization. It will encompass and enrich the relationship between company leadership, advisors, and customers, supporting our advisors as they extend the H&R Block community to clients. As more [intranet] services are built using WebParts, the interchangeability and seamless integration of information will become self-evident. And by demonstrating the direct business benefit of unlocking bits of data on corporate information stores and converting it into revenue generating information, other business units and executive management will recognize the business opportunity. Overall this can only help showcase the complete range of our financial service capabilities and conclude with [us] successfully achieving our corporate mission of positioning the company as America's tax and financial partner.

Banco Nacional de Costa Rica Enhances Productivity

Banco Nacional de Costa Rica used the Microsoft Solution for Intranets as a strategic tool to empower its employees with information anywhere at any time, while also improving employee productivity and achieving new operational efficiencies. Implementing a standards-based framework for the corporate intranet enabled the bank to migrate from its former hierarchical structure for content publishing to a flattened management structure, thereby reducing the publishing time from five weeks to less than an hour. The Microsoft Solution for Intranets enabled the bank to easily create new divisional portals customized to meet specific user needs and thereby increase customer satisfaction. The bank is already achieving a return on investment by leveraging and sharing information that had been locked in isolated databases and is optimizing its return on people by creating a truly usable knowledge base.

Executive Summary

As the largest bank in Costa Rica, offering a full range of personal and corporate financial services, and one of the most important banks in all of Central America, Banco Nacional de Costa Rica knows how to use information technology (IT) for strategic advantage. An early adopter of automatic teller machines (ATMs) in Central America, the bank optimized its growth in rural and urban areas by using technology as a substitute for walk-in services. Now Banco Nacional de Costa Rica is leveraging the latest advances in intranet technology to optimize its intellectual capital by ensuring that its employees have information anywhere, anytime. Utilizing the Microsoft Solution for Intranets, the bank expects to increase employee productivity and improve operational efficiency by better collaboration, better knowledge sharing, and a reduction of isolated silos of information throughout the bank.

Warren Castillo Fernández, Chief Information Officer for Banco Nacional de Costa Rica, exclaimed:

> As one of the first banks in Central America to use the Internet as a tool for delivering financial services, we have a distinct obligation to our customers, shareholders, and employees to maintain our market position by providing superior service and innovative products. We must use our corporate intranet for developing a usable knowledge base and improving operational efficiency in the same way as we embraced the Internet for servicing our customers: proactively and with undivided attention to achieving business goals. Using the Microsoft Solution for Intranets, we have been able to transform multiple, nonintegrated intranets and isolated databases into a cohesive, integrated, and consistent corporate portal that is easily used by any bank employee. As a result of better collaboration and improved knowledge sharing, we have increased our insight into the needs of our customers and are now better able to develop products and offer services that truly add value.

The Microsoft Solution for Intranets is the next generation intranet designed to enable the knowledge workplace through Web-based collaborative team services, a portal for information management and discovery, and broadcast communications to employee desktops.

Under the direction of Castillo Fernández, the bank defined five goals for its new corporate intranet, divisional portals, and team-related intranet sites:

- Create a centralized information repository
- Develop a common user interface
- Create a common and easy-to-use search capability
- Decentralize the ability to publish
- Improve employee productivity

As of the publication of this book, Banco Nacional de Costa Rica has implemented the overall corporate portal and has populated two of the divisional portals—IT and finance—with content enabling employees to test fundamental capabilities and achieve basic functionality of the Windows Broadcast Media component in under one month. Additionally, hundreds of team sites using Microsoft SharePoint Services have been successfully established, thus enabling employees to search the existing portals, improve collaboration, share information, and improve job performance. The bank is in process of deploying the remaining divisional portals, which should be completed by the first quarter of 2002.

Divisional Portals Empower Employees with Easy Information Access

A consistent user interface and rapid enterprise search are key criteria for success of the intranet at Banco Nacional de Costa Rica and its over 4500 employees. The bank defined six divisional portals that were critical for developing a cohesive knowledge base and for ensuring that the corporate intranet succeeded in improving worker productivity and operational efficiency. These six portals included IT, human resources, finance, loans, management, and bank business.

The structure of the divisional portals is simple. They were based on the primary functional areas within the bank that offered information needed by every bank employee. Previously, the bank had numerous intranets, developed by different functional groups and independent of IT resources and standards, including technology, graphics, content, and publishing authority. A key goal of the new Microsoft-based solution was the use of Microsoft SharePoint Portal Server and SharePoint Team Services to provide a framework within which all intranet developers could work in concert. This would improve the end user experience, shorten the learning curve, and enable more effective use of intranet resources.

Sigifredo Fonseca Mora, Corporate Manager of Technology and Operations for the Banco National de Costa Rica, said it most succinctly: "We are very happy now that we have a standard framework to build our intranet. The guidelines are focused and simple. And the Microsoft technology is easy to set up, populate with content, refresh, and maintain."

One of the most important characteristics of the Microsoft Solution for Intranets is the functional simplicity of the underlying technology. The key components of the Microsoft Solution for Intranets are as follows:

- **A central corporate portal** provides one-stop searching of and linking to a wide variety of other content, such as divisional portals, a broadcast media portal, formally managed team sites, ad hoc team sites, and external content. It serves as a common source of company-wide information, including announcements, news stories, calendar items, and a catalog of other Web sites. It can also provide user subscriptions for a variety of new information, in which users receive notifications of the arrival of new documents pertaining to subjects in which they are interested.

- **Divisional portals** surround the central corporate portal in this hub-and-spoke arrangement. Each divisional portal is targeted to address the needs of up to 1000 users. Divisional portals provide document management services, search and subscription services to related team sites and external content, categorized views of content, and an application platform for integrating Web parts that provide access to a number of business applications (for example, news, events, links, or line-of-business integration).

- A **single-purpose team site** is at the outside of this model and is designed for small groups or specific projects targeting 10 to 100 users. They are linked to, and indexed by, the divisional portals around which they revolve and are also indexed by the corporate portal.

As with many organizations, Banco National de Costa Rica already has standards in place for the development of its intranet. Unfortunately, business growth outpaced the resources necessary to maintain the standards. Because prior intranet development throughout the entire organization was decentralized, standards were not commonly used. Implementing the standards-based Microsoft solution enables the bank to maintain its decentralized approach to intranet development yet also provides a consistent look and feel to every divisional and/or team site that is developed. Equally as important, it also provides a basic roadmap that is easily modified as business conditions change or as modifications in organizational structure mandate.

José Mario Bolaños Alvarado, Intranet Administrator for Banco Nacional de Costa Rica sums it up nicely:

Employees can now find and share information using a common source. They don't have to install or configure anything in their workstations. By using the intranet, in essence, they have the whole bank in their hands, with access to information useful for all internal bank projects. From an administrator's perspective, the Microsoft solution is better than conventional Web architecture because all the necessary elements are contained in a basic set of easy-to-understand and simple-to-deploy templates.

Decentralized Publishing Model: Efficiency Yields More Productivity

The bank's prior publishing model was inefficient in two ways: (1) isolated silos of information that were not accessible or easily searchable and (2) the length and complexity of the publishing process. Most importantly, there was only one central administrator responsible for all the intranet sites that were created. With neither adequate time nor resources, individual site "owners" were left to their own means to develop and maintain their sites. As a result, the former intranet development and publishing process took approximately five weeks from initial idea to first release.

First the user had to take a one-week class in Microsoft FrontPage, the Microsoft Office Web site creation and management solution, or some other Web site building application. The instructor was usually the intranet administrator, taking that person away from critical site management functions. Then the user spent most of the remaining four weeks actually building the site, adding content, and, if he or she had the capability, conducting site testing. Site development removed users from their daily job responsibilities, thereby decreasing their normal productivity and impacting the productivity of those people upstream and downstream from them in the value chain.

With literally thousands of documents spread randomly across the bank's organization; no uniform technology, graphic design, or navigation standards; and no comprehensive search capability, the knowledge stored on the Bank's prior intranets were really nothing more than individual data points, which lacked relationship and hence relevance to user needs.

According to Oscar Cambronero Molina, System Engineer at Banco Nacional de Costa Rica and a member of the content team for the Microsoft solution,

The new Microsoft Solution based on a SharePoint Portal Server with built-in content indexing and search capabilities and SharePoint Team services form the technology standards crucial for developing a next generation intranet that we can use today.

New policies mandate that every new site, whether a divisional portal or a team site, must conform to technical and graphic standards and must reside within the [Microsoft] solution. We are currently migrating old sites and conforming them to the new standards. Now that site creation is as simple as using a standard template, and document publishing is as simple as several mouse clicks and configuration, we have reduced site creation and content publishing time to less than one hour. This improves everyone's productivity and enables the overall site administrator to focus on what he or she does best, dealing with scalability and extensibility issues and ensuring that the intranet roadmap is adhered to so that future intranet services come on line when they are needed and expected.

Even with only two divisional portals currently online, the bank is already experiencing increased productivity from its employees, resulting in the development of better products and services.

Robust Functionality and Customizable Solution Improves IT Efficiency

With only a single administrator for the bank's intranet, human and technical resources are stretched thin. The IT department is busy operating the corporate network and ensuring that infrastructure components, essential to the bank's daily operations, keep running smoothly. That's why the key to delivering the functionality and performance of the Microsoft solution lies in the deployment of servers to deliver four specialized functions:

- **Corporate portal** functionality is provided by a combination of two machines. The central portal server is a single physical server running SharePoint Portal Server 2001 with Service Pack 1. This server hosts the portal homepage and all the prescribed WebParts, corporate-wide search, and subscriptions. It does not directly index any content sources but instead receives regular index updates from the content index server. It provides no document management services of its own, although some of its WebParts provide direct links to the divisional portals and team sites hosted on other servers.

- The **content index server** makes up the other half of the corporate portal function. It indexes all content across the various intranet and Internet servers and forwards its results to corporate portal. It is one physical server running SharePoint Portal Server 2001 with Service Pack 1. It can be configured to index file shares, Web sites (secure and anonymous), Microsoft Exchange public folders, Lotus Notes databases, and SharePoint Team Services sites. While it is kept quite busy, all of its activity occurs in the background relative to the activities of the other servers in this scenario.

- A **divisional portal** is one physical server running SharePoint Portal Server 2001 with Service Pack 1. It hosts the dashboard-based portals used by division members, processes search requests for local content as well as content in federated team site servers, and provides document management services. This server is configured to support 1000 users performing a variety of tasks. Other WebParts and subdashboards may be customized after deployment to provide division-specific application functionality.

- **Team sites** for a division are delivered using one physical server running SharePoint Team Services and SQL Server 2000. This server stores the content for all of the team sites. It is configured to support up to 1000 users spread across 100 team sites.

According to Sigifredo Fonseca Mora,

The time required to administer and maintain our new intranet solution is radically decreased from our prior intranet. This enables our administrator to focus on more value-added functionality to the overall intranet rather than troubleshooting individual team sites or divisional portals.

We are in process of implementing the Windows Broadcast Media component of the [Microsoft] intranet solution because we think it will contribute immensely to the bank's ability to quickly and relatively painlessly disseminate company-wide audio and video information direct to each employee's desktop. And we are also exploring using broadcast video to each user's PC as way to improve training and productivity while lowering out-sourced training costs.

The Windows Broadcast Media component of the Microsoft solution for Intranets makes it easy for the IT group to implement streaming media on their corporate network.

- **Event scheduling and management** can be offloaded to knowledge workers or administrative assistants, enabling the IT group to remain focused on its core activities. All event information entered is automatically logged in SharePoint Portal Server and displayed on the intranet portal for easy end user access.
- **Turn-key production and delivery** uses Windows Media with a four-step wizard to validate server availability, connect to audio and video devices, launch the broadcast, and automatically archive on the SharePoint Server portal at the conclusion of the event.

Enabling Business Agility Through a Successful Knowledge Workplace

Meeting the business goals of Banco Nacional de Costa Rica through the use of technology to transform data into knowledge is only part of the equation. The other part is employee empowerment. The bank is using information technologies across all business units to achieve operational efficiencies and boost employee productivity to facilitate the development of new products and services.

Castillo Fernández noted:

We are betting that by using IT as a strategic tool to enable business goals, the bank will maintain its position as leader in financial services for all of Costa Rica. The ease of design, low cost of maintenance, and simplicity in deployment provided by the Microsoft Solution for Intranets allows us to be proactive in our approach to solving business problems. We anticipate increasing our market share through the development and adoption of new forms of electronic products and services for our commercial and personal clients.

Tracy Unified School District Improves Student Learning and Reduces Administration

The Tracy Unified School District (TUSD) of Northern California used the Microsoft Solution for Intranets as a strategic tool to fundamentally restructure the means by which its district-wide administrators and teachers collaborate and communicate. Using the Microsoft solution, the district implemented an electronic document repository that enabled the district's human resources (HR) department to more effectively store and retrieve information. Improved access to education materials and better collaboration between teachers and administrators is expected to improve overall effectiveness in curriculum development. Using the Windows Media Broadcast component of the Microsoft Solution for Intranets allows the district to decrease the number of in-person meetings, thereby enabling teachers to spend more time with students and develop curriculum. The district anticipates that the net result of better collaboration and communications will be an improved curriculum and better student scores on California's standardized exams.

Executive Summary

Situated at the southern edge of the San Joaquin-Sacramento River delta, Tracy, California, is the gateway between the Central Valley and the San Francisco Bay area. Growing at an annual average of nearly 800 new students for each of the last five years, the school district was an early user and advocate of information technologies (IT) to improve student learning, both in topical subject areas and in the use of technology. While student scores on standardized statewide exams were improving, the district's administrative functions were in need of similar technology advancements. The district established a goal of improving communications and collaboration between school administrators and teachers with the intent of enhancing curriculum development and hence student achievement and preparation for their after high school years.

"As a school district, our effectiveness is measured by how well we prepare our students to meet the challenges of an ever demanding world, both in terms of their role in the labor force as well as in their personal development," said Dr. Keith T. Larick, Ed.D., Superintendent of Schools for the Tracy Unified School District.

Our students have made great academic strides. Now we need to use technology to facilitate the professional development of our teachers and administrators. By utilizing the Microsoft Solution for Intranets, we have made a significant shift in the way we collaborate and share information. We have improved efficiency and productivity and in the process reduced teacher burnout and attrition. The Microsoft Solution for Intranets allows us to push broadcast media to the teacher's desktop and in so doing will enable them to spend more time with students and in developing lesson plans. This represents a major change in the way we consume and share information, which we believe will reap tremendous benefits for our students.

The school district looked to the Microsoft Solution for Intranets to help create a single, uniform intranet that enabled administrative functions to take place in an electronic, rather than paper-based, environment. The Microsoft solution will also enable administrators and teachers to spend less time in meetings and more time developing curriculum and attending to students. The Windows Media Broadcast component of the Microsoft Solution for Intranets will enable cross-district messaging from the superintendent's office as well as that of the school board and other key administrators. A portable video production studio will enable live broadcasts of special events from locations throughout the district.

The Microsoft Solution for Intranets distinguishes itself as the most recent advance in intranet technology that offers a complete solution with immediate robust functionality. Comprehensive in scope, the solution empowers the knowledge workplace by providing Web-based collaborative team services, a gateway for information management and discovery, and broadcast communications direct to each desktop.

Dr. Larick continued:

In implementing the Microsoft Solution for Intranets, we are simply following the motto of our school district, "The future belongs to the educated." We interpret this literally and think that our students will directly benefit if their teachers and the administrators who make up the educational backbone of our schools are also using the same technologies that enable improved learning in the classroom. The Microsoft Solution for Intranets is the culmination of a vision for educational administration that started over seven years ago, and which today we are on the verge of fulfilling.

With 1500 total employees, the school district has already implemented a document repository of over 60,000 hard-copy records for its HR department and is in process of scanning these records and inserting them in a living electronic archive of over 17 GB. Expansion of the document repository structure into a collaboration and communications portal for administrators and teachers is currently in process, as is the capability for live and on-demand broadcast video direct to the desktop. Implementation of the communications portal and the broadcast capability is anticipated to be completed by the close of 2001.

Digitizing the HR Department-Document Management for the Twenty-First Century

With an educational history spanning more than 80 years, the district's HR department has accumulated a hard-copy archive of over 60,000 records that were in continuous use. Recognizing that constant hand processing, search, and retrieval of these paper-based documents was an inefficient use of human resources and required an inordinate amount of file storage in limited office space, the Information Services and Education Technology group of the Tracy Unified School District embarked on an ambitious program to digitize all the records and put them on compact discs (CDs) that could then be easily retrieved via network access to a CD storage device.

Kerry Johnson, Director of Information Services and Education Technology for Tracy Unified School District, explained:

> Implementing a document management solution for the department of human resources was part of the first stage of implementing a single point of access to records that would eventually become the basis for a district-wide communication and collaboration portal for all administrators and teachers.

With more than 70 servers spread across 20 sites, providing a variety of district functions, including file and print, tracking school schedules, and meeting the ever-increasing requirements of state and federal school authorities, it was increasingly difficult for users to find the information they required. Although the network was centrally administered, the content was not. Since content existed on personal servers and network file shares, a user often had to review multiple versions of the same document with the same file name but with different content before being able to locate the desired file. As a result, a great deal of time was spent searching through multiple domains and servers to locate the correct file. Not only was this inefficient in terms of time and resources, it also inhibited the full professional development of the users.

Johnson continued:

> This problem was compounded by a district-wide policy of enabling remote access to all teachers and administrators. We needed a solution that could work on a dial-up connection, could easily scale, and would be secure no matter who tried to access the site through the Tracy Education Network. We also required search capability that would span the entire district and the numerous stores of content that were constantly being revised and updated. We used Microsoft SharePoint Portal Server as the foundation upon which we could build a comprehensive knowledge infrastructure, based on the Microsoft Solution for Intranets, because it was simple to implement yet offered a flexible and extensible architecture that could be readily adapted to a more sophisticated site as our needs and capabilities expanded.

As a result of initiating the District's new intranet with SharePoint Portal Server, the school district positioned itself to take advantage of the complete Microsoft Solution for Intranets as it progressed to its next level of developing an all-inclusive communications and collaboration portal.

Collaboration and Enhanced Communication Yields Improved Professional Development

With 99 percent of the classrooms in the district wired and connected to the Internet, and 75 percent of the teachers doing student attendance on networked computers, it was a natural evolution to bring the efficiencies of a comprehensive intranet solution to the more than 1500 staff members who support the nearly 15,000 students in the school district. Further, hiring more than 180 new teachers in each of the last several years and bringing them up to speed in educational technology and curriculum specific to their classes was a daunting task using conventional tools.

Michael Lau, the Technology Training Manager for the Tracy Unified School District, explained:

> Professional development usually takes place in multiple meetings and over a long period. This is neither an efficient use of time nor professional resources. We needed a new way to share information and enable a dialogue to take place no matter where people were located or what they schedule they were on. We wanted everyone to have access to same information so that they could make more informed decisions when developing curriculum, discussing student performance, or mentoring new teachers on state and federal accountabilities.

The district did not have a consistent method for document collaboration and versioning nor was there an effective search capability across the entire network. The district needed a more effective way to disseminate and share critical information as well as to conserve time and valuable professional resources.

Sara Windsor, Senior Network Engineer with Information Services and Education Technology for the Tracy Unified School District, noted:

> We were already in process of implementing the document repository of over 17 GB of scanned data for the human resources department, so we were familiar with what SharePoint Portal Server could provide in context of a complete intranet solution. We needed to be sure that the collaboration platform we implemented would integrate with and complement our new HR document management system. The logical next step was to use SharePoint Team Services as a component within the Microsoft Solution for Intranets to facilitate professional development through improved collaboration and better communication.

With the assistance of Compaq Global Services, the TUSD designed a comprehensive intranet solution built on the district's Windows 2000 server-based network. It could supply a full range of communications and collaboration services that would enable the district to decrease the amount of time that teachers and staff spent in in-person meetings by providing

- Seamless, secure access to documents and information via a common interface from both the intranet and extranet

- Comprehensive district-wide document search and retrieval

- Document versioning, check-in, check-out, and subscriptions

- A customizable digital dashboard interface with the ability to integrate with other key district information sources, such as the student information system

By implementing a comprehensive intranet solution, the district now has the ability to host forms and track and approve documents. A digital dashboard, developed as a custom application, will integrate with student information systems and dynamically update and present key student data, such as attendance, enrollment, or grades, to staff and administrators. And the subscription feature of the Microsoft Solution for Intranets enables teachers and administrators to subscribe to a range of time-sensitive e-mail notices, bulletins, progress reports, and other topic-specific updates that otherwise would come to them in paper-based memos or newsletters, often arriving after the effective date.

The new intranet will also provide a complete platform for the quick and seamless exchange of student, curricula, and administrative-related data. The district anticipates that this will decrease the amount of time that teachers and administrators need to spend in meetings, which in turn will enable them to spend more time developing curricula and in face-to-face meetings with students.

Broadcasting to the Desktop: Improving Productivity in Real Time

Using technology to provide today's learners with the knowledge and skills of tomorrow is nowhere more evident than with the district's initiative to create a video broadcast capability direct to the desktop of every teacher and administrator. The combination of video and PC technologies broadcast over the intranet is expected to help the district eliminate meetings, decrease interdistrict and intradistrict travel (and attendant costs), and improve the productivity of teachers and administrators by enabling them to remain at their desks and multitask. The need for ongoing curriculum development meetings could be reduced due to the ability to log on from within the intranet or externally via remote access and view a broadcast.

Technology Training Manager, Michael Lau, noted:

> Providing a portable [video] production station for use throughout the district will enable everyone to view live broadcasts in real time. This will enable each person to be current with the latest information wherever they are located. And, by installing a production station adjacent to our superintendent's office, we can watch the latest developments in curriculum development and educational administration unfold before us.

The Windows Media Broadcast component of the Microsoft Solution for Intranets has several unique features that enable even a developing network administrator to effectively set up and use the tool. Selected features include the following:

- **Event scheduling and management** can be offloaded to teachers or administrative assistants, enabling the IT group to remain focused on its core activities. All event information entered is automatically logged in SharePoint Portal Server and displayed on the intranet portal or integrated into the Microsoft Outlook messaging and collaboration client for easy end user access.

- **Turnkey production and delivery** using Windows Media with a four-step wizard to validate server availability, connect to audio and video devices, launch the broadcast, and automatic archival on the SharePoint Server portal at the conclusion of the event.

Lau continues:

> Most important for professional development is the ability to easily access archived programs in the comfort of a school or home office. The Windows Media Broadcast component enables each of us to effortlessly set up a team services function for collaborative efforts that cross site boundaries, for example, groups of teachers working on a collaborative curriculum project, and stream the video in real time so that everyone can participate. This is educational technology at its best.

Immediate Functionality and Low Maintenance Eases Job of IT

According to Sara Windsor,

> IT groups in most K-12 educational environments operate in a patch-work of technology with limited technical resources. We've been exceedingly fortunate to have the skill and expertise of Compaq Global Services in whom we could entrust our needs and feel assured that they would deliver what was required on time and within budget. They helped us identify the ways in which the Microsoft Solution for Intranets could assist the district and then they helped design and implement the solution using Compaq hardware. The absolute reliabili-ty of the ProLiant servers and the immediate access to support resources-engineers who have cut their teeth on bigger enterprise intranet engagements-was invaluable to getting the design and struc-ture of the document library and solution completed and implemented. Compaq's huge base of experience with Microsoft's products and net-work operating systems provides an invaluable technical resource from the perspective of an organization which has actually implemented the solutions being supported.

Helen McNeal, Solution Architect with Compaq Global Services, noted:

> Customizing the portal to the specific information and collaboration needs of the Tracy Unified School District was a critical decision point. Although the Microsoft Solution for Intranets has very robust out-of-the-box functionality, we needed to orient it to meet the specialized educational needs of the district. We expect that the district will con-tinue to customize its portal, with the plan to eventually offer role-specific digital dashboards designed to meet the needs of specific user groups. For example, principals might get a dashboard that includes WebParts which dynamically present their school's attendance and enrollment data, GPA [grade-point average] information, and site administrative announcements. School board members might get a dashboard that includes WebParts which dynamically present summa-ry attendance/enrollment/GPA data for the entire district, as well as subscriptions to board meeting agendas with links to the supporting documents. The ease with which the district can customize its portal

and tailor it specifically to reflect its needs, even if those needs change on a relatively frequent basis, is one of the great attributes of the Microsoft solution. Nothing is written in stone; everything can be modified to reflect the way any business works. The built-in flexibility and extensibility makes this a very powerful tool for organizations of any scope or size.

Changing the Way the District Does Business: From the Ground Up and the Top Down

According to Michael Lau,

> As a direct result of using the new intranet, I'm spending less time with paperwork and more time evangelizing the use of technology with teachers and administrators throughout the district. I help teachers develop curricula, and I assist site administrators understand the power of this technology in helping them improve their own efficiency as well as that of their staff and teachers. Plus, I get to see how it has changed the daily work patterns of clerks, teachers, managers, and site administrators throughout the district. No longer are people caught in meetings or racing to catch up with their daily tasks. Now they get information pushed to them through subscriptions, can configure a digital dashboard specific to their own needs, or can watch the superintendent's latest executive briefing in real time, with the ability to replay the archive if there is something important they need to review. The Microsoft Solution for Intranets is impacting the way we do our work every day. In fact, it is even helping us redefine our jobs as we move to more value-added activities as a result of being more efficient with our assigned tasks.

Compaq Global Services Increases Revenue and Lowers Costs

Compaq Global Services, the services arm of Compaq Computer, used the Microsoft Solution for Intranets as a strategic tool to reshape the way the organization organizes its knowledge assets. Compaq Global Services anticipates winning new business as a direct result of better access to information, and the company has unlocked hidden gems of data that are now considered valuable intellectual capital and essential to leveraging new income. Compaq Global Services has also experienced a reduction in direct costs associated with intranet publishing, conservatively estimated at $1.5 million as a result of using the Microsoft Solution for Intranets. Clients are benefiting from the added value that Compaq Global Services brings to their intranet implementation from having deployed and successfully used the Microsoft solution in Compaq Global Services' own environment.

Executive Summary

As a worldwide, geographically dispersed services organization for a leading global hardware manufacturer, Compaq Global Services provides a wide variety of technology solutions to meet the business needs of enterprise, middle-tier, and small businesses. Information about these solutions and services, and how to sell and deliver them, is vital to the effectiveness and continued success of the organization.

Having successfully developed intranets for themselves and their customers, Compaq Global Services realized that the actual creation of knowledge occurs in teams. This intellectual capital, contained in e-mails, reference or technical documents, hallway conversations, or postmortem discussions, is often never captured or is "lost" by the time a final project deliverable is published on an intranet. Capturing this information and converting it to knowledge by effectively sharing it throughout its global organization is a key element of Compaq Global Services' knowledge strategy.

Compaq Global Services looked to the Microsoft Solution for Intranets to help them create a flexible yet consistent environment so that teams could more effectively capture the knowledge they create. The program team was also seeking an intranet solution that automated the actual physical management and presentation of documents from an internal publishing perspective.

Craig Samuel, Chief Knowledge Officer for Compaq Global Services, explained:

> We serve our customers best when we can positively and enthusiastically tell them that a solution works because we are using it day in and

day out in a production environment. The Microsoft [intranet] solution works! We know this because we have already experienced enhanced productivity as a direct result of unlocking hidden knowledge and sharing information that with our prior intranet model might not have been captured nor effectively shared.

The Microsoft Solution for Intranets represents the latest advances in a solutions-focused intranet technology that enables the knowledge workplace through Web-based collaborative team services, a portal for information management and discovery, and broadcast communications to employee desktops.

Samuel continues:

The Microsoft solution has a straightforward architecture, is relatively uncomplicated to set up, intuitive to use, and simple to maintain. Based on an information architecture design and with some customization, we're already using it with over 3000 people internally and are in process of rolling it out to our global organization.

The new knowledge infrastructure is already in use. White papers, knowledge briefs (Compaq Global Services internal white papers), and solution components are already in field use, and WebParts, such as the DownLoad Manager, have been deployed by various customers. WebParts-reusable Web objects that are part of the Microsoft.NET Framework—are custom components that speed service delivery within the Compaq Global Services intranet. The fundamental building block of a corporate knowledge base—intellectual capital created in team environments-has been accelerated by the aggressive development of community-based "micro-portals"[2] throughout the organization.

As a result of a successful pilot project within Compaq Global Services, the Microsoft Solution for Intranets is being deployed throughout its worldwide organization. Additionally, Compaq Global Services is working with enterprise customers to solve their knowledge management

2. Compaq Global Services refers to community-based Web sites as "micro-portals." For additional information on micro-portals and Microsoft intranet technologies, you can read the white paper *The Use of Portals in Corporate Intranets* published by Compaq in March 2001. This white paper is available in the SharePoint Technologies section of the Compaq Web site (*www.compaq.com/sharepoint*) or you may go to *http://activeanswers.compaq.com/ActiveAnswers/Render/1,1027,5195-6-100-225-1,00.htm.*

problems using a similar federated micro-portal model based on Microsoft technology.

Hidden Information Unlocked: The Value of Team-Created Intellectual Capital

According to Chief Knowledge Officer Samuel,

> Information is the lifeblood of our business. If we cannot quickly and effectively disseminate information to the various parts of our organization that require it in a timely manner, then we don't have the capability to respond to opportunities, win new business, and achieve the level of customer satisfaction we seek. An enterprise client once told me, "If we *really knew* half of what we know, we'd be twice as profitable, and that doesn't include what we don't know!" Therefore, our key objective is to eliminate the barriers to the development of knowledge and then facilitate its distribution and use within the organization.

A core challenge in running a global services business is sharing intellectual capital and knowledge among the various geographies, global practices, and professional communities. Compaq Global Services' prior intranet had created virtual silos of information, and with over 400,000 pages of information, most were difficult to find. Further, with 20 content editors maintaining various subfolders, most of their time was spent in the basic mechanics of posting files, finding and removing old files, editing HTML pages for consistency, and manually maintaining pages of links to content.

Samuel continued:

> Our prior intranet was a huge cost to us. Not just direct costs, such as the time spent in creation, archival, search, and maintenance. But, more importantly, the indirect costs, such as the opportunity cost of not having information at our fingertips with which we could win more business or facilitate current projects by leveraging our existing knowledge. We think indirect costs could be as much as 103 greater than our direct costs. Using the Microsoft Solution for Intranets we expect to reduce costs and increase revenue by ensuring that the intellectual capital we create becomes globally accessible and useful knowledge.

Under the guidance of Chief Knowledge Officer Samuel and Chief Technology Officer Tony Redmond, Compaq Global Services embarked on a knowledge infrastructure based on three tiers using the Microsoft Solution for Intranets for the creation, management, and presentation of intellectual capital. This same model can be readily applied in any enterprise environment:

- **Tier 1, corporate intranet**—core organizational information such as services, contact information and more delivered as static Web pages.

- **Tier 2, communities of practice**—functional groups within Compaq Global Services who develop or deliver solutions to customers. Compaq Global Services uses Microsoft SharePoint Portal Server to provide each community with a self-managed virtual community space. Members create and manage the technical content through Web folders, while the SharePoint Portal Server Web interface provides a digital dashboard integrating internal content with other content sources and applications of interest to the community that can be freely shared throughout the intranet.

- **Tier 3, teams**—Teams are where the work occurs and where raw intellectual capital is created and refined. SharePoint Team services is one of the solutions that Compaq Global Services is using to provide the secure, shared spaces that teams need to complete tasks effectively. The space is used only until the task is complete and the resulting intellectual capital is ready to be published.

With this architecture, information moves up from the team space in which it is created to the community-of-practice space, where it is shared, reviewed, and refined. Finally, it moves to the corporate intranet site when it becomes a standard practice or solution offering.

Compaq Global Services chose the Microsoft Solution for Intranets for the communities of practice for three fundamental reasons:

- **Document management,** including check-in/check-out, approvals, and profile attributes

- **Security** by using standard Microsoft Windows authentication that does not require separate accounts or passwords

- **Customizable Web interface** that automates the presentation of content to both members of the community and to the organization as a whole

SharePoint Portal Server provides both document management and search functions, accessible either from a Web browser or the desktop. Because of its integration with the Microsoft Office product suite and its automated Web interface, SharePoint Portal Server can be configured as a portal at all levels of the enterprise, from a departmental collaboration server to a corporate search engine.

According to Samuel,

> By using SharePoint Portal Server to provide self-managed spaces for the communities, we are segmenting the content to make it easier to maintain, as well as reducing the role of the practice editor. The savings, strictly in terms of cost reduction are conservatively estimated to be over $1.5 million. More importantly, we envision earning new revenue from the fluid exchange of organizational knowledge that enables us to respond to new business opportunities as they arise.

Out-of-the Box Functionality Yields Productivity Benefits

According to Chief Technology Officer Redmond,

> We had a huge amount of information on diverse Web sites, in many [Microsoft] Exchange public folders, and on network file shares. Finding anything was like looking for diamonds in haystacks. The Microsoft Solution for Intranets, using [Microsoft] SharePoint Portal Server, has allowed us to bring information together in one place to create one-stop shopping for our technical community. It is now a fundamental element of our overall knowledge management strategy.

According to Andrew Gent, Lead Knowledge Architect for Compaq Global Services,

> We want to empower our community members by making it easy to publish. We are very rapidly phasing in the establishment of new communities and needed to make this as painless as possible. Using the

best practices we've learned from our first communities, we've created a cookie-cutter framework for the core elements of each community micro-portal so that a basic site can be generated in only a few hours. Then we can customize and populate the site as needed.

Since Compaq Global Services is by nature a global organization, scalability and reliability were key concerns for SharePoint Portal Server.

Gent continues:

SharePoint Team Services snaps right into our knowledge management strategy for using secure team spaces as the incubator for intellectual capital within the organization. Because it is part of [Microsoft] Office XP, which is SharePoint aware, it is simple to integrate with our Office-based personal productivity platform. Using SharePoint Team Services, team members can post documents, check schedules, participate in threaded discussions, send out meeting minutes or do file sharing. Team members can also subscribe to content categories, or subscribe to documents or to particular authors. Once the intellectual capital is ready for publishing, it can be moved up to the communities-of-practice micro-portal.

Comments from the Compaq Global Services Microsoft technical (MSTech) community, a pilot group of only 3300 individual users who are already hitting the site at an average of 300 to 400 unique visitors per day, demonstrate a positive response. Recent user comments include, "This site is brilliant, don't ever take it away." Another user in the MSTech community practice site said, "Indexing the other resources is one of the features on MSTech I really like. Now, I only need to search from one central place to discover all the information I could possibly need." And a third user noted, "Results relevancy is unusually good, and needed documents can be easily identified." The first several months of usage showed an aggregate of over 80,000 hits, demonstrating that even with little internal promotion, site usage is growing organically. Feedback provided to the knowledge-management team is used to improve the site(s).

"I work with multiple communities-of-practice sites on a daily basis, and I find the default page very useful," noted another user of the MSTech site. "In fact, I rarely need to go beyond the default page for most searches." The micro-portals are architected so that the home page of each portal displays the most current documents. The user continued, "I've found the subscription feature to be extremely useful as well. More like push media, I use subscriptions to prompt me to look for something interesting or new. This is a great way to keep current with all my areas of interest."

Lead Knowledge Architect Andrew Gent added:

> The key learning here is to do whatever we must to enable effective collaboration and sharing of information and in the process not re-create silos of information or isolated bits of data. The knowledge management framework we've built using the Microsoft solution provides the structure and the tools to let us create whatever we need.

The first phase of deployment includes the creation of 20 to 25 communities of practice, such as "Wireless," "Global Wins," "References," "Business Sites," and more, while phase 2 is expected to double that amount to 50 to 100 communities within 12 to 18 months.

Broadcasting Knowledge to the Global Desktop

Keeping employees current with the latest corporate information, training, and executive messaging can be challenging when operating across every time zone in the world. And with budget constraints and safety and security issues paramount, corporate travel is being deemphasized. To meet this challenge, Chief Knowledge Officer Samuel envisions using the Windows Media Broadcast component of the Microsoft Solution for Intranets in the future to push live and on-demand video and audio broadcasts direct to a user's desktop.

> The current desktop video space is immature. Every vendor has a different process for setting up a broadcast, some even requiring that the files to be broadcast are sent days in advance to be loaded onto production servers. This just isn't practical from a business perspective. The Microsoft solution is simple to set up and use—for both administrators and end users—and operates on standard streaming protocols without requiring large server farms.

Most importantly, the broadcast component is flexible. It will allow Compaq Global Services to schedule a broadcast or an update whenever it is needed. The solution integrates with the Microsoft Outlook messaging and collaboration client, letting Compaq Global Services schedule a broadcast the same way as it would schedule a meeting. Most important for a global organization, the broadcast server automatically specifies the appropriate streaming server for people in different regions, allocating bandwidth on a per user basis, and saving the company a lot of time and administrative headache as well as user support.

Samuel noted:

We anticipate that the Windows Media Broadcast component will bring value to Compaq Global Services by improving employee productivity and helping us reduce costs. Our executives will be able to reach our dispersed employee base in real time with critical business communications. Employees will be able to participate from their desktops, eliminating the need to travel or commute to a meeting location. Not only will productivity be improved, but we anticipate that we'll be able to save money that would otherwise be allocated to travel and events. As a result, we expect a rapid return on our technology investment.

Leveraging .NET to Empower IT and End Users

In most organizations, finding development resources to build an intranet is at best an open book and at worst a tug-of-war between senior executives, the IT group, or a line-of-business manager. The Microsoft Solution for Intranets tries to mediate this challenge by providing robust out-of-the-box functionality that can be easily customized to meet the specific needs of any organization. While it is ideal for any organization to initiate its intranet vision from the executive office, the Microsoft solution also enables action at the grassroots level for either basic functionality or a more comprehensive implementation gained through customized code.

For example, Compaq Global Services used C#, a programming language of the Microsoft .NET Framework to create a variety of WebParts, each with unique functionality that can be integrated into a user's digital dashboard, enabling it to be customized according to his or hers professional needs and preferences. WebParts can also be linked to other systems, even those of application service providers (ASPs) or other third parties. The key reason for developing WebParts is that they can improve the speed and efficiency of accessing and sharing information, whether a user is on-site or off-site. Examples of custom WebParts that were developed at Compaq Global Services are as follows:

- **Last documents published** enables the home page of a communities of practice or team Web site to stay fresh by enabling a user to readily identify current documents from a preselected list of categories.

- **Download manager** is targeted to field consultants who often are required to download multiple files using a dial-up connection. The download manager allows the user to select files from various dashboards, such as search, categories, and documents, and put them in a shopping basket. When the user is ready to download the files, the download manager automatically zips all the documents into a single zip file and automatically sends it to the user. Users also have the option of having the zip file delivered to their Outlook inbox.

- The **knowledge rating system** enables a user to rank any individual piece of knowledge, whether a white paper, knowledge brief, or case study, and share that rating in a public space. Similar to a movie rating schema, other users can then identify if that document could be useful for their needs.

- **Pocket PC renderer** allows remote users of handheld devices, such as the Compaq iPAQ Pocket PC, or laptops to access search and browse categories in a portal. Active Server Pages (ASPs), developed by Compaq Global Services, automatically scale the image to screen size of whatever device or laptop is being used.

Veli-Matti Vanamo, Consultant in the Technology Leadership Group of Compaq Global Services, noted:

You can readily take advantage of previous investments in Microsoft infrastructure and leverage your experiences for rapid development and a faster time-to-market, as well optimizing maintenance and support. The point is this is a very integrated environment in which every Microsoft product will work.

Equally as important for an IT services organization is the ability to demonstrate that the design and strategy being developed for a client has already been tested and debugged in a real-time enterprise environment.

Chief Technology Officer Redmond adds,

The time and energy invested in developing knowledge in any organization is phenomenal. With personnel turnover and the rapid evolution of technology in today's business environment, continuity of content can be challenging. The Microsoft Solution for Intranets is helping us resolve this dilemma by enabling us to easily and cost-effectively implement our knowledge strategy. And because we can leverage our expertise in the solution architecture and deployment of other Microsoft products that build on the Windows infrastructure, such as Microsoft Exchange Server, we are able to readily transfer this knowledge to our customers when we are engaged to develop their knowledge management solutions.

Empowering the Knowledge Workplace: Real Help for Real Problems

According to Chief Knowledge Officer Samuel,

We are using the Microsoft Solution for Intranets to unlock the hidden business value within Compaq Global Services' organization. What's the real purpose here? Fundamentally, it's about real business issues: enabling a global organization to truly operate globally and breaking down the barriers to knowledge generation, sharing, and reuse. It's a three-part process: technology, business process, and, most significantly, cultural changes that the organization must adopt. We're using the Microsoft Solution for Intranets to help us achieve the technology part, which because of the way the solution is designed—open standards, integrated architecture, and as a snap-in with other Microsoft products— we are able to influence business processes as well. The cultural part? Well, every organization that makes the decision to be a knowledge organization has already made a significant cultural change. And when they are ready to implement a knowledge management solution, Compaq Global Services will lead them through the process and add value at every step along the way.

Summary

The case studies presented in this chapter illustrate the considerable value of intranets. Irrespective of whether deployed in financial services, banking, educational, or technology businesses, these examples further demonstrate how a successful intranet can deliver substantial benefit to organizations in the form of increased productivity and, in many cases, reduced costs achieved through enhanced collaboration, empowerment of employees, process efficiencies, and the provision of rapid access to business information.

Making Intranets Work: Planning and Beyond

Of course, the bottom line is, "How do you make the intranet work? How do you ensure that it will add value to the organization and become a reliable business tool?"

Chapter 10 provides practical guidance to business decision makers with regard to planning and managing an intranet deployment. It examines the key factors and attributes of both successful and unsuccessful intranets and builds on lessons learned by others. In Chapter 11 we consider what the future holds, for society in general and the knowledge workplace in particular, for this is the realm in which intranets must continue to power productivity.

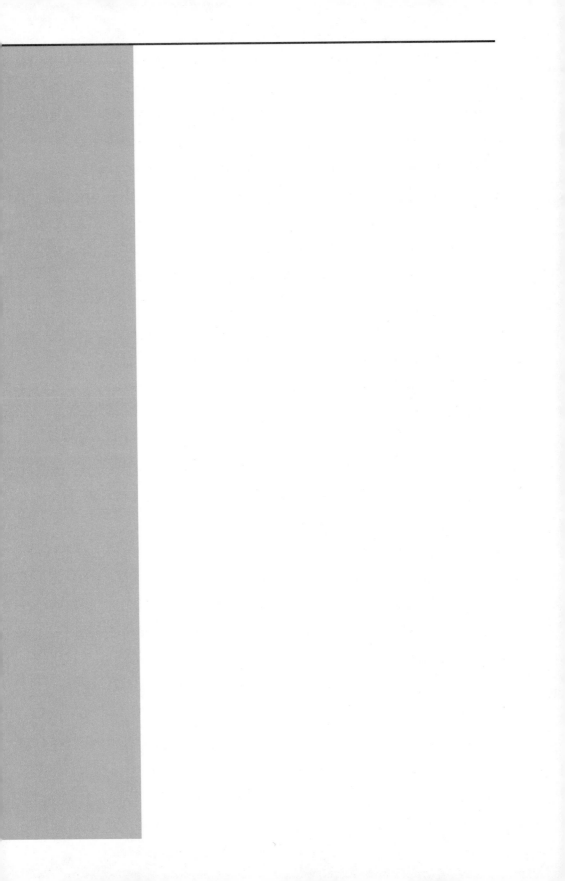

CHAPTER 10

Strategies for Planning and Deploying a Successful Intranet

In a recent article in *Darwin Magazine,* the key success factors of intranets were examined and reference was made to Hewlett Packard's positive experience. The executive committee of this computer manufacturer asked all employees to take a voluntary payroll reduction in June 2001. The decision was posted immediately on the company's intranet, called @HP, along with a tool enabling the 90,000 employees in 125 countries to volunteer for the reduction. The first day 10,000 employees signed up. Within three days 30,000 employees had volunteered. Instead of relying on rumor and word of mouth, employees were able to check the current tally of volunteers. As the count grew steadily, it convinced increasing numbers of employees to volunteer. Ultimately, more than 90 percent of HP's employees volunteered for the reduction in pay. [1]

This is just one illustration of the power of a successfully deployed intranet. This book is brimming with other examples, yet many organizations invest in what appears to be a straightforward project only to fail. Although it can be difficult to measure the financial impact of a failed intranet, the losses are often considerable. And let's not forget the unrealized expectations and wasted time that have resulted in frustrated employees and skeptical management. Although there are several ways to approach the development of a knowledge-enabled and learning organization, there are a number of recurring variables that can be attributed to the deployment of a well-planned and executed intranet.

Before we delve into the details, here are the top intranet challenges, as identified by Tim Horgan, Vice President for CIO Communications, in *CIO Magazine:*

---

1. Daintry Duffy, "Why Do Intranets Fail?" *Darwin Magazine* (November 1, 2001), 57.

- *Integrate* data from diverse sources.
- Provide *access* to data by all stakeholders.
- *Present* information in a format that is appropriate for each stakeholder.
- *Guarantee* performance, availability, serviceability, and security.[2]

Horgan also identified the top intranet business issues for organizations:

- What is the value of an intranet to an organization?
- How much will it cost?
- Will the intranet change current business processes?
- How will the organization and its employees organize for the intranet? Will there be new roles and functions?
- Will the corporate culture be favorable to the intranet?
- How will employees use it to achieve benefits?
- What training will be needed for employees?
- How will success be measured?
- What are competitors doing with intranets?[3]

These challenges and business issues should be considered at the beginning of the intranet planning process to make the best-informed decisions about content, services, design, and deployment. In this chapter we examine what distinguishes a successful intranet from a failure. We build on valuable lessons learned from others and describe what we think are the attributes of a great intranet.

What Went Wrong?

Let's take a closer look at why some intranets fail. Unsuccessful intranets typically happen because of

---

2. Tim Horgan, *Developing Your Intranet Strategy and Plan*
   (*http://www.cio.com/WebMaster/strategy/*, November 25, 2001).
3. Ibid.

- A lack of foresight-ignoring the changing economic and business landscapes in the planning process

- Deficient strategic planning-the intranet deployment was not mapped to organizational goals and visions

- Inattention to user experience-the needs, skills, and expectations of the user were overlooked in favor of other considerations

- Poor organization of the content and intranet staffing that leads to inefficiencies in the use of resources-both time and money

- Inconsistent content management, which results in a lack of demonstrated value and credibility to the user community

- Inadequate executive sponsorship-management's commitment is not continuously and overtly communicated throughout the organization

- A deficient network infrastructure that cannot handle necessary capacity, resulting in user frustration due to slow speed of access and too much "down time"

According to Jakob Nielsen, an intranet pioneer who is currently a principal of the Fremont, California, consulting firm of Nielsen Norman Group, failed intranets are drains on an organization's resources in two ways.

- Poorly organized intranets are a huge time waster. Every time a user has to download a change of address form or attend to any of those small things that takes 30 minutes rather than 5 minutes, resources are poorly used. If you multiplied the time losses—say 25 minutes—across an organization of 5,000 employees, there is a very direct and explicit loss. Nielsen estimates that the value of time lost around the world because of suboptimal intranets is a $1 trillion problem.[4]

- Countless poor decisions are made each day based on inadequate and incomplete information because intranet users cannot locate what they need or if the information is static, outdated, and therefore irrelevant. The cost to the organization in rework, mistakes, and lost opportunity is unfathomable.

---

4. Duffy, 57–58.

No Big Picture View

The very technology that made the Internet a revolutionary information and communications tool was supposed to revolutionize the organization as well, but this has not always been the case. The very ease of use that makes the Web so attractive was the undoing of many intranet projects. Initial excitement was overtaken by a lack of discipline. Web publishing tools made it possible for intranet content to be created and posted with a single mouse click; there were no consistent design templates, style guides, navigational tools, or structured databases-a gigantic albatross. With little or no governing authority, employees were wasting a great deal of time, often giving up in frustration.

Now add to this mix the growing popularity of public Web sites as a vehicle for outward facing customer communication. Why invest limited resources on a site that only employees will use when there are valuable customers to be wooed by the glitzy Internet site? Consequently, many intranets suffer the "stepchild" fate: ignored and underfunded. Many are obligatory shells that lack direction and support; thus, they are of little or no value.

Poor Planning

In order to achieve value, an intranet must be aligned with the strategic goals of the organization, division, or business group it is designed to support, but this business principle is often overlooked by those enamored with the possibilities introduced by this powerful medium. Without examining how the intranet supports the strategic goals of the organization, the expectations of management and employees will not be met

For example, at Los Angeles-based Occidental Petroleum, adopting a framework that was clearly driven by the company's goals made the third attempt at building an intranet successful. Previous iterations were characterized as chaotic—each department built its own site, and there was no central control or unified vision. According to Bill Dykes, Director of Communications and Web Development, each internal site—and there are hundreds—must now conform to similar navigational and structural guidelines. As well, each intranet proposal must include a development plan that analyzes the value it will bring to the organization, specifies strategic objectives, and describes the content.[5]

Poor User Experience

Many intranets don't succeed because user experience is frustrating or confusing. When an intranet fails to deliver immediate real or perceived value to busy end users, it will be unsuccessful. Users reject sites that are time consuming, complex, and make their tasks more cumbersome. In some cases there is also a lack of trust because of a perceived lack of security around personal or proprietary information, a lack of relevance, or poor data quality (out-of-date, inaccurate, or incomplete information).

Give employees tools that will help them be more productive and watch usage skyrocket. Content that is out of date, a lack of meaningful service offerings, and wasted time are all guaranteed to turn off the user. (See the sidebar Intranet Success and Failure for tips on the applications that tend to help an intranet succeed.) The best way to determine the optimal blend of content and services is to go to the users directly. Canvas them for ideas and suggestions on what they need and how to organize it. At Allied Van Lines, Annette Pierson, Senior Vice President of Strategy and Development, stressed the importance of involving Allied's 600-plus agents in every intranet product. Their new intranet was designed based on feedback incorporated from their agents.[6]

There is a great deal to consider when designing intranets for optimal user experience, including the appropriate information architecture, as well as interface, navigation, and functionality considerations. There are also cultural factors, such as how to get employees who are rewarded for their individual research and ideas to share information with associates and the organization at large.

---

5. Duffy, 59.
6. Duffy, 60.

Intranet Success and Failure[7]

A intranet consulting company, Enticy Group of Northern California, has developed a list of the applications that are typically successful and those that are not. We have included this here in the hopes it will be of value in the intranet planning process and will contribute to more of the former and less of the latter.

Which applications tend to succeed?

Information distribution:

    Policies and procedures manuals

    Underwriting guidelines

    Policy rating and quoting

    Organization charts

    Benefits and human resource information

    Stock options

    Phone, e-mail, and company directories

    Publications and newsletters

    Helpdesks

    Reports

    Software distribution

Information sharing:

    Project management and status

    Calendars

    Discussion groups

    Newsgroups

(continued)

---

7. Enticy Group LLC (*http://www.enticygroup.com,* December 21, 2001).

Intranet Success and Failure   *(continued)*

Data capture:

    Surveys and questionnaires

    Equipment and facility booking

    Time and expense recording

Interactive training

What applications tend to fail?

Computer-assisted design (CAD)

Image processing

Applications that require local hardware, such as scanning

Poor Organization

The value of knowledge is largely tied to the way in which it is structured, categorized, indexed, and organized. If information cannot be discovered, it is not of much use. A structure for identifying and describing how bits of information are related is particularly powerful when applied to business processes. Intranets should enable rapid access to knowledge. It should not be a game of hide-and-seek, yet organizations often complicate the task through poor information architecture design. For example, a company had a pension calculator on its intranet but no one could find it because someone in the Information Systems department had created it and published it on the IS pages, rather than the benefits or HR pages.[8] Poor information structure also arises when intranets are built based on organizational charts. This perpetuates the existence of individual silos or stovepipes of information in marketing, finance, human resources, and the like and can wreak havoc with intranet sites when there is a reorganization.

As intranets grow in breadth and scope, the challenge of separating the "wheat" from the "chaff" becomes more difficult as it becomes more critical. Successful intranets have sophisticated indexing and taxonomic capabilities

---

8. Duffy, 60.

to organize knowledge so that search time is minimized and appropriate information is discovered. Without such a conceptual framework, document management systems, corporate portals, and other collaborative online environments are mere dumping grounds for information.

Another common cause of failure is the lack of policies and guidelines to enable the intranet to scale beyond its small beginnings. At issue is nothing less than the effectiveness of the intranet. If content policies are not established, trust and reliability are compromised. If technology standards are not created, functionality is compromised. If navigational standards are not followed, productivity is impaired. These statements do not even begin to account for the substantial waste of time and money attributable to reworking errant efforts. Nor do they account for the reduced efficiency and increased frustration suffered by both users and content owners. Standards and guidelines make it easier to publish on the intranet, provide a framework of identity for disparate sites within an organization, facilitate navigation, and expedite search and discovery of business information.

Many organizations fail to incorporate metrics into their intranets; thus, they have no way of knowing what kind of content is being accessed, what databases are consulted most frequently, or what tools are most popular. Before Occidental Petroleum installed its site analysis tool, the company's best guess was that a few hundred employees out of a few thousand were visiting the site. This guess was based on the number of telephone calls received when the intranet went down. It turned out that more than half of all the employees were using the intranet at least once per day.[9]

Who Should Lead?

Multiple departments must cooperate to make an intranet successful, but at the same time governance is an important issue. How do you determine who will be in charge? Companies often delegate ownership to a single department that may not be fully equipped to handle the project. Another scenario is splitting ownership among a triumvirate of departments, usually IT, corporate communications, and marketing. This sharing of ownership can frequently lead to infighting, finger-pointing, and tasks falling between departments. [10]

---

9. Duffy, 60.
10. Duffy, 61.

Lisa Sulgit, founder and self-styled "e-vangelist" of lisa@sulgit.com, a New York City-based Web consultancy who has worked with Con Edison, Pitney Bowes, and Time Inc., suggests that the strongest department, or the one closest to the core content, should lead the project.[11] She also suggests creating an oversight council or team composed of stakeholders from all departments that will direct the establishment of guidelines, procedures, and other policies that impact the whole project.

Many intranets fail because one department assumes exclusive responsibility for content management. Deciding whose job it is to update which intranet content and when can be a complex and thorny one because the decision impacts multiple individuals and parts of the organization. The challenge of content ownership can be summed up as follows:

> Though we've had overtures to functional areas within the company to claim real estate for their own missions, we've had few instances where ownership has been successfully established and maintained. When content owners discover that the new baby needs to be fed, hugged, and changed frequently, they rapidly discover the "joys" of child neglect and abandonment.[12]

Lack of Executive Buy-In

Perhaps the most important but least appreciated aspect of a successful intranet is support and endorsement from the organization's leadership. Many companies fail to achieve this kind of buy-in because project leaders have not communicated the goals, objectives, progress, and successes of the organization's intranet to the management team and throughout the organization. Executives do not want to hear about the bells and whistles of intranet functionality; they want to know that it will make new products market-ready one month sooner, speed up the hiring process by 15 days, or save $75,000 in annual printing costs.

The great quality guru, Dr. W. Edwards Deming, always insisted on seeing the corporation's chief executive officer (CEO) and his or her staff for a first meeting. He believed that without buy-in from the top, his

---

11. Duffy, 60.

12. Michael Rudnick and Patterson Shafer, "Debunking the Intranet: Tales from the Front," *Communication World* (March 1, 1999), 27.

recommendations would gather dust on some office shelf. Likewise, successful intranet development needs full cooperation and support from the organization's leaders. Every technology that has survived the test of the early adopters has had to obtain executive commitment before it is deployed in the organization. Not only do executives hold sway over the purse strings, their early and well-publicized endorsement sends a signal to the rest of the organization about the value of the intranet.

If an intranet is successful, senior management is often unprepared for the resulting cultural changes. Empowering employees by providing rapid and direct access to business information has some radical implications. It tends to flatten the corporate hierarchy and can be threatening to executives who are not prepared for instant and direct feedback from employees or engaging in team-based collaborative initiatives.

Recalling a study of principal regrets that CEOs had upon leaving office, Sal Rasa, a former consultant with Watson Wyatt in New York, said that many dismissed the notion of communications as "soft," only to realize later that the biggest barrier to value creation was the under utilized knowledge of employees.[13] To unlock this valuable asset and derive the greatest value from the organization's intranet, CEOs must actively and publicly support it. An intranet stands little chance of success if there is no champion. CEOs, or their appointees, need to probe for the concrete business value of the project and communicate it to senior management in a language they understand, act as a cheerleader to get people involved and interested in the intranet, and reach out beyond politics to gather a team that will really invest and believe in the intranet.

Despite a surfeit of failed intranets, the case studies and return on investment (ROI) profiles presented in previous chapters prove that devoting appropriate resources and commitment to intranets can provide organizations with valuable tools for greater productivity through collaboration, knowledge sharing, and streamlined business processes. Now that we have described how *not* to approach intranet deployment, let's move forward and discover what can be done to achieve positive outcomes.

---

13. Duffy, 62.

Attributes of a Successful Intranet

A successful intranet requires careful planning, collaboration, and teamwork. Equally, it necessitates an organic, flexible, and adaptive approach. Like all guidelines and best practices the ones provided here have to be tailored to meet the unique needs of the organization that it will serve.

Knowing the Audience

The key to any successful product is knowing the consumer, and intranets are no exception. This means identifying the audiences that will use the intranet, understanding what information and applications are needed, and how they will be applied. The more you know about why the audience needs what it needs, and how the information is used, the better you can deliver relevant content to employee desktops.

In addition to defining the "who" of the audience, successful implementations have also considered the "whats." What is the level of computer and Web literacy? What prior knowledge does the audience have of legacy databases and the content possibilities these bring to the intranet? What will lead the audience to draw the same conclusions that you have with regard to the quality of the information and the value of the services?

User-Centered Design

Organizations that have focused on the user during intranet planning, design, and deployment have been successful. Users should feel as though the system was designed specifically for them. This is achieved with user training and tools, profiling, and personalization. Profiling recognizes that different people need different information and applications to do their jobs. An organization might establish 5 or 10 profiles that tailor the intranet to job functions, such as communications, human resources, sales and marketing, finance, and so forth. Personalization then allows individuals to further customize their desktops. This is not about screen savers; it is about giving users what they need to do their jobs and getting rid of the rest.[14]

---

14. Rudnick and Shafer, 30.

Interestingly, the winners of the "10 Best Intranet Designs of 2001" were exceptionally user centric, emphasizing simplification (for example, fewer graphics for a clean look and feel) and creating unified navigation as well as implementing methods that simplify the search process and feature it prominently.[15] In addition, there was an increased concentration on designs that facilitated collaboration and communication, with easy-to-use features that encouraged employees to post news and other information of interest. On average, companies saw intranet use increase by 98 percent following their user-centric redesigns.[16]

Look and Feel

Is there a connection between the success of an intranet and the consistency of its "look and feel"? Different approaches adopted regarding an intranet's presentation range from total anarchy embraced by a global technology firm in the United States to strict uniformity of design adopted by a global manufacturer headquartered in Switzerland.[17] We believe that an intranet's look and feel should reflect the culture of the organization, especially on the homepage. The implied communication should be aligned with its mission and vision. Some degree of functional and navigational uniformity means that content creators and owners can expend more energy on improving process and content and less on flashy design.

Having said that, guidelines should not be so restrictive as to limit the identity or sense of purpose of individual workgroups and local sites in terms of aesthetics. In her book *Virtual Leadership: Secrets from the Roundtable for the Multi-Site Manager,*[18] Jaclyn Kostner describes the elements of success for project teams. She emphasizes the importance of identity as a key enabler, especially in an online world, and recommends that functional intranet sites have some kind of identity reinforcing their specific missions, much the same way astronauts design a unique emblem for each mission.[19]

---

15. *http://www.useit.com/alertbox/20011125.html* (November 28, 2001).

16. Ibid.

17. Rudnick and Shafer, 29.

18. New York: Warner Books (1996).

19. Kostner, 30.

Content Management

There is a direct link between information organization and how quickly the intranet is adopted as a business tool. Successful intranet implementations recognize this and continue to build around it. Content is critical; it must be created, gathered, organized, profiled, linked with similar resources, and then delivered to the desktop. However, implementation of a successful intranet is ultimately driven by balancing two opposing forces: autonomy and control. On the one hand, content providers must be able to respond quickly to needs and events without being hampered by bureaucracy. On the other hand, the intranet requires design, discipline, and order.

Much of what makes an intranet successful relates directly to the information it provides, thus enabling the content providers is a critical part of this process, for they will be responsible for managing the content and keeping it up to date. The challenge is to direct them to align content with the goals and objectives of the intranet and the organization as a whole. With specific reference to content, organizations with successful intranets have

- Promoted an environment wherein content providers can share and exchange what they know and do best. Because they are closer to the information than anyone else, content providers should be engaged early in the process.

- Rewarded innovation and creative solutions. The individuals responsible for the processes can best analyze what worked well or what went wrong, based on knowledge and experience.

- Made available to the content providers the newest tools, templates, libraries, and plug-ins. Then the content providers are left to create.

- Resisted the urge to overmanage content providers. A little Web anarchy can be a good thing. After all, isn't that how the Internet started?[20]

Organizations that are aware of the importance of entrusting the control and management of content to those closest to it are enjoying positive intranet experiences. In order to create topic experts, employees need to be

---

20. Randy Hinrichs, *Intranets: What's the Bottom Line?* (Englewood Cliffs, NJ: Prentice Hall, 1997), 278-279.

encouraged to contribute and maintain content on the intranet. At Chicago-based Andersen, a global management consulting firm, where the knowledge gleaned from consulting assignments is captured, retained, and shared, contributions to the intranet comprise an element of the performance review.[21]

Another critical element of content management relates to the development and application of taxonomies and indexing to describe, organize, and group similar documents. Everyone has experienced the frustration of receiving search results with thousands of mostly useless links. Pitney Bowes, an office products manufacturer, manages a great deal of regulatory paperwork, so it created an intranet taxonomy that is specific to its business, a corporate vernacular that is incorporated into its document management, and information search and discovery components so employees can zero in on what they need.[22]

The third essential ingredient in sound content management is the establishment and communication of guidelines and procedures for creating and maintaining the content. Information mayhem may exist on some intranets, where only part of the answer is there, or what is available is not up to date or is simply wrong. However, while chaos can create content—this is how much of the content of early intranets was created when local groups just published what they needed or made available what they had—at some point it can become problematic. The intranet will never become a trusted business tool if out-of-date information is provided or redundant sources are posted.

Ongoing Intranet Management

Many books have been written on how to manage an intranet. It is beyond the scope of this book to delve too deeply into this topic; however, we wanted to identify some of the management issues that need to be addressed once the intranet is up and running.

In many ways the intranet will manage itself. The infrastructure established in the planning process will allow for the free flow of information and

---

21. Duffy, 60.
22. Duffy, 61.

a collaborative workspace but there is still a need for "management." This vast resource of corporate knowledge must be coordinated with an information architecture that makes it valuable to employees and ultimately to suppliers and customers.

In periods of transformation a tendency to resist change arises as individuals attempt to recover a sense of stability by re-creating the seeming security of a prior time. Going backward, however, is clearly impossible. What worked well before is unlikely to work now. In these days of accelerated change, we need to uncover the new strategies and tactics suitable to the time in which we find ourselves. Leading an organization before and after intranet deployment is really an exercise in change management. Change is announced, planned, designed, built, and launched. By integrating corporate knowledge and legacy data, and providing rapid access to business critical information, the intranet's presence is pushing change in the culture and behaviors of the workplace. It comes down to managing communications, training, and, most of all, expectations.

In order for the intranet to thrive, there must be growth; managed growth in some ways, but growth that comes from constant invention and innovation. By allowing the intranet to develop in stages, a time for unrestrained growth and a time for creating a single organizational voice are realized. Too many intranet projects get stalled, sidetracked, or even terminated because the organization viewed it as too experimental or tried to impose the same old rules and regulations on its command and control.[23]

Part of the continuous development process intranets encourage is user community engagement. This is essential for intranet self-improvement. Feedback loops furnish opportunities for employees to ask questions, offer suggestions, and help facilitate the collaborative environment that the intranet supports. Forms, e-mail, online discussions, broadcasts, and interactive games are just a few examples of feedback mechanisms.

How do organizations ensure content is business critical? This is the challenge. It requires finding a balance between autonomous content development and central quality control and creating an environment that values the contributions of the content developers. It also means that recruitment

---

23. Hinrichs, 234.

criteria may need to include subject expertise and content management skills. Talented people with business savvy and some technical acumen are needed to craft and maintain an information infrastructure that supports a productive and competitive organization. Identifying any gaps in employee skills and working to address these in training and future recruitment efforts will ensure that an organization has the human resources it needs.

Technology will continue to advance. Whether it is network, application, or intranet technology, there is a need to monitor what is happening. Management should be aware of development and decide if, when, and how to introduce such technology.

The satisfaction of the user community is crucial to the success of the intranet. In addition to content, database integration, and access, how else can you manage the user's intranet experience? "Management" is needed to control the look and feel of the solution; ensure employee access; integrate intranet training with orientation programs for new staff; provide intranet training and intranet-based training; and invite participation in the review of the processes, content, features, and functionality of the intranet.

Summary

This chapter has examined what needs to be done to set the stage for a successful intranet. Like all guidelines, the ones enumerated here need to be adjusted to accommodate the particulars of the organization that it will serve. There is no right way, and no one has all the answers. However the lessons gleaned from both successful and unsuccessful efforts can assist business decision makers as they plan and deploy their intranets. As a strategic business tool, intranets have great potential, and the best intranets are a direct result of thorough planning, focusing on the needs of the user, solid organization and information architecture, and executive sponsorship. In the final chapter we indulge in a little crystal-ball gazing and try to envision some of the conditions and technologies that will impact our society and workplace. After all, that is the context in which intranets must continue to serve their organizations.

Do's and Don'ts of Intranet Development[24]

DO:

- Have a vision for the intranet and align it with the strategic initiatives of the organization.
- Get senior executive support for the intranet.
- Sell the intranet to the user on an ongoing basis.
- Provide intranet training.
- Hold regular user reviews.

DON'T:

- Assume everyone will want to use the intranet just because it is there. The benefits need selling.
- Overlook a clear analysis of both qualitative and quantitative benefits.
- Rush the development. Make sure you are getting all the value from the initial project implementation before going on to the next stage.

24. Rudnick and Shafer, 31.

CHAPTER 11

The Future

One thing is certain in the rapidly changing world of information technology and knowledge sharing: evolving societal, work, and technological movements will play a central role in shaping the knowledge workplace. This chapter looks into the future and outlines the primary factors that will impact the evolution of intranets.

Changes in Society

Nothing is constant in this world except change. Our lifestyles are changing; our economies are changing; and our society is changing. Economic, social, and technological forces are at work to change the world in which we live, work, and play. Peter Drucker (one of the most respected management gurus of our time) has described and characterized what he calls the "next society."

The next society will be a knowledge-driven society, where knowledge is the key resource, and knowledge workers are the dominant work group. The three main characteristics of this knowledge society will be borderlessness (knowledge travels even more effortlessly than money), upward mobility (knowledge will be available to everyone through broadly available and advanced education), and the potential for failure as well as success (anyone will be able to acquire the knowledge, but not everyone will be able to use it to win).[1] Information technology will continue to have a significant effect by facilitating the spread of knowledge almost instantly to vast numbers of people in different parts of the world.

Historically, the foundation of the multinational enterprise has been rooted in ownership—domestic firms with subsidiaries abroad, each self-contained and relatively autonomous. Multinational enterprises in the next society will be unified more by strategy than by bricks and mortar and ownership. Of course, the concept of control will continue, but alliances, partnerships, minority stakes, know-how agreements, and contracts will

---

1. Peter Drucker, "The Next Society," *Economist* (November 1, 2001), 3.

increasingly be the building blocks of a confederation. In this scenario the role of knowledge and the technologies that facilitate its creation and sharing will be even more important than they are today. Additionally, a new form of senior management will be required—one that is not just an extension of operating management but a separate and distinct organ.[2]

Technology in the Workplace

Computing and information technologies have advanced at a dizzying pace in the last 25 years. Personal computers (PCs) have become increasingly faster, smaller, and cheaper. If the automobile industry moved at a similar pace, observers say we would all be driving disposable, jet engine Ferraris by now. Judging by current evidence, computing and information technologies will continue to accelerate and change at an unprecedented pace. Here are some of the devices and features that we can expect to see in the near future.

No one knows for certain what the future desktop landscape will be. In the short run you can expect to see PCs become smaller and more powerful, with thinner and lighter screens, and developments in voice and advanced face-recognition systems could change the look of workstation attachments. In the long run it is predicted that people will be using a number of other types of computing devices along with desktops, including handheld devices and even miniature "wearable" computers. According to the Gartner Group, a giant IT consulting firm, by 2007 more than 60 percent of the U.S. population ages 15 to 50 will carry or wear a wireless computing and communications device at least 6 hours a day.[3]

Processing power will continue to increase—Moore's Law[4] states that processing power doubles every 18 months—and storage technology research will continue. The silicon chip's storage capacity will reach its limit; nanotechnology and quantum computing are two areas of research that are

---

2. Drucker, 5.

3. David Coursey, "The Four Biz-Tech Trends of the Coming Decade," *Anchordesk* from ZDWire (October 8, 2001).

4. This law is named after Gordon Moore, the founder of Intel, who made this prediction in 1965, but it continues to hold true today.

attempting to supplant the chip in the storage technology world. Robert Morris, Director of IBM's Almaden Research Center, envisions storage in another dimension. IBM is very interested in the idea of holographic storage. Instead of storing magnetic bits on a disk's surface, IBM is experimenting with lasers and their interference patterns to store information in a crystal and read it at a rapid speed.[5]

Additionally, network technology will keep improving. Just as fast ethernet moved from copper to fiber-optic cabling, gigabit ethernet, terabit ethernet, and layer 3 switches will allow for greater amounts of data to be carried.

Bandwidth will become increasingly abundant and inexpensive; dial-up Internet access will become something of the past. The concept of "going online" will disappear, as people will always be connected. More data will be able to travel across increasingly smaller lines, and new technologies will allow us to squeeze more data through smaller pipes. And with voice and visual recognition capabilities requiring enormous processing, it will be a welcome addition.

While advances in mobile and wireless technology are beginning to impact our lives, the next few years will bring even more change. The Yankee Group predicts that the number of wireless Internet users-connecting mainly through wireless telephone networks-will grow from 3 million in 2000 to 50 million by 2004.[6]

Companies will move to integrate their mobile workforce via some form of wireless infrastructure to their intranets. However, as with wired communications, bandwidth and security will continue to be of concern, along with service reach, reliability, cost, and performance. Expect this to be resolved with the introduction of new technologies in the next few years. Standardization and fast packet-switched public networks are making it easier and cheaper to add wireless capabilities to mainstream business applications. IDC, a global market intelligence and advisory firm, claims that these applications are set to increase. By 2005 we should see widespread intranet access, Web browsing, vertical applications, and e-mail access via laptops or personal digital assistants (PDAs).[7] Additionally, Deloitte & Touche Consulting

---

5. Glen McDonald and Cameron Crotty, "The Digital Future," *PC World* (January 1, 2000), 117.

6. McDonald and Crotty, 118.

7. "Mobile Applications Revenues Set to Rise, Says IDC Report," *Telecomworldwire* (June 19, 2001).

reports that there are signs of more sophisticated enabling technologies, such as Bluetooth, which will capture our attention. Bluetooth has the ability to wirelessly link digital devices as diverse as digital cameras and computer printers.[8]

A recent study from Meta Group reports that one fifth of the business-to-business transactions will be undertaken by wireless systems in 2003. The report admits that budgets for wireless projects are still very low but predicts that they will grow rapidly within the next 14 months.[9] Many equipment developers have pilot projects in progress with prospective wireless intranet and applications users; it looks like business users, rather than consumers, will be the focus for wireless services. Organizations want wireless solutions that can cope with multiple mobility needs and ubiquitous access to business applications in which they have already invested.[10]

Intranets Continue to Evolve

Intranets are set to emerge as a key aspect of the nascent knowledge work-place, empowering employees, integrating business partners, and connecting customers. The right intranet solution will tie together all content and business process applications within the enterprise: employee information from old mainframe applications that were previously stand alone, data that used to be stored in "data warehouses," and access to process applications. Intranets, extranets, and the Internet may cease to become separate entities as the boundaries blur between private and public networks.

Increased Functionality

Intranets will include "process managers"—engines that learn and then manage/facilitate business processes. For example, a sales representative would be guided through the steps required for qualifying a lead, using

8. *2001 Technology Trends Annual Report,* Deloitte & Touche Consulting (May 2001), 5.

9. "Mobile Intranets—Have You Got the Message?" *Management Consultancy* (November 8, 2001), 10.

10. Joanne Elachi, "The Wireless Enterprise Opportunity," *CommWeb.com* (July 27, 2001, *http://www.commweb.com/article/COM20010727S0001*).

information about the account to determine the next steps. Intranets will also allow context-based personalization. A user's profile would determine the type of information retrieved to avoid information dumps. The profile might contain various descriptors, such as the user's job or role, the task he or she is working on, the time of day, his or her location, and what kind of device he or she is using to access the intranet. In sum, the intranet will become an intelligent immersive productivity workspace.

There will be an increasing demand for voice support. According to the Telecommunications Industry Association, the Internet telephony or voice-over internet products (VoIP) equipment market has nearly doubled from 2000 to 2001. Sales for 2001 have been estimated at $853 million and at $11.6 billion by 2004. VoIP is defined as voice-over managed networks, such as intranets and extranets.[11]

According to the Intranet Content Management Strategy Conference held in September 2001, in London, England, content management is a key survival strategy.[12] To succeed in electronic business, companies must adopt a best-of-breed approach to intranet site architecture and taxonomy, especially as content grows. In a Fortune 1000 survey, respondents reported an average of 77,000 pages per site, and one third of the respondents expected their content to at least double by the end of 2001.[13] This is supported by a study from the School of Information Management and Systems at the University of California, Berkeley, that claims humankind will generate more original information over the next 3 years than was created in the previous 300,000 years combined.[14]

Increasingly, applications will become seamlessly integrated with the intranet. The sheer volume of data in a multitude of formats will mandate advancements in content management technologies and policies. There must be efficient ways to access large quantities of unstructured text. The role and function of metadata will take on more significance as pressure builds to

11. "New Media," *Communications Daily* (June 4, 2001).

12. Simon Williams, "The Intranet Content Management Strategy Conference," *Management Services* (September 1, 2001), 16.

13. Williams, 16.

14. *Technology Industry Evolving to High-Performance, Security-Driven Mobile Marketplace, Says 2001 Technology Trends Annual Report from Deloitte & Touche Consulting* (press release, *http://www.dc.com/obx/pages?Name=prtechtrends2001*, May 1, 2001).

identify deep relationships in the organization's unstructured knowledge. In addition to text, this will include methods for creating and applying metadata to multimedia files and other digital media

Summary

As we discovered in Chapter 1, knowledge work is not new. What is new is our level of consciousness about it and the broad availability of powerful and affordable enabling technologies. Our relationship with information throughout history inspired the development of writing systems, storage devices, and methods of organizing it to make it accessible. Intranets have been, and will continue to be, based on these same human behaviors and will reinforce the concept of the value of knowledge in the workplace.

As we move through the twenty-first century, the need for rapid access to relevant knowledge—the right information at the right time at the right place—has never been greater. The world of business is progressively more competitive, and the demand for innovative products and services will continue to expand. Governments and private sector organizations alike struggle with the need to respond to customers whose level of sophistication and awareness grows every day.

The winners in the next society will be the individuals and organizations that adapt to and embrace the knowledge workplace as it unfolds before us. This is the productivity imperative of our time. Next generation intranets effectively harness individual knowledge and make it available to the collective team, group, or organization, thus revealing the knowledge workplace. The promise inherent in this transformation is immense. This brave new century overflows with the potential for human creativity and innovation. Knowledge is *the* enabling force of this time; it is to the twenty-first century what the internal combustion engine was to the twentieth century. The knowledge workplace is *the* engine of twenty-first century organizational productivity.

An Intranet Glossary[1]

activeX controls   Reusable software components that add specific functionality quickly, such as a stock ticker.

ADSL (asymmetric digital subscriber line)   A method for moving data over regular telephone lines that is much faster than a regular telephone connection. A common configuration of ADSL allows a subscriber to download at speeds of up to 1.544 megabits per second and upload at speeds of up to 128 kilobits per second. *See also* baud, bps, ISDN, *and* modem.

anonymous FTP   To connect to an FTP server without providing a personal login name and password. Often permitted by large host computers who are willing to openly share some of their system files to outside users who otherwise would not be able to log in. *See also* FTP, login, *and* password.

API (application program interface)   A set of routines, protocols, and tools for building software applications. A good API makes it easier to develop a program by providing all the building blocks.

applet   A small Java program that can be placed (embedded) in an HTML page. Applets differ from full-fledged Java applications in that they are not allowed to access files and serial devices (modems, printers, and so forth) on the local computer and are prohibited from communicating with other computers across a network. *See also* HTML, Java, *and* network.

application   Any computer program designed to accomplish a specific task or related set of tasks.

Archie   An early Internet search tool not used very much since the advent of the Web browser in 1994. It is an archive of filenames maintained at Internet FTP sites. *See also* browser *and* Veronica.

ARPANet (Advanced Research Projects Agency Network)   The precursor to the Internet. It was developed in the late 1960s by the U.S. Department of Defense as an experiment in wide-area networking that would survive a nuclear war. *See also* Internet.

ASCII (American Standard Code for Information Interchange)   The worldwide standard of code numbers used by computers to represent all the uppercase and lowercase Latin letters, numbers, and punctuation. There are 128 standard ASCII codes, each of which can be represented by a 7-digit binary number, 0000000 through 1111111. *See also* binhex.

ASF (active streaming format)   A format developed by Microsoft Corporation that allows you to develop streaming multimedia presentations using sound, video, and other formats.

ASP (application service provider)   A third-party entity that manages and distributes software-based services and solutions to customers across a wide area network from a central data center.

ASP (active server page)   A way of storing information on a Web server that uses server-side scripting to deliver finished pages to a Web browser. The script runs at the time the page is called and delivers finished HTML to the browser.

authentication   Verifying members of a team to allow participation in Web-based collaboration or users against an internal employee database.

AVI (audio/video interleaved)   A common video file format (.avi). Video quality can be good at smaller resolutions, but files tend to be large.

---

1. Adapted from *http://domainavenue.com/faq_glossary.htm* and Webopedia (*http://www.webopedia.com*).

backbone   A high-speed line, or series of connections, that forms a major pathway within a network. This term is relative, as a backbone in a small network may be much smaller than nonbackbone lines in a large network. *See also* network.

bandwidth   The transmission capacity of the lines that carry the Internet's electronic traffic. The greater the bandwidth, the more data that can be moved at one time. A lack of bandwidth can impose severe limitations on the ability of the Internet to quickly deliver information. *See also* bps *and* bit.

baud rate   How many bits a modem can send or receive per second. *See also* bit *and* modem.

BBS (bulletin board system)   An online meeting and information system that allows people to carry on discussions, make announcements, and transfer files. There are thousands of BBSs around the world, varying in size from those running on a single machine with only 1 or 2 phone lines to massive networks such as CompuServe.

binhex (binary hexadecimal)   A method for converting nontext files into ASCII files, which is required because Internet e-mail can only handle ASCII files. *See also* ASCII, MIME, *and* UUENCODE.

bit (binary digit)   A bit is the smallest unit of computerized data, composed of either a 0 (off) or a 1 (on). Bandwidth is usually measured in bits per second. *See also* bandwidth, bps, *and* byte.

BITNET ("Because It's Time NETwork" or "Because It's There NETwork")   A network of educational sites separate from the Internet. Listserv, the most popular form of e-mail discussion groups, originated on BITNET.

bookmark   A pointer to a Web site of interest. Within browsers, pages can be "bookmarked" for quick reference, rather than remembering and typing the complete Internet address in the address bar. *See also* Microsoft Internet Explorer, Mosaic, *and* Netscape Communicator.

bps (bits per second)   A measurement of how fast data is moved from one place to another. A 28.8 modem can move data at 28,800 bits per second. *See also* bandwidth, bit, *and* modem.

browser   A software program that is used to view Web sites and other Internet resources on the World Wide Web. *See also* Internet, Microsoft Internet Explorer, Mosaic, Netscape Communicator, homepage, URL, *and* World Wide Web.

BTW (by the way)   A shorthand term appended to a comment in an online forum or e-mail. *See also* IMHO *and* RTFM.

byte   A set of bits that represents a single character. There are usually 8 bits in a byte. *See also* bit, kilobyte, megabyte, gigabyte, *and* terabyte.

cache   A section of memory or the hard drive where data can be stored for rapid or frequent access.

CAUCE (The Coalition Against Unsolicited Commercial e-mail)   An organization dedicated to removing spam from the Internet. *See also* spam.

CERN   The European Particle Physics Laboratory in Geneva, Switzerland, where the original protocols for the World Wide Web were first developed and implemented.

certificate authority   An issuer of security certificates used in secure sockets layer (SSL) connections. *See also* security certificate *and* SSL.

CGI (common gateway interface)   A programming language used to convert data gathered from a Web page into another form. A CGI program might turn the content of a feedback form into an e-mail message or search a server's database with user-entered keywords. *See also* cgi-bin, e-mail, *and* World Wide Web.

cgi-bin   The most common directory in which to store CGI programs on a Web server. The "bin" part of "cgi-bin" is an abbreviation of "binary," dating back to when programs were referred to as "binaries." *See also* CGI, server, *and* World Wide Web.

CGI script   A short, uncompiled computer program written using a scripting language (typically PERL) that handles communication with Web servers and other applications.

client   The client part of a client/server architecture. Typically, a client is an application that runs on a personal computer or workstation and relies on a server to perform some operations. For example, an e-mail client is an application that enables you to send and receive e-mail. *See also* client/server *and* server.

client/server   Computer technology that separates computers and their users into two categories. When you want information from a computer on the Internet, you are a client. The computer that delivers the information is the server. A server both stores information and makes it available to any authorized client who requests the information. *See also* client *and* server.

compression   Data files available for upload and download are often compressed in order to save space and reduce transfer times. Typical file extensions for compressed files include .zip (DOS/Windows) and .tar (UNIX). *See also* download, PKZIP, *and* upload.

cookie   A piece of information (login name, password, online "shopping cart" items, user preferences, and so forth) sent by a Web server to a Web browser and saved to the computer. These "cookies" can then be used at a later date to restore the information when the same Web server is accessed again. Cookies are usually set to expire after a predetermined amount of time. *See also* browser, login, password, *and* server.

CPU (central processing unit)   The CPU is the brains of the computer. Sometimes referred to simply as the processor or central processor, the CPU is where most calculations take place. In terms of computing power, the CPU is the most important element of a computer system.

cyberspace   Coined by William Gibson in his novel *Neuromancer,* cyberspace is currently used to describe the whole range of information available through computer networks. *See also* Internet.

database   Any file or set of files containing data stored in an original format.

DBML (Database Markup Language)   A language used to embed database access commands inside HTML documents in the same way HTML is used to embed document publishing and hyperlinking commands inside plain text documents.

desktop   The local computer environment that sits on a user's desk. It is also the set of applications available on a user's local computer, including the operating system.

desktop publishing   Using a personal computer or workstation to produce high-quality, printed documents. A desktop publishing system allows you to use different typefaces, specify various margins and justifications, and embed illustrations and graphs directly into the text.

dial-in   An Internet account that connects a personal computer directly to the Internet. These accounts use a software application to connect to an Internet service provider and establish a link to the Internet. To access a dial-in connection, a computer needs either a modem to connect via a regular phone line or a terminal adapter to connect via an ISDN phone line. *See also* ISDN, modem, TCP/IP, *and* terminal adapter.

directory   A term used in UNIX and early computer operating systems to describe a location on a hard drive where files are stored. This is equivalent to the term *folder* in Macintosh and Windows systems.

discussion group   A section within USENET dedicated to a particular topic or interest. Discussion groups are also known as newsgroups. *See also* newsgroup *and* USENET.

DNS (domain name server)   A computer running a program that converts domain names into internet addresses and vice versa. Domain name servers (also known as name servers) are the backbone of the Internet. *See also* domain name, IP address, *and* server.

domain   A way of organizing the Internet, characterized by the suffix of the domain name. For example, *.com* is the commercial domain that includes organizations such as Microsoft Corporation (*www.microsoft.com*); *.edu* is the education domain that includes educational institutions such as Rutgers University (*www.rutgers.edu*) and Harvard University (*www.harvard.edu*). Other domains include *.org* (organizations), *.gov* (governments), and *.net* (networks). Special graphical domain suffixes are provided for Internet services that are specific for a country, such as *.us* for the United States, *.ca* for Canada, *.fr* for France, or *.de* for Germany.

domain control panel   A password access section of a site that domain registrants and partners use to make domain modifications, receive proprietary scripting code, and use our management system. Each panel's content is different and depends on your status in relation to Registrars.com.

domain name   A unique name that identifies an Internet site. A domain name is the Internet's way of translating a numeric Internet address into an easy-to-remember combination of words and numbers. A given machine may have more than one domain name, but a given domain name points to only one machine. For example, the domain names "example.com," "mail.example.com," and "sales.example.com" can all refer to the same machine, but each domain name can refer to no more than one machine. *See also* IP address.

download   The process of transferring data from a remote computer to a local computer. When you copy a file from the Internet to your computer, you are "downloading" that file. *See also* upload.

dynamic HTML   New features added to HTML that allow control over layering and positioning of objects on a Web page. Dynamic HTML also allows scripts to be embedded on a Web page, which cause the page to change based on user actions, without requiring additional calls to the server.

e-mail (electronic mail)   Messages sent from one person to another via the Internet. Electronic messages can also be sent to many addresses at once through a mailing list. *See also* Internet, list server, *and* mailing list.

ethernet   The common method of networking computers in a local area network. An ethernet connection will handle about 10,000,000 bits per second. *See also* bandwidth, bps, *and* LAN.

Extensible Markup Language   *See* XML.

extranet   A new buzzword that refers to an intranet that is partially accessible to authorized outsiders. An intranet resides behind a firewall and is accessible only to people who are members of the same company or organization, while an extranet provides various levels of accessibility to outsiders. You can access an extranet only if you have a valid username and password; your identity determines which parts of the extranet you can view and/or access.

FAQ (frequently asked questions)   An FAQ document lists and answers the most common questions on a particular subject. It is considered good netiquette to check for FAQs and read them. *See also* netiquette.

finger   An Internet tool for locating people on other sites. A finger can also be used to give access to nonpersonal information, but the most common use is to see if a person has an account at a particular site. The most famous finger site was a soda machine at Carnegie-Mellon University that students had wired to the Internet. They could then finger the machine and find out how many bottles remained and how long they had been in the machine so they wouldn't walk all the way there and find an empty machine or warm soda.

firewall   A combination of hardware and software that separates a local area network into two or more parts for security purposes. A firewall is commonly used to separate a network from the Internet. *See also* LAN *and* network.

flame   To "flame" originally meant to debate in a passionate manner, often involving the use of flowery language. More recently, however, "flame" has come to refer to any kind of derogatory or inflammatory comment, no matter how witless or crude. *See also* flame war *and* netiquette.

flame war   When an online discussion degenerates into a series of personal attacks against the debaters, rather than a discussion of their positions, it is referred to as a flame war. *See also* flame *and* trolling.

form   A hypertext document containing various graphical fields and devices, including text boxes, pull-down menus, radio buttons, and check boxes.

FQDN (fully qualified domain name)   The official name assigned to an individual computer. Organizations register names, such as "example.com," then assign unique names to their computers, such as "mail.example.com." *See also* domain name.

freeware   Software that is available for download and unlimited use without charge. *See also* register *and* shareware.

front end   The client interface. In other words, the "front" side of a client/server application that directly communicates with the user.

FTP (File Transfer Protocol)   A common method of moving files between two Internet sites. Most FTP sites require a login name and password before files can be retrieved or sent. *See also* anonymous FTP, login, *and* password.

gateway   Hardware or software set up to translate between two different protocols.

GIF (Graphics Interchange Format)   A graphics file format commonly used on the Internet to provide images on Web pages. GIF images are 8-bit (256-color) graphics. *See also* JPEG *and* TIFF.

gigabyte   A thousand megabytes. *See also* bit, byte, kilobyte, megabyte, *and* terabyte.

gopher   A searching tool that was once the primary tool for finding information on the Internet before the Web became popular. Gopher is now buried under massive amounts of Web pages. *See also* client, hypertext, server, *and* World Wide Web.

groupware   Software that allows multiple users to work as a group on the same set of data or documents. Groupware often includes integrated e-mail, scheduling, and other group-oriented communication features.

GUI (graphical user interface)   A program interface that takes advantage of the computer's graphics capabilities to make the program easier to use. Well-designed graphical user interfaces can free the user from learning complex command languages.

helper application   A program that allows you to view multimedia files (images, audio, video) that a Web browser cannot handle internally. The file must be downloaded before it will be displayed. Some plug-ins allow you to view the file over the Internet without first downloading it. *See also* browser *and* plug-in.

Hit   A "hit" is a single request from a Web browser for a single item from a Web server. For example, a page displaying three graphics would require four hits: one for the HTML document and one for each of the three graphics. "Hits" are often used as a rough measure of load on a server; however, because each hit can represent a request for anything from a tiny document to a complex search request, the actual load on a machine from a single hit is impossible to define.

homepage   Originally, a homepage was the Web page that a browser is set to use when it starts up. The more common definition refers to the main Web page for any business or personal site. *See also* browser *and* World Wide Web.

host   Any computer on a network that is a repository for services available to other computers on the network. It is common to have one host machine provide several services, such as World Wide Web access and USENET. *See also* node *and* network.

HTML (Hypertext Markup Language)   The language used to build hypertext documents on the Web. Hypertext documents are nothing more than plain ASCII-text documents interpreted (or rendered) by a Web browser to display formatted text and fonts, color, graphic images, and links. *See also* browser, Microsoft Internet Explorer, Mosaic, Netscape Communicator, *and* World Wide Web.

HTTP (Hypertext Transfer Protocol)   The protocol for moving HTML files across the Internet. This requires an HTTP client program on one end and an HTTP server program on the other end. HTTP is the most important protocol used on the Web. *See also* client, server, *and* World Wide Web.

hyperlink   An element in an electronic document that links to another place in the same document or to an entirely different document. *See also* hypertext.

hypertext   Text in a document that contains a link to other text. Hypertext is used in Windows help programs and CD encyclopedias as well as Web pages to link and reference related information across documents. *See also* hyperlink.

IMHO (in my humble opinion)   A shorthand term appended to a comment in an online forum or e-mail. IMHO indicates that the writer is aware that he or she is expressing a debatable or dissenting view. *See also* BTW *and* RTFM.

Internet   The vast collection of interconnected networks that evolved from the ARPANET of the late 1960s and early 1970s. *See also* ARPANET, Internet, *and* network.

intranet   A private network within an organization that uses Internet protocols and technologies. It may consist of many interlinked local area networks, desktop computers, Web sites, and portals. *See also* Internet, network, *and* portal.

IP address (Internet protocol address)   A unique number consisting of four parts separated by dots. 123.45.678.9 could be an IP number. Every machine that is on the Internet has a unique IP number or address. Most machines also have one or more domain names that are easier for people to remember. *See also* DNS, domain name, Internet, *and* TCP/IP.

IRC (Internet relay chat)   A large multiuser, live chat facility. There are a number of major IRC servers around the world that are linked to each other. Anyone connected to IRC can create a channel or chat room, and all others in the channel see everything that everyone types. *See also* mailing list.

ISDN (integrated services digital network)   A high-speed medium to move data over existing phone lines. In theory, it can provide speeds of roughly 128,000 bits per second; in practice, most people are limited to 56,000 or 64,000 bits per second.

ISO (International Organization for Standardization)   Founded in 1946, this international organization is composed of national standards bodies from over 75 countries.

ISO 9000   This family of standards defines a quality assurance program approved by the International Organization for Standardization. Companies that conform to these standards can receive *ISO 9000 certification*. This doesn't necessarily mean that the company's products have a high quality; it only means that the company follows well-defined procedures for ensuring quality products.

ISOC (Internet Society)   Based in Reston, Virginia, the Internet Society promotes the Internet and coordinates standards. Visit their site at *http://www.isoc.org* to learn more about the society or become a member.

ISP (Internet service provider)   An organization that provides access to the Internet and the World Wide Web in some form, usually for a fee. *See also* Internet *and* World Wide Web.

Java   A network-oriented programming language invented by Sun Microsystems specifically designed for creating programs that can be downloaded to a computer from a Web page and immediately run. Using small Java programs ("applets"), Web pages can include features such as animations, calculators, and other fancy or interactive tricks. *See also* applet.

JavaScript   A scripting language developed by Netscape Communications Corporation that can be added to Web pages to perform special programming functions. Microsoft Corporation created a similar language called *Jscript*.

JPEG (Joint Photographic Experts Group)   The committee that designed the photographic image-compression standard. The format (.jpg) is optimized for compressing full-color or grayscale photographic images, but it does not work well for line drawings or black-and-white images. JPEG images are 24-bit (16.7 million-color) graphics. *See also* GIF *and* TIFF.

just-in-time information   Information available and delivered to the user only when it is needed.

kilobyte   A thousand bytes. *See also* bit, byte, megabyte, gigabyte, *and* terabyte.

LAN (local area network)   A computer network restricted to a limited area, usually the same building or a floor of a building. Office computers are typically connected to a local area network. *See also* ethernet *and* network.

leased line   A telephone line that is rented for an exclusive 24-hour, 7-day-a-week connection from your location to the Internet. The highest speed data connections require a leased line. *See also* T-1 *and* T-3.

legacy data   Data stored on older computer systems or in older file or database formats that often remains behind as the *legacy* of older technologies.

legacy system or application   An application or computer system in which a company or organization has already invested considerable time and money. Typically, legacy applications are database management systems running on mainframes or minicomputers. An important feature of new software products is the ability to work with a company's legacy applications or at least being able to import data from them.

list server   The most common kind of mailing list. List servers originated on BITNET but are now common on the Internet. *See also* BITNET, e-mail, *and* mailing list.

login   The user or account name used to gain access to a computer system. Also the act of entering or "signing on" to a computer system. *See also* password.

lurking   To read through mailing lists or newsgroups and get a feel of the topic before posting your own messages. It is considered good netiquette to "lurk" a while before joining an online discussion. *See also* netiquette, netizen, spam, *and* trolling.

mailing list   An e-mail-based discussion group. Sending one e-mail message to the mailing list sends that e-mail to all members of the group. Mailing lists are usually joined by subscribing and can be left by unsubscribing. *See also* e-mail.

mainframe   A very large and expensive computer capable of supporting hundreds or even thousands of users simultaneously.

masking   To conceal a Web site's address (URL) in some manner, normally by using a domain name. For example, if an address shows up as "http://www.example.com/" but the Web site is actually located at "http://www.somewhere-else.com/example/," that address is said to be "masked." *See also* domain name *and* URL.

megabyte   A million bytes or a thousand kilobytes. *See also* bit, byte, gigabyte, kilobyte, *and* terabyte.

metadata   Data about data. It describes how, when, and by whom a particular document or set of data was created or collected and how it was formatted. Metadata is essential for understanding information stored in databases.

metasearch engine   A search engine that simultaneously searches the search engines.

Microsoft Internet Explorer   A Web browser developed by Microsoft Corporation. *See also* browser, Mosaic, *and* Netscape Communicator.

MIDI (musical instrument digital interface)   A high-quality audio file format (.mid). *See also* QuickTime.

MIME (multipurpose Internet mail extension)   The Internet standard for attaching nontext files to standard e-mail messages. Nontext files can include graphics, spreadsheets, word processor documents, sound files, and so forth. An e-mail program is said to be "MIME compliant" if it can both send and receive files using the MIME standard. *See also* binhex, browser, e-mail, *and* UUENCODE.

Mirror   To "mirror" something is to maintain an exact copy of it. The most common use of the term on the Internet refers to "mirror sites": FTP or Web sites that maintain exact copies of material originally stored at another location. Another common use of the term *mirror* refers to writing information to more than one hard disk simultaneously to prevent its loss or destruction. *See also* FTP *and* World Wide Web.

modem (modulator-demodulator)   An electronic device that lets computers communicate with one another, much as people communicate with telephones. The name is derived from "modulator-demodulator" because of its function in processing data over analog phone lines. Terminal adapters are often (and mistakenly) referred to as modems. *See also* terminal adapter.

Mosaic   The first Web browser that was available for Macintosh, Windows, and UNIX machines with the same interface for each. The popularity of the Web began with Mosaic. *See also* browser, NCSA, Netscape Communicator, Microsoft Internet Explorer, *and* World Wide Web.

MPEG (Motion Picture Experts Group)   A video file format (.mpeg) offering excellent quality in a comparatively small size. Video files found on the Internet are frequently stored in the MPEG format. *See also* compression.

multimedia   A combination of media types in a single document, such as text, graphics, audio, and video.

NCSA (National Center for Supercomputing Applications)   One of the five original centers in the Supercomputer Centers Program and a unit of the University of Illinois at Urbana-Champaign. Founded in 1986, NCSA developed Mosaic, the Web browser responsible for launching the multibillion dollar dot-com explosion. *See also* browser *and* Mosaic.

netiquette   The desired mode of manners and conduct for the Internet. *See also* flame, netizen, spam, *and* trolling.

netizen   A citizen of the Internet or someone who uses networked resources. The term connotes civic responsibility and participation. *See also* netiquette, Internet, spam, *and* trolling.

Netscape Communicator   A Web browser created by Netscape Communications Corporation. This browser was originally based on the Mosaic program developed at the National Center for Supercomputing Applications. It provided major improvements in speed and interface over other browsers but also engendered debate by being the first to create browser-specific elements for HTML. *See also* browser, Mosaic, Microsoft Internet Explorer, server, *and* World Wide Web.

network   A network is created whenever two or more computers are connected together to share resources. When two or more networks are connected, it becomes an Internet. *See also* Internet *and* intranet.

newsgroup   The name for a discussion group on USENET. *See also* USENET.

NIC (Network Information Center)   A unique ID code issued by Registrars.com to identify contact persons associated with a domain name. There can be up to three NIC handles per domain, referred to as "ADMIN/TECH/BILL," each having its own area of responsibility. *See also* domain name.

NIC (Networked Information Center)   Any office that handles information for a network can be referred to as an NIC. The most famous of these is the InterNIC, the original office of domain registration. Another definition of NIC is network interface card, which plugs into a computer and adapts the network interface to the appropriate standard. *See also* domain name *and* network.

NNTP (Network News Transfer Protocol)   The protocol used by client and server software to move a USENET posting over a network. Most common Web browsers use an NNTP connection to participate in newsgroups. *See also* browser, newsgroups, TCP/IP, *and* USENET.

node   A single computer connected to a network. *See also* Internet, intranet, *and* network.

OC-3 and OC-12   High-speed data lines capable of transferring data at 155 and 622 Megabits per second, respectively. OC-3 and OC-12 lines are replacing the T-3 as the backbones of the Internet. *See also* backbone, bps, Internet, *and* T-3.

online   When someone is connected to the Internet, he or she is considered to be "online." *See also* Internet.

object code   Instructions in a program written in a language that the computer's central processing unit can read and interpret, in contrast to source code, which is written and understood by a software engineer. *See also* source code.

online publishing   Publishing information in such a way that it can be viewed online.

operating system   Software used to handle the underlying infrastructure of a computer. The operating system provides a way of running other computer applications and accessing disk drives and other peripheral devices.

packet   A chunk of data. The TCP/IP protocol breaks large data files into smaller "packets" for transmission over the Internet. When the data reaches its destination, the protocol makes sure that all packets arrived without error. *See also* TCP/IP.

packet switching   A method of moving data around the Internet that allows many people to use the same lines at the same time. In packet switching, all data being transferred from a machine is broken into packets, with each packet having the address of its origin and destination. This enables packets from different sources to be simultaneously transferred, sorted, and directed on the same line. *See also* Internet *and* packet.

password   A code used to gain access to a locked system. Effective passwords should contain both letters and numerals (that is, alphanumeric) and not be common or easily guessed words. *See also* login.

PC (personal computer)   A small, relatively inexpensive computer designed for an individual user. The price of personal computers ranges from a few hundred dollars to over five thousand dollars. All are based on the microprocessor technology that enables manufacturers to put an entire processing unit on one chip.

PDF (Portable Document Format)   A file format developed by Adobe Systems. PDF captures formatting information from a variety of desktop publishing applications, making it possible to send formatted documents and have them appear on the recipient's monitor or printer as they were intended.

peripheral   A device connected to a computer, such as the disk drive or the printer.

PERL (Practical Extraction and Report Language)   A scripting language commonly used to handle the input from sed forms (stream editor command language) in early Web stages.

ping   A program for determining if another computer is presently connected to the Internet.

pixel   Shorthand for "picture element," a pixel is the smallest unit of resolution on a monitor. It is commonly used as a unit of measurement.

PKZIP   A widely available shareware utility that allows users to compress and decompress data files. *See also* compression.

platform   A specific combination of operating system and hardware that dictates the operating requirements of a computer application.

plug-in   A small piece of software that adds features to a larger software application. Common plug-ins are those for Web browsers (RealAudio, QuickTime, and so forth) or graphics programs (Kai's Power Tools, DigiMarc, and so forth). *See also* browser.

POP ("point of presence" or "Post Office Protocol")   A point of presence usually refers to a city or location where a network can be connected to. For example, if an Internet company says they have a POP in Vancouver, this means they have a local telephone number in Vancouver and/or a place where leased lines can connect to their network. A second definition, Post Office Protocol, refers to the way e-mail software (such as Eudora) retrieves mail from a mail server. Almost all SLIP, PPP, or shell accounts come with a POP account as well. *See also* SLIP, PPP, *and* leased line.

port   First and most frequently, a "port" is where information goes into and/or out of a computer, such as the serial port. Secondly, a "port" often refers to the number appearing after the colon in a domain name, such as "http://www.example.com:7000/." Thirdly, to "port" something refers to translating a piece of software from one computer platform to another (for example, from Windows to Macintosh). *See also* domain name *and* URL.

portal   The primary Web-based gateway to most, if not all, tools and information on an organization's intranet. The portal can be all-inclusive and provide access to the entire intranet or specific business units or functions, such as a portal for sales or human resources. *See also* Intranet *and* vortal.

posting   A single message entered into a newsgroup, mailing list, or other communications system. *See also* newsgroup, mailing list, thread, *and* USENET.

PostScript   A page-description language that offers flexible font capability; primarily a language for printing documents on laser printers, it can be adapted to produce images on other types of devices. PostScript is the standard for desktop publishing.

PPP (Point-to-Point Protocol)   The protocol that allows a computer to use a phone line and a modem to make TCP/IP connections and connect to the Internet. *See also* IP address, Internet, SLIP, *and* TCP/IP.

PPTP (Point-to-Point Tunneling Protocol)   A communications protocol used to connect computers across a TCP/IP network while actually tunneling through the security mechanisms on a firewall.

Protocol   Computer rule that provides uniform specifications so that all computer hardware and operating systems can communicate with each other.

QuickTime   A common video file format created by Apple Computer. Video files found on the Internet are often stored in this format and require a browser plug-in to be viewed (.mov). *See also* MIDI *and* plug-in.

RAM (random access memory)   This is the same as main memory. When used by itself, the term RAM refers to read *and* write memory; that is, you can both write data into RAM and read data from RAM. This is in contrast to ROM, which permits you to read data only. Most RAM is *volatile*, which means that it requires a steady flow of electricity to maintain its contents. As soon as the power is turned off, whatever data was in RAM is lost. *See also* ROM.

register   To pay a software company for a product to receive the full working copy. Registration is most often required for shareware programs, which may be partially disabled or contain "nags" until registered. *See also* shareware.

RFC (Request for Comments)   The process for creating a standard on the Internet and the name of the result. New standards are proposed and published online as a Request for Comments. Any new standards that are established retain the acronym RFC. For example, the official standard for e-mail is RFC 822. *See also* e-mail *and* Internet.

robot   A program that automatically searches the World Wide Web for files and catalogues the results. *See also* World Wide Web.

router   A computer or software package that handles the connection between two or more networks. Routers spend all their time looking at the destination addresses of the packets passing through them to decide which route to send them on. *See also* network, packet, *and* packet switching.

ROM (read-only memory)   Computers almost always contain a small amount of read-only memory that holds instructions for starting up the computer. Unlike RAM, ROM cannot be written to. *See also* RAM.

RTFM (read the f***ing manual)   A commonly used abbreviation in online forums and e-mail in response to foolish questions or questions already answered in the FAQ. *See also* FAQ.

SAN (storage area network)   A high-speed subnetwork of shared storage devices. A storage device is a machine that contains nothing but a disk or disks for storing data.

scripts   A list of commands that can be executed without user interaction.

search engine   A tool for locating information on the Internet by topic. Some of the popular search engines include MSN Search, Google, Altavista, and HotBot.

security certificate   Information that is used by the secure sockets layer (SSL) protocol to establish a secure connection. Security certificates contain information about its ownership, issuer, valid dates, and an encrypted "fingerprint" that can be used to verify the contents of the certificate. In order for an SSL connection to be created, both sides must have a valid security certificate. *See also* SSL, protocol, *and* certificate authority.

server   A computer or device on a network that manages network resources. For example, a file server is a computer and storage device dedicated to storing files. Any user on the network can store files on the server. A print server is a computer that manages one or more printers, and a network server is a computer that manages network traffic. *See also* client/server *and* network.

SGML (Standard Generalized Markup Language)   A system for organizing and tagging elements of a document. SGML was developed and standardized by the International Organization for Standardization in 1986. SGML itself does not specify any particular formatting; rather, it specifies the rules for tagging elements. These tags can then be interpreted to format elements in different ways.

shareware   Software that is available on a limited free trial basis. Some shareware applications are fully featured products, while others may have disabled features to encourage purchase of the full ("registered") version. *See also* freeware *and* register.

shell account   A software application that allows use of another machines' Internet connection. Users do not have a direct Internet connection; instead, an Internet connection is made through a host computer's connection.

signature file   An ASCII text file containing the text for someone's signature. Most e-mail programs will automatically attach a signature file to all messages sent, eliminating the need to repeatedly type a closing. *See also* ASCII *and* e-mail.

site   A single Web page or a collection of related Web pages.

SLIP (Serial Line Internet Protocol)   A standard for using a telephone line (or serial line) and a modem to connect a computer to the Internet. SLIP is gradually being replaced by PPP. *See also* Internet *and* PPP.

SMTP (Simple Mail Transport Protocol)   The main protocol used to send e-mail on the Internet. STMP consists of a set of rules for how the sending and receiving programs should interact. *See also* client, server, *and* protocol.

SNMP (Simple Network Management Protocol)   A set of standards for communicating with devices connected to a TCP/IP network, such as routers, hubs, and switches. Software for managing devices via SNMP is available for every kind of commonly used computer and is often bundled along with the device it is designed to manage. *See also* network, protocol, router, *and* TCP/IP.

source code   Instructions in a program written by a software engineer, in contrast to object code, which is those same instructions written in a language the computer's central processing unit can read and interpret. *See also* object code.

spam   A message or advertisement sent to a large number of people who did not request the information or to repeatedly send the same message to a single person. "Spamming" is considered very poor netiquette. The Coalition Against Unsolicited Commercial e-mail is an organization dedicated to removing spam from the Internet. *See also* netiquette, netizen, *and* trolling.

spider   A program that automatically fetches Web pages. Spiders are used to feed pages to search engines. It's called a spider because it crawls over the Web. Another term for these programs is webcrawler. *See also* search engine *and* webcrawler.

SQL (Structured Query Language)   A specialized programming language for sending queries to databases. Each application will have its own version of SQL-implementing features unique to that application, but all SQL-capable databases will support a common subset of SQL.

source code   Instructions that are written and understood by a software engineer in contrast to object code, which is written in a language the computer's central processing unit can read and interpret.

SRS (Shared Registry Server)   The central system for all accredited registrars to access and register/control domain names. *See also* domain name.

SSL (secure sockets layer)   A protocol designed by Netscape Communications Corporation to enable encrypted, authenticated communication across the Internet. SSL is used mostly, but not exclusively, in communications between Web browsers and Web servers. An Internet address that begins with "https" instead of "http" indicates an SSL connection will be used. *See also* browser, server, security certificate, *and* URL.

streaming audio/video   A method of delivering multimedia data so that it can be read or played back in near real time, while that data is still being downloaded.

style sheet   A method of defining certain page layout elements, such as headings, body text, numbered lists, and bullet lists, so that they can be easily applied by assigning a style tag to each paragraph. For instance, if you apply the *body text* style tag to a certain paragraph, it looks like body text, If you apply the *numbered list* style to the same paragraph, it becomes an element in a numbered list.

subdirectory   A term used in UNIX and early computer operating systems to describe a location on a hard drive where files are stored. This is equivalent to the term *folder* in Macintosh and Windows systems.

subscribe   To become a member of a mailing list, newsgroup, or other online service. *See also* mailing list *and* newsgroup.

sysop (system operator)   Someone responsible for the physical operations of a computer system or network. A system administrator (or sysadmin) decides how often system maintenance should be performed, and the sysop performs those tasks. *See also* network.

TAR (tape archive)   A compression format commonly used in the transfer and storage of files on UNIX computers (.tar). *See also* compression, PKZIP, *and* ZIP.

taxonomy   The science of classification.

T-1   A leased-line connection capable of transferring data at 1,544,000 bps. At maximum capacity, a T-1 line could move a megabyte in less than 10 seconds. *See also* bandwidth, bit, bps, byte, ethernet, leased line, *and* T-3.

T-3   A leased-line connection capable of transferring data at 44,736,000 bps. This is fast enough to view full-screen, full-motion video, which requires a transfer rate of at least 10,000,000 bits per second. *See also* bandwidth, bit, bps, byte, ethernet, leased line, *and* T-1.

TCP/IP (Transmission Control Protocol/Internet Protocol)   TCP/IP is the suite of protocols that defines the Internet. Originally designed for the UNIX operating system, TCP/IP software is not available for every major computer operating system. To connect to the Internet, a computer must have TCP/IP software. *See also* IP address, Internet, protocol, *and* UNIX.

telnet   An Internet protocol allowing a personal computer to connect to a host computer and use that computer as if you were locally connected. This often provides the ability to use all the software and capabilities of the host computer. *See also* host.

terabyte   A thousand gigabytes. *See also* bit, byte, kilobyte, megabyte, *and* gigabyte.

terminal adapter   An electronic device that interfaces a personal computer with a host computer via an ISDN phone line. Terminal adapters are often called "ISDN modems"; however, they are not actually modems. *See also* ISDN *and* modem.

terminal server   A special-purpose computer with places to plug in several modems on one side and a connection to a local area network or host machine on the other side. The terminal server does the work of passing connections to the appropriate node. Most terminal servers can provide PPP or SLIP services if connected to the Internet. *See also* host, LAN, modem, node, PPP, *and* SLIP.

thread   An ongoing message-based conversation on a single subject. *See also* mailing list, newsgroup, *and* posting.

TIFF (Tag Image File Format)   A popular graphic image file format (.tif). *See also* GIF *and* JPEG.

trolling   The act of deliberately posting false or inflammatory information in order to start a flame war or cause aggravation to others. *See also* flame, flame war, netiquette, *and* spam.

UNIX   The most common operating system for servers on the Internet. UNIX systems are designed to be used by many people at the same time and have built-in TCP/IP. *See also* server *and* TCP/IP.

upload   The process of transferring data from a local computer to a remote computer. When you copy a file from your computer to the Internet, you are "uploading" that file. *See also* download.

URL (Uniform Resource Locator)   The standard method of giving the address for any resource on the World Wide Web. A URL might look like this: "http://www.example.com/examples.html." The most common use of a URL is to enter it in a Web browser to access a certain page on the Internet. *See also* browser, HTTP, *and* World Wide Web.

USENET   A distributed bulletin board system that runs on news servers, UNIX hosts, online services, and bulletin board systems. Collectively, USENET is composed of all the users who post to and read newsgroup articles. The USENET is the largest decentralized information utility available today. *See also* newsgroup, posting, *and* thread.

user authentication   The process of requiring a user to enter an authorized name and password before entering a Web site.

UUENCODE (Unix to Unix encoding)   A method for converting files from binary format to ASCII text so that they can be sent across the Internet via e-mail. *See also* ASCII, binhex, *and* MIME.

Veronica (Very Easy Rodent-Oriented Netwide Index to Computerized Archives)   Developed at the University of Nevada, Veronica is a constantly updated database of the names of almost every menu item on thousands of gopher servers. *See also* Archie *and* gopher.

VBScript (Visual Basic Scripting)   A scripting language developed by Microsoft Corporation and supported by Microsoft Internet Explorer. VBScript is based on the Visual Basic programming language but is much simpler to use. Similar to JavaScript, it enables Web authors to include interactive controls, such as buttons and scrollbars, on their Web pages.

VM (virtual machine)   A self-contained operating environment that behaves as if it is a separate computer. For example, Java applets run in a Java virtual machine (VM) that has no access to the host operating system.

VoIP (Voice-Over Internet Protocol) . Voice-over Internet products or Internet telephony applications.

VRML (Virtual Reality Modeling Language)   A specification for displaying three-dimensional objects on the World Wide Web. It is a three-dimensional equivalent of HTML.

vortal   A vortal is a portal Web site that provides information and resources for a particular topic. *See also* portal.

WAIS (wide area information server)   A commercial software package that allows the indexing of huge quantities of information and then makes those indices searchable across networks and the Internet. A prominent feature of WAIS is the ranking (scoring) of the search results according to how relevant the hits are. *See also* search engine.

WAN (wide area network)   Any network that covers an area larger than a single building or campus. *See also* Internet, LAN, *and* network.

WAV (waveform audio)   A common audio file format for DOS and Windows computers (.wav).

webcrawler (spider)   A program that automatically fetches Web pages. Webcrawlers are used to feed pages to search engines. It's called a spiderweb crawler because it crawls over the Web. *See also* search engine *and* spider.

winsock (windows socket)   An application programming interface for developing Windows programs that can communicate with other machines via the TCP/IP protocol. *See also* API, browser, FTP, Internet, *and* TCP/IP.

World Wide Web (WWW)   The technical definition is the global network of hypertext servers that allows text, graphics, audio, and video files to be mixed together. A second, more loosely, used definition is the entire range of resources that can be accessed using Gopher, FTP, HTTP, telnet, USENET, WAIS, and other such tools. *See also* FTP, gopher, HTTP, telnet, USENET, *and* WAIS.

WYSIWYG (what you see is what you get)   A WYSIWYG application is one that enables you to see on the display screen exactly what will appear when the document is printed. This differs, for example, from word processors that are incapable of displaying different fonts and graphics on the display screen even though the formatting codes have been inserted into the file.

XHTML (Extensible Hypertext Markup Language)   A hybrid between HTML and XML specifically designed for Internet device displays. XHTML is a markup language written in XML; therefore, it is an XML application. *See also* XML.

XML (Extensible Markup Language)   A specification developed by the World Wide Web Consortium (W3C). XML is a pared-down version of SGML and designed especially for Web documents. It allows designers to create their own customized tags, thus enabling the definition, transmission, validation, and interpretation of data between applications and organizations.

ZIP   A compressed file format (.zip). Many files available on the Internet are compressed or "zipped" in order to reduce storage space and transfer times. *See also* compression *and* PKZIP.

Resource List

Here is a selective list of Internet sites that offer news, advice, case studies, tips and tricks, and conference and trade show information relating to intranets and portals. The primary focus is North America.

CIO's Intranet/Extranet Research Center (*http://www.cio.com/research/intranet/*): One of the many "research centers" offered on *CIO Magazine's* site (*www.cio.com*), this Web site provides selected and fairly current information with a "business perspective" rather than a technical one.

Complete Intranet Resource (*http://www.intrack.com/intranet*): This site contains some rather dated material, but a relaunch of this site is expected soon. (As this book went to press, it had not been relaunched.) The range of the material on the site is excellent, with good lists (for example, Top 10 Intranet Myths) and best practice material.

Enterprise News (*http://www.internetnews.com/ent-news/*): Provided by INT Media Corporation, Enterprise News is a frequently updated news site that tracks products, services, and companies in the area of Internet technologies.

Enterprise Portals Letter (*http://www.ucgtech.com/portals/*): Home of the monthly Corporate Portals Letter, this site is designed to promote the newsletter. The newsletter contains good, in-depth case studies of portal deployment, thus its content is limited. However, there is a useful range of items available from previous issues of the newsletter.

Infoconomy: Information and Intelligence for the Technology Elite (*http://www.infoconomy.com*): This Web site is operated by Infoconomy Ltd., a company based in the United Kingdom and focused on the European Union. It aims to provide technology executives with a level of detail and perspective that is not available elsewhere. It is well-designed with good content.

Intranet Journal (*http://www.intranetjournal.com*): The Intranet Journal is a very good site with information for both business decision makers and IT professionals. It includes market research, case studies, and links to conferences and trade shows.

Intranet Professional: Managing Knowledge Ecosystems (*http://www.infotoday/IP*): Intranet Professional is a newsletter created for library and information professionals who are planning, designing, implementing, or managing intranet solutions and knowledge management practices.

Intranets 2001 (*http://www.intranets2001.com*): Many of the papers that were given at the Intranets 2001 conference in Santa Clara in April 2001 covered portal developments. The Microsoft PowerPoint versions of some of these papers can be downloaded from the conference site.

Intranets 2002 (*http://www.intranets2002.com*): As this book went to press, not much has been added to the site, but it is recommended that readers check often for conference outlines, keynotes, and so forth.

Iorg.com (*http://www.iorg.com*): A good site that, despite some dated content, includes intranet-related white papers and articles of interest.

Microsoft—Intranets (*http://www.microsoft.com/technet/treeview/default.asp?url=/technet/itsolutions/intranet/default.asp*): This is a clearinghouse of resources to help you deploy, maintain, and support your intranet.

Microsoft SharePoint Technologies (*http://www.microsoft.com/sharepoint/*): Microsoft SharePoint technologies give users the ability to organize information, readily access that information, manage documents, and enable efficient collaboration-all in a familiar, browser-based and Microsoft Office-integrated environment. This site also provides information on SharePoint Portal Server and SharePoint Team Services.

Network World Fusion (*http://www.nwfusion.com/*): This site is packed with news, events, white papers, and case studies related to enterprise networking.

Web and Intranet Development Forum (*http://www.clearlight.com/~dmc/board/index.html*): This forum is intended to be a place for discussion about web development; web servers; and CGI programming, tools, and techniques.

Webtrends Network-the Portal site for Internet and Intranet Professionals (*http://www.alerttrack.com*): An interesting combination of news, good technical resources, links to events, and a bookstore.

Bibliography

Abbate, Janet. 1999. *Inventing the internet.* Cambridge, Mass.: MIT Press.

Adobe Corporation. 2001. History of the Adobe Corporation. *http://www.adobe.com/aboutadobe/pressroom/pdfs/timeline_090501.pdf.*

Air Products and Chemicals, Inc. 2001. Air Products gets to market faster with SharePoint Portal Server. *http://www.microsoft.com/servers/evaluation/casestudies/AirProducts.asp.*

Baker, Sunny. 2000. Getting the most from your intranet and extranet strategies. *Journal of Business Strategy* (July): 40.

Bernard, Ryan. 1997. *The corporate intranet: Harness the power of the next-generation intranet,* 2d ed. New York: John Wiley & Sons, Inc.

Berreby, David. 1999. The hunter-gatherers of the knowledge economy. *Strategy and Business,* No. 16:52.

Birkinshaw, Julie. 2001. Making sense of knowledge management. *Ivey Business Journal* (March): 32.

Computer Museum History Center. 2001. *http://www.computerhistory.org.*

Cortada, James. 1998. Introducing the knowledge worker. In *Rise of the Knowledge Worker.* Boston: Butterworth-Heinemann.

Cortese, Amy. 1996. Here comes the intranet and it could be the simple solution to companywide information-on-demand. *Business Week* (February): 76.

Coursey, David. 2001. The four biz-tech trends of the coming decade. *Anchordesk* from ZDWire.

Coy, Peter. 2000. The creative economy. *BusinessWeek* (August 28): 78.

DeBell, Camille. 2001. Ninety years in the world of work. *Career Development Quarterly* (September): 77.

Deloitte & Touche. 2001. *2001 technology trends annual report.* Deloitte & Touche Consulting.

Drucker, Peter F. 1959. *Landmarks of tomorrow.* New York: Harper & Row.

Drucker, Peter F. 1974. *Management: Tasks, responsibilities, practices.* New York: Harper & Row.

Drucker, Peter. 1995. *Managing in a time of great change.* New York: Dutton.

Drucker, Peter F. 1999. *Management challenges for the 21st century.* New York: HarperBusiness.

Drucker, Peter. 2001. The next society. *Economist* (November): 3-5.

Duffy, Daintry. 2001. Why do intranets fail? *Darwin Magazine* (November).

Dyer, Greg. 2001. The state of KM. *Knowledge Management* (May): 31.

Elachi, Joanne. 2001. The wireless enterprise opportunity. *CommWeb.com. http://www.commweb.com/article/COM20010727S0001* (July 27).

Ellis, Kristine. 2001. Sharing best practices globally. *Training* (July): 32.

Fisher, Kimball, and Maureen Duncan Fisher. 1998. *The distributed mind.* New York: Amacom Books.

Ford, Henry, and Samuel Crowther. 1923. *My life and work.* Garden City, N.Y.: Garden City Publishers.

Galt, Virginia. 2001. Firms seen stifling key employees. *Globe and Mail*, 3 July, final edition.

Gantz, John. 2000. Controlling the coming chaos of intranets. *Computerworld* (March 6): 33.

Gates, Jean Key. 1968. The story of libraries. In *Introduction to librarianship.* New York: McGraw-Hill.

Intranet-related hardware, software and services: A U.S. market trend report. 2001. San Jose, Calif.: Global Industry Analysts.

Goff, Leslie. 1999. And the winner is.... *Computerworld* (January 25): 86.

Hamilton, Joan O'C. 1996. The new workplace: Walls are falling as the office of the future finally takes shape. *BusinessWeek* (April 29): 106.

Harrison, Frederick. 1943. *A book about books.* London: John Murray.

Hinrichs, Randy. 1997. *Intranets: What's the bottom line?* New York: Prentice Hall.

Hobbes' Internet Timeline, v5.5. 2001. *http://www.zakon.org/robert/internet/timeline.*

Horgan, Tim. 2001. Developing your intranet strategy and plan. *http://www.cio.com/WebMaster/strategy.*

Horibe, Frances Dale Emy. 1999. *Managing knowledge workers: New skills and attitudes to unlock the intellectual capital in your organization.* Etobicoke, Ont., Can.: John Wiley & Sons.

Intranet/extranet fact book 2000. Framington, Mass.: IDC.

Intranet ROI: Appraising the value of intranet investments. 2001. Toronto: Prescient Digital Media.

Inventors. 2001. *http://inventors.about.com/library/weekly/aa070798.htm.*

Kaplan, Robert, and David P. Norton. 1992. The balanced scorecard: Measure that drive productivity. *Harvard Business Review* (January-February): 71–79.

Kersten, Gregory. 2001. Knowledge workers feed an organization: Special report on mastering information management. *National Post,* 18 September, final edition.

Knowledge worker manual. 2001. *http://navcenter.borgess.com/KworkerManual/ePages/front_page/kw_def.html.*

Knowledge worker state of the market. 2000. Gartner Group.

Kohlhepp, Robert J. 1996. Intranets: Getting there from here. *Network Computing* (September): 39.

Krell, Eric. 2001. The knowledge race. *Training* (July).

Kristula, Dave. 2001. History of the internet. *http://www.davesite.com/webstation/net-history.shtml.*

Laiserin, Jerry. 2000. The pre-history of internet collaboration. *Cadence* (December): 59.

Leiner, Barry M., Vinton G. Cerf, David C. Clark, Robert E. Kayn, Leonard Kleinroch, Daniel C. Lynch, John Poster, Lawrence G. Roberts, and Stephen S. Wolff. 1997. The past and future history of the internet. *Communications of the ACM* (February): 102.

Lemos, Robert. 1999. ENIAC: Calculated history of the computer. *ZDNET News* from ZDWire.

Len, Maksim. 2002. Memory of the Future: Two directions. *Digit Life (http://www.digit-life.com/articles/memory/twodirections/index.html).*

Lewis, David. Boeing portal to serve employees, partners. *InternetWeek* (July 30): 36.

The list: Valuable content. 2001. *Computerworld (http://www.computerworld.comroi/july/0,3277, STO61902,00.html).*

Lucent Technologies. 2001. "Bell Labs Innovations: History. *http://www.bell-labs.com/history.*

Machlup, Fritz. 1998. Knowledge production and occupation structure. In *Rise of the knowledge worker.* Boston: Butterworth-Heinemann.

Maney, Kevin. 1997. Debate stirs over origin of computers. *USA Today*, September, final edition.

McDonald, Glen, and Cameron Crotty. 2000. The digital future. *PC World* (January): 116.

Mears, Jennifer. 2001. Portals: The new business desktop. *Network World* (May): 34.

Mecham, Kimberley. 2001. How Microsoft built a cost-effective HR portal. *HR Focus* (August): 4.

Microsoft Encarta Encyclopedia 2000 Deluxe. "Atanasoff-Berry Computer (ABC)."

———. "Babbage, Charles."

———. "Chinese Language."

———. "Computer Memory."

———. "Gutenberg Bible."

———. "Hypertext."

Mobile applications revenues set to rise, says IDC report. 2001. *Telecomworldwire.*

Mobile intranets—have you got the message? 2001. *Management Consultancy* (November 8): 10.

Myers, Mark. 2001. How do you know what you know? *Computer Technology Review* (April 1): 54.

Nielsen, Jacob. 2001. 10 best intranet designs of 2001. *Alertbox (http://www.useit.com/alertbox/20011125.html).*

Nickols, Fred. 2001. "What is" in the world of work and working: Some implications of the shift to knowledge work. *http://home.att.net/~nickols/shifts.htm.*

New Media. *Communications Daily* (June 4).

Nucleus Research, Inc. 2001. ROI Profile: Aanza, Inc. *Research Note,* No. B25.

Nucleus Research, Inc. 2001. ROI Profile: Microsoft SharePoint/Anderson Power Products. *Research Note,* No. B30.

Nucleus Research, Inc. 2001. ROI Profile: Microsoft SharePoint/Children's Hospital Boston. *Research Note,* No. B28.

Nucleus Research, Inc. 2001. ROI Profile: Microsoft SharePoint/Legal Firm, United States. *Research Note,* No. B26.

Oboler, Eli M. 1983. *To free the mind: Libraries, technology and intellectual freedom*. Littleton, Colo.: Libraries Unlimited.

PBS life on the internet. 2001. *http://www.pbs.org/internet/timeline/index.html.*

Powers, Vicki J. 1999. Ford creates clearinghouse, virtual network, web site to support its benchmarking efforts. *Benchmarking in Practice,* No. 15.

Prusack, Laurence. 1998. Why knowledge why now? In *Rise of the knowledge worker.* Boston: Butterworth-Heinemann.

Rosenheim, Mimi. 2001. How to comb through jumbled data and ideas and produce an intranet that serves as a valuable corporate resource. *Web Techniques* (July): 20.

Runyan, Linda. 1991. 40 years on the frontier. *Datamation* (March 15): 34.

Santosus, Megan. 1998. The trouble with numbers: Why the Harvard Business School doesn't worry about its intranet's ROI. *CIO Magazine (http://www.cio.com/archive/webbusiness/100198_hbs.html).*

Schement, Jorge Reina, and Terry Curtis. 1995. *Tendencies and tension in the information age: Production and distribution of information in the United States.* New Brunswick, N.J.: Transaction Publisher.

Seattle Times. 1997. Editorial, 30 June.

Stellin, Susan. 2001. Intranets Nurture Companies from the Inside. *New York Times,* 29 January, final edition.

Stockwell, Foster. 2000. *A history of information storage and retrieval.* Jefferson, N.C.: McFarland & Company.

Stiroh, Kevin J. 2001. Investing in information technology: Productivity payoffs for U.S. industries. *Current Issues in Economics and Finance* (June): 1.

Sullivan, Dan. 2001. Five principles of intelligent content management. *Intelligent Enterprise* (August 31): 28.

Taylor, Kit Sims. 1998. *The brief reign of the knowledge worker.* Paper presented at the International Conference on the Social Impact of Information Technologies, 12-13 October, St. Louis, Mo.

Technology industry evolving to high-performance, security-driven mobile marketplace, says 2001 technology trends annual report from Deloitte & Touche Consulting. 2001. Press Release, *http://www.dc.com/obx/pages?Name=pr techtrends2001.*

Thill, Brent, and John Torrey. 2001. *Corporate portals: Leveraging 5+ years of software investments.* Boston: Credit Suisse First Boston.

Tissen, Rene, Daniel Andriessen, and Frank Lekanne Deprez. 2000. *The knowledge dividend.* London: Financial Times/Prentice Hall.

Wah, Louisa. 2000. Workplace of the future. *Management Review* (January): 9.

Waltner, Charles. 1999. Intranet ROI. *Information Week* (May 24): 90.

Waters, Malcolm. 1996. *Daniel Bell.* London: Routledge.

Wesley, Doug. 2000. Retaining workers in the knowledge economy. *Information Outlook* (October): 34.

Williams, Simon. 2001. The intranet content management strategy conference. *Management Services* (September): 16.

Woods, Bob. 2001. Taking stock of what you know. *Chief Executive(U.S.)* (July): 6.

Yockelson, David. 2001. ROI can be found in enterprise portals. *InternetWeek* (October 8): 28.

Young, Debby. 2000. An audit tale. *CIO Magazine* (May): 150.

Zimmerman, Andrew B. 1997. The evolution of the internet. *Telecommunications,* (June): 39.

Index

Get a **Free**
e-mail newsletter, updates,
special offers, links to related books,
and more when you

register on line!

Register your Microsoft Press® title on our Web site and you'll get a FREE subscription to our e-mail newsletter, *Microsoft Press Book Connections.* You'll find out about newly released and upcoming books and learning tools, online events, software downloads, special offers and coupons for Microsoft Press customers, and information about major Microsoft® product releases. You can also read useful additional information about all the titles we publish, such as detailed book descriptions, tables of contents and indexes, sample chapters, links to related books and book series, author biographies, and reviews by other customers.

Registration is easy. Just visit this Web page and fill in your information:

http://www.microsoft.com/mspress/register

Microsoft®

Proof of Purchase

Use this page as proof of purchase if participating in a promotion or rebate offer on this title. Proof of purchase must be used in conjunction with other proof(s) of payment such as your dated sales receipt—see offer details.

Collective Knowledge: Intranets, Productivity, and the Promise of the Knowledge Workplace
0-7356-1499-7

CUSTOMER NAME

Microsoft Press, PO Box 97017, Redmond, WA 98073-9830

EDUCATIONAL TESTING SERVICE

000013832